THE OPENING KICKOFF

THE OPENING KICKOFF

The Tumultuous Birth of a Football Nation

DAVE REVSINE

LYONS PRESS
Guilford, Connecticut
An imprint of Globe Pequot Press

Lyons Press is an imprint of Globe Pequot Press.

Project editor: Meredith Dias
Layout: Justin Marciano

Library of Congress Cataloging-in-Publication Data is available on file.

ISBN 978-0-7627-9177-4

Printed in the United States of America

To my father, Professor Lawrence Revsine, who shared with me his passion for college sports. That he is not here to read this book is sad beyond words.

Contents

Contents

AUTHOR'S NOTE

"DAD, WHAT'S A DROPKICK?"

It was a rainy, cold fall afternoon sometime in the early 1980s—a miserable day. I was seated with my father, a college professor, in our own semiprivate hell: Dyche Stadium in Evanston, Illinois—home of the hapless Northwestern Wildcats. On the field, my father's alma mater and employer was getting smacked around, as it did every Saturday. The Wildcats were in the midst of what would turn out to be a thirty-four-game losing streak, the longest in major college football history.

In order to distract myself from the carnage on the turf, I had begun flipping through the game program, eventually stumbling across a page entitled: "NU/Opponent Records." There, in the midst of the 90-yard passes and 300-yard rushing days, was an entry for the longest field goal ever kicked against the Wildcats. "62 yards," it read. "Pat O'Dea, Wisconsin, 1898 (dropkick)." It was that parenthetical "dropkick" that prompted my question.

Seemingly pleased to have something to talk about aside from the matter at hand, my dad explained all he knew about the early days of football, describing an antiquated kicking method, where a player would allow the ball to hit the ground before booting it. The entire conversation couldn't have taken more than five minutes. I stored the name "Pat O'Dea" in my head and didn't think about him again for roughly thirty years.

In the late summer of 2010, I encountered O'Dea again. I was thumbing idly through the *ESPN College Football Encyclopedia*, anticipating the start of a new season. In the Wisconsin section, there was a one-paragraph mention of O'Dea, describing not just his remarkable skills, but also a fascinating and somewhat bizarre personal story. Memories of that long-ago conversation with my now deceased father flooded back. I began to search the Internet for more information about O'Dea.

I was captivated. What a remarkable tale: a 110-yard punt, a record-setting dropkick in the middle of a blizzard, and a riveting mystery to boot! How had I, a passionate college football fan and studio host of a network devoted to covering the Big Ten, not been aware of this?

Coincidentally, I was headed to Wisconsin's campus in Madison the next week to give a speech. I made an appointment with the university archivist, who pulled O'Dea's file for me. I spent the rest of the day poring through the amazing details of his life and the period in which he played. I had always assumed that the nineteenth-century game was an afterthought—a series of sparsely attended contests between undergraduates who were looking for a distraction from their studies. As I learned, that couldn't have been further from the truth. O'Dea, I discovered, had been a full-fledged superstar long before Red Grange or Jim Thorpe. He helped raise the national profile of a university, put fans in the stands, and left journalists searching for new adjectives to describe his feats. And, like many of today's top athletes, he encountered a fair amount of controversy along the way. I left campus that day determined to find a way to tell the story.

During my free time over the next couple of years, I read everything that I could about O'Dea's era and the early development of college football. I discovered that the sport wasn't that much different in the late nineteenth and early twentieth centuries than it is in the early twenty-first. The issues were largely the same. Only the scope had changed.

I came to realize that, as interesting as O'Dea was, he was really just a mechanism for telling a much bigger story—the story of the most pivotal time in the development of college football.

What has been will be again, what has been done will be done again; there is nothing new under the sun.

—ECCLESIASTES 1:9

Preface

THESE ARE CHALLENGING TIMES FOR COLLEGE FOOTBALL. I HAVE WATCHED the challenges escalate for nearly two decades, while sitting at the anchor desk at ESPN and the Big Ten Network. It's the scandals that grab most of the headlines. And, while I was writing this book, there was plenty of scandal to go around.

The University of North Carolina was rocked by the revelation that one of its professors was catering his courses to the school's football players, offering limited work and unauthorized grade changes.

At Miami a convicted Ponzi-schemer named Nevin Shapiro admitted to showering that school's football players with everything from cash to prostitutes. *Sports Illustrated* ran a series claiming that Oklahoma State had engaged in similarly sordid tactics.

And, of course, there was the shocking story of Penn State, where a university president, an athletic director, and a legendary football coach allegedly protected a child abuser so as not to jeopardize their school's lucrative football program.

But the problems went beyond these abominations. Greed rules. The University of Texas practically allowed a conference to disintegrate around it so it could have a greater share of television revenues.

Debates raged over amateurism. Reigning Heisman Trophy winner Johnny Manziel's playing status was up in the air for weeks as the NCAA investigated whether he had violated the organization's rules by profiting from autographs. *Time* magazine put Manziel on its cover, accompanied by a headline reading, IT'S TIME TO PAY COLLEGE ATHLETES.

Meanwhile, concern about safety at all levels of the game grabbed headlines, as the effects of years of traumatic head injuries manifested themselves in dementia and, in some cases, suicide. Two-time NFL MVP Kurt Warner told a national radio show that he'd prefer it if his sons didn't play football. Warner said the notion of his kids absorbing violent hits, "scares me as a dad." Former Detroit Lions cornerback Lem Barney publicly referred to the game as "deadly." The Hall of Famer expressed the belief that "in the next 10 to 20 years society will alleviate football altogether," due to concerns over violence and concussions. It was such a big issue that even President Barack Obama weighed in, telling the *New Republic* that the violence in the game needs to be reduced, adding, "I tend to be more worried about college players."

It is a period, we've been told, unprecedented in the history of the sport. But what if I told you that it *did* have precedent? In fact, what if I told you that the current problems in college football might actually be viewed as an improvement—that, in some regards, the college game was once far worse than it is today?

That is partly the story of *The Opening Kickoff,* which explores college football in the years between 1890 and 1915. It was during this time that many of the game's current problems first manifested themselves.

The North Carolina academic scandal, for instance, had its precedent at the University of Chicago. That school's greatest star of the early twentieth century, Walter Eckersall, was allowed to compete for three years despite making almost no progress toward a degree. He was enabled along the way by legendary coach Amos Alonzo Stagg, whose friends on the faculty did all they could to keep the All-American eligible.

Nevin Shapiro is nothing more than a modern-day version of the Yale boosters of 1905, who gave their star, James Hogan, a free Caribbean vacation at the end of the season.

Though no one committed offenses nearly as horrifying as those alleged at Penn State, the concept of the athletic tail wagging the academic dog is certainly not a new one. The administration of Princeton president Francis L. Patton in the late nineteenth and early twentieth centuries is just one example. One university history noted that Patton's desire for winning teams and increased alumni donations led him to promote the school's athletic program with a "shocking apathy of conscience."

Texas's greed? No different than that of Chicago under Stagg's leadership in the late 1890s. Finding itself in an advantageous financial position due to its location in a major city, the school refused to share football gate receipts equally with its conference foes, nearly causing the dissolution of what is now the Big Ten.

Amateurism has been a source of contention since the earliest era of the sport. Universities often spent the days leading up to games filing sworn affidavits charging that their opponents had benefitted from illegal inducements. And, in fact, many had, as schools routinely shopped the open market for so-called "tramp" athletes.

And the violence? In 1905 a Harvard star named Karl Brill retired prematurely from the sport, saying, "I believe that the human body was not made to withstand the enormous strain that football demands." He dismissed the game as "a mere gladiatorial contest." In that same year, eighteen players died at all levels of football from injuries suffered on the gridiron. President Teddy Roosevelt went so far as to call the game's leaders to the White House for an emergency summit, and a number of schools dropped the sport.

The game's problems, though, are only part of the college football narrative, as the modern-day challenges are accompanied by immense popularity. College football ranks behind only professional football and baseball on a list of Americans' favorite sports. It is thrilling to watch—an extravaganza full of pageantry and passion. It brings people together—uniting grads and nongrads alike behind a common cause and filling stadiums from coast to coast. It is a sport that moves rational people to drive through the night to attend a game, unload significant portions of their income on bowl trips, or spend countless hours on websites devoted to speculating about the college choices of eighteen-year-olds. It spawns new television networks. And it makes money. ESPN paid $5.64 billion for the right to broadcast the first twelve seasons of the new College Football Playoff.

The seeds of that popularity were sown in the same twenty-five-year period covered in this book. Between 1890 and 1915, the modern spectacle of the game began to emerge. It was the byproduct of a combination of factors, many of which were only tangentially related to football itself. The sport's rise was far from inevitable. College football was simply in the right place at the right time, quickly rising to the forefront of the burgeoning sporting consciousness.

Grandstands overflowed for the biggest games, with school spirit whipping campuses into a frenzy, and the media breathlessly covering it all—creating new superstars along the way. Though the game may have looked very different, it felt the same. Even then, college football was a big deal—captivating the nation, and changing the tenor of the campus experience.

The story of the game's rise begins in the East. Those who wonder why we can't "just go back to the way it used to be," might be surprised to find that, in fact, we have.

CHAPTER ONE

"FOOTBALL DAY"

As Thanksgiving Eve, 1893, turned to Thanksgiving Day, Billy Edwards prepared to leave his post and head home. He made one last pass through his palatial workplace, the elegant bar at New York's exclusive Hoffman House hotel, briefly reflecting on what had been one of the busier and more remarkable nights of his career as the famous establishment's bouncer.

He walked past the gorgeous carved mahogany bar, momentarily pondering his reflection in the massive mirrors that lined the walls, mirrors that were said to be the largest in the nation. Standing less than 5'5", the forty-eight-year-old Edwards was an impeccably dressed and strikingly handsome man. He fit in perfectly with the Hoffman House's high-end clientele. Despite his advancing age, he had a perfect physique. An Englishman by birth, he had once been the lightweight boxing champion of America—an indefatigable fighter, who, twenty-two years earlier, had gone a remarkable ninety-five rounds in a championship match.

On his way out the door, Edwards paused beside an out-of-towner transfixed in front of the bar's most famous attraction. It was a massive painting, the scandalous "Nymphs and Satyr," the work of celebrated Frenchman William-Adolphe Bouguereau. The man stood before the twelve-foot-high canvas, mouth slightly agape, staring longingly at the four frolicking naked women at the centerpiece of the work. As the tourist absentmindedly attempted to light a cigarette, Edwards quipped, "Say, young fellow, don't light your nose," and walked out onto Broadway.

Edwards was immediately struck by the almost overwhelming din, standing in stark contrast to the more dignified scene inside the Hoffman House. Even at this late hour, the streets were jammed with people—many of them collegians, wearing huge overcoats and fashionable yellow shoes and carrying canes wrapped in either blue or orange ribbons. College cheers rang through the air, the "rah, rah" of Yale answered by the "sis boom bah" of Princeton.

Edwards quickly got lost in the crowd. It was probably for the best. Though he was certainly more than capable of defending himself, the former boxer felt a little trepidation in the early hours of this Thursday morning. At a time when the average American made less than ten dollars per week, he was carrying roughly fifty thousand. It was the day of the biggest sporting event of the year, the annual championship football game, and Edwards was New York City's best-known bookie.

Intercollegiate football was still in its infancy, less than a quarter of a century removed from its humble beginnings—an 1869 match between Princeton and Rutgers. The early games were sparsely attended and had a collegial feel. A visiting team might roll into town on game day, stroll around with its hosts—perhaps play some billiards—and then head off to the field for the contest, the result of which was a veritable afterthought. When the game ended, the two teams often dined together, sharing toasts and laughter.

Within a decade, though, the games became a more serious matter. Princeton, Yale, Harvard, and Columbia formed a football association in the mid-1870s and began crowning an annual champion. The tenor changed. The emphasis on camaraderie was replaced by an emphasis on winning. Students rallied around the team as an expression of loyalty to their school. Its fortunes helped determine the university's reputation.

The championship game was moved to New York City in 1880, though, in the first few years, it remained largely a curiosity. That first big-city game was played in front of just 5,000 fans, netting each school the modest sum of $320.42. A little more than a decade later, the crowd had increased by a factor of ten, while the gate receipts had grown by a staggering 5,600 percent. Near riots broke out on the day the reserved tickets went on sale, and students resold them for more than five times their face value. Football had become a big business.

That business was driven largely by the social elite. One of the year's most-anticipated social events, the championship game was a place for high-society New Yorkers to see and be seen. It was an age when conspicuous displays of wealth were becoming more and more acceptable, and the Thanksgiving game was the perfect time to show off, as the Vanderbilts and the Whitneys used the contest as a convenient excuse to spend and celebrate. Their activities were breathlessly described in New York's powerful and ubiquitous newspapers, which spread the gospel of the event to the masses.

"No one who does not live in New York can understand how completely it colors and lays its hold upon that city," famed journalist Richard Harding Davis wrote in 1893 of the Thanksgiving Day game. "[I]t, in short, became 'the thing to do,' and the significance of that day which once centred in New England around a grateful family offering thanks for blessing received and a fruitful harvest now centres in Harlem about twenty-two very dirty and very earnest young men who are trying to force a leather ball over a whitewashed line."

The *New York Herald* echoed that thought. "No longer is the day one of thanksgiving to the Giver of all good. The kicker now is king and the people bow down to him." The rival *New York Times* opined of the day, "It is not what the Puritans made it, and while the traditional name cannot be easily displaced . . . it has plainly lost its old meaning. Suggestions of a new designation would be timely, but football day will not do."

❧

Game day morning was a gloomy one—windy and cloudy with an occasional misty drizzle. It did nothing to dampen the enthusiasm. Those without tickets set out early. For most, the destination was the so-called "Deadhead Hill," also known as "Coogan's Bluff," after real estate owner James J. Coogan. The bluff rose abruptly over Manhattan Field and, in past years, had given spectators like them a free, albeit distant, view of the game: The earlier the arrival, the better the seat. They piled on the Sixth and Ninth Avenue elevated railroads and made their way up to 155th Street.

The aristocrats headed to the game far more luxuriously. They met at the most exclusive hotels—the Plaza, the Fifth Avenue Hotel, and the aforementioned Hoffman House. There, they boarded carriages, many of which had been reserved up to a year in advance. As many as twenty men and women piled atop the largest ones, known as "Tally-hos," six horses pulling the elaborately decorated coaches northward. Depending on the allegiance of the occupants, cloths of either orange or blue draped all four sides of the carriages. Similarly-hued ribbons lined the spokes.

The riders were decked out from head to toe in college colors, massive blue or orange chrysanthemums pinned to their clothing. They waved flags; they screamed; they sang. They jumped up and down, bouncing the coaches as they went, good-naturedly taunting any carriage they encountered that was covered in rival colors. As the procession moved along, the city's occupants jammed the streets to watch, often standing three or four deep. Houses all along the way were covered with bunting and flags. It was a joyous celebration, and the riders enjoyed every minute of it. They were in no great hurry. The journey was part of the fun, and, besides, they had a spot reserved at the game. The carriages would be pulled right up to the field.

Meanwhile, the train passengers arrived in Harlem, greeted by a bit of a surprise. Coogan had rented his land to a speculator, who, for the staggering sum of $2,000, had exclusive domain over the bluff for the day. He had cordoned it off and was charging fifty cents a head to get inside the ropes. Some gladly paid, while those who couldn't made their way up higher to the newly constructed viaduct, which loomed over the bluff, even farther away from the field.

As game time grew closer, the trains began to overflow. Passengers hung from the steel gates between the cars as the conductors attempted to maintain some semblance of order. The vehicles creaked slowly and agonizingly along, finally reaching the terminus as the relieved employees cried, "One Hundred and Fifty-Fifth Street! All Out!" In the final hour or so before the game, trains arrived every two minutes, with each pouring upwards of five hundred rooters into the chaotic scene.

As the fans surged through the doorway of the station, they were greeted by sheer pandemonium. The street was teeming with men, women, children, and horses. One fan carried a frightened poodle, its fur dyed a faint Princeton orange. All around them, hawkers sold every manner of souvenir—banners, flags, ribbons, buttons, and horns. The air was a cacophony fueled by every noisemaker imaginable—from drums and cymbals to human vocal chords.

When the spectators finally made their way inside Manhattan Field, they were awed by what they saw. "It was exactly as though you were in a pit or in the mouth of a monster crater lined to its edges with human beings," a *New York Sun* reporter observed. "It would be worth coming to Manhattan Field on Thanksgiving Day even if one had to turn around and go out and away before a single play was made."

The field was ringed by a four-foot fence. Just beyond it was a mass of humanity, all standing, with a poor, albeit comparatively cheap, view of the playing surface. Behind them the grandstands rose majestically, jammed to the gills. On the north end of the field, the stands had been divided into more luxurious covered boxes, the domain of some members of the aristocratic set. Below them were the carriages and Tally-hos, their occupants on the roofs, dining on scrumptious meals of chicken, cranberry sauce, and mince pies—while washing it all down with champagne. Some dignitaries, including New York mayor Thomas Gilroy, mingled in a clubhouse on the east side of the field. The bluff and viaduct dwellers loomed in the distance. There were people as far as the eye could see—a crowd estimated at 50,000.

As kickoff neared, the weather steadily improved. The sun peeked through the clouds and temperatures climbed into the upper forties. In the standing-room areas, fans jostled for position. On the bridge near the viaduct, men fought each other to look through a narrow hole in the boarding. The reward? A view of part of a single goalpost. This was deemed worth fighting for. An enterprising group of fans on the field broke down a portion of the fencing and quickly constructed a make-shift platform, thus obstructing the view of those standing behind them. Understandably, this didn't go over so well, and another group knocked the legs out from under the structure, sending the men sprawling to the grass. Just when it seemed a fight might break out, the crowd erupted in an earsplitting roar. The players had taken the field.

The Princeton men charged out from their dressing quarters with great enthusiasm. One player, David Balliet, was so excited that he did cartwheels as he ran out with his teammates. Three other Tigers per-formed a pre-orchestrated dance of sorts, which ended with the trio all burying their noses in the grass, as if savoring its fine aroma. They were decided underdogs in the game. Not only had they not defeated the pow-erful Elis since 1889, they hadn't even managed to score a point against them in that span—dropping the three games by a combined tally of 63–0. They weren't the only ones who had struggled with Yale, though. The Elis had won a remarkable thirty-seven games in a row. In that span, they had outscored their opponents by an amazing total of 1,285 to 6.

The Yale men came out in a more sedate and businesslike man-ner. Not surprisingly, they conveyed an air of great confidence. The public shared that sentiment. The bets that Billy Edwards had taken at the Hoffman House all week favored Yale by odds of better than two to one.

The players emerged for warm-ups in their full uniforms. On top they wore snugly fitting canvas jackets that laced up the front—similar to the so-called "smocks" introduced in 1877 by Tiger halfback Ledu Smock. Below that they sported canvas pants that went down to the knees, where they met the players' socks. Over the socks, some players wore shin guards made of cork and covered with leather or canvas, a piece of equipment that had been introduced earlier in that very same year. Padding under the uniforms, made of layered cotton or wool, had become more prominent in recent seasons, though it was by no means universal. Players donned whatever amount they felt comfortable with. Many of the men wore rubber nose guards, which were held in place by a rubber band that was strapped around the back of the head. It was a device that had been introduced by the cartwheeling Balliet three years earlier when he played for Lehigh, and subsequently refined by Edgar Allan Poe, former Tiger captain and grand-nephew of the famous poet.

The most distinctive feature of the players, though, was their hair. Though a few gridiron men had begun to wear headgear, it would not come into widespread use for several years. Instead, footballers grew their hair long, in the belief that their flowing locks would provide the padding necessary to protect them. "That of 'Phil' King of Princeton has been envied by every football player in the country," the *New York Times* had written that morning of the Tiger quarterback's hair style. "His golden locks resemble a huge chrysanthemum; they cover his eyes and ears, and he claims that he can butt a stone wall without the least fear of fracturing his skull or causing a concussion of the brain."

King was more than just a newspaper scribe's modern-day Samson, though. He was also Princeton's best player. "If the Tigers down old Eli today, King will be in the thickest of the fray," the *Times* wrote of Princeton's 5'7", 159-pound star. "That chrysanthemum head will be seen everywhere, tackling, interfering, punting, and making runs toward the blue goal. A fair-minded lover of the game, who has had years of experience, said last night that King is the superior of any football player in the country."

In the days before radio and television, football fans, the majority of whom never got to see the players in action, counted almost entirely on the opinions of newspaper men to help them understand and appreciate the game. And the papers were up to the task, painting prose pictures of dramatic action and larger-than-life heroes. The *New York Sun*, which sent seventeen reporters to the game and would devote roughly 20 percent of the next day's paper to its coverage, didn't disappoint. It conveyed the mammoth task that faced King and his teammates. "They were all there," the *Sun* reported of the Elis team, "the giants, Hickok and

Stillman; Hinkey, the silent captain, whose visage scarred and seamed told of deeds of daring on many field; Butterworth, the full back, upon whom Yale counted so much; Thorne, swathed in bandages and wearing a nose mask. . . ." On and on it went, building the drama.

And the truth was, it was dramatic. The anticipation was so great that as Princeton prepared to kick off to Yale, a remarkable hush came over the throng. They had waited for this for so long, talked about it so much, and now, it was finally here. The tension was almost too much to bear.

Almost immediately, it became apparent that the powerful Elis were in for a battle. The first handful of possessions saw only minimal gains for both sides. It was a time when the forward pass was still illegal, meaning there were only two ways to move the ball—running it and kicking it. Teams had three downs to make five yards, but if their field position was poor, they often chose to punt on first or second down. The reasoning was simple. Fumbles were commonplace, and the penalty for many of the rules infractions was a loss of the ball at the spot of the foul. Coupled with a scoring system that gave more value to a field goal than a touchdown, the decision to run a play close to your own goal line was a risky one.

As the first half moved along, it was the Tigers who were getting the better of the battle, ripping off several long runs. They had discovered two weak points in the Yale line—the tackle spots manned by Fred Murphy and Anson Beard. They capitalized by using one of the game's newest and most brutal innovations—the flying wedge, in which a mass of players would start well behind the line of scrimmage in a V formation, timing their arrival at the line with the snap of the ball and concentrating the impact on one unfortunate opponent. The ball carrier would then run through the vacated spot. As football historian Parke Davis remarked many years later, "the impact was such that the objective point usually remembered it for years."

Indeed, injuries became part of the story of the game. About midway through the first half, Princeton's J. R. Blake, racing with his head down on a dead run in an attempt to scoop up a punt, was leveled by Yale captain Frank Hinkey. Hinkey got the worst of the collision. "The shock," the *Sun* reported, "was enough to break the neck of a bull." Yale's star lay dazed on the field as blood cascaded out from his head and his right ear.

Almost instantly, a medical brigade from the Yale sideline ran onto the field. One man carried a bag of instruments, another had a satchel full of medicines. Others sprinted out with water and sponges. After briefly laying on the turf in a daze, Hinkey staggered to his feet. He could barely walk and shook his head from side to side as he was helped to the sidelines. The doctors feverishly went to work on him. Under the rules of the day, they had five minutes to get him back on the field. If Hinkey was replaced by a substitute, he would not be allowed to return to the game at any point. Most in the crowd assumed the medical effort would be in vain.

And yet, a few minutes later, Hinkey reappeared. His head was wrapped tightly in a bandage, which had been covered in plaster in an effort to stem the flow of blood from his ear, the lobe of which had been torn away from his head. His neck and jersey were covered in crimson stains. At the sight of their star, the Yale fans erupted with cheers and chanted, "Hinkey! Hinkey! Hinkey!" while the 157-pound dynamo made his way back toward his teammates. A man of few words, he gathered the Yale players around him and said simply, "Come, boys, let us get to work."

But it was the Tigers who seized the momentum. After an exchange of several kicks and fumbles, a short Yale punt gave Princeton the ball at their opponent's 25-yard line. A series of runs by halfbacks William Ward and Frank Morse, aimed at Murphy and Beard, gave Princeton a first down at the Yale four-yard line. The Tigers' supporters were in a frenzy. A small group near the goal line began to chant, "Four, four, four yards more!" Soon, the yell spread throughout the stadium. The seemingly invincible Elis were in serious trouble.

Two straight runs by Ward netted a shade more than three yards. The Tigers had one last chance, from a bit more than two feet away. The sound of 50,000 screaming voices was nearly deafening. The snap went to King, who lateraled it to Ward. His teammates, in a completely legal maneuver, grouped behind him and pushed him over the goal line.

The celebration was instantaneous and ear piercing—a roar that began close to the field and quickly spread up to the bluff and the viaduct. Princeton orange was everywhere, with fans waving their flags and banners in sheer jubilation. On the sidelines, the substitutes turned somersaults while the coaches broke into massive grins and vigorously shook one another's hands. The four-point touchdown was followed by the equivalent of the modern extra point—a two-point goal kicked by King.

While pandemonium reigned in Harlem, 75 miles away in New Haven, the mood was one of shock. A local telephone company had erected a special scoreboard outside its offices. The results of each play were wired in from Manhattan. When he received them, the device's operator maneuvered puppets that had been suspended on a wire rigged between two goalposts to provide a visual summary of the action. Hundreds had gathered there to witness this modern marvel, and, "when the Princeton puppet juggled the ball behind the Yale goal, dead silence prevailed."

Though Princeton was unable to score again, the second half played out largely like the first. The Tigers had the only real scoring threats. Twice they drove deep into Yale territory, only to lose the ball on downs. Later, they missed a short attempt at a goal from the field—the modern equivalent of a field goal, which, had it been dropkicked through, would have given the Tigers five points.

While Princeton had blown several opportunities to put the game away, Yale was unable to take advantage of the miscues. The Tigers held the field-position advantage for most of the half, forcing the Elis to punt early on several possessions. When Yale did try to move the ball, it met fierce resistance from the strong Princeton line, "and the Yale team fell back baffled and chagrined." On top of that, the Elis repeatedly shot themselves in the foot with a series of penalties and fumbles that hindered their progress.

The game was stopped numerous times in the second half in order to treat the growing list of wounded. After a wedge play that sent a Princeton back into the Yale line for two yards, Balliet remained on the turf, as blood "poured in a torrent down the neck and chest of the big Princeton centre." It was an injury highly reminiscent of the one that Hinkey had suffered in the first half, and, like Hinkey, after a few minutes of treatment, Balliet was able to continue. "[T]he game went on as though torn ears were a necessary adjunct," observed the *Sun*.

Darkness began to descend on the field. It became difficult for the fans to make out the players. For those on Coogan's Bluff and the viaduct, the game at this point was nothing more than a rumor. Though time still remained on the clock, the referee, former Harvard captain W. A. Brooks, decided to call the contest due to darkness. Yale had lost a football game for the first time in more than three years.

Instantly, the Princeton fans descended on the field and mobbed their Tiger heroes—many of them plowing into distraught Yale players as they went. The Tigers would celebrate with their rooters that night, but at this moment, they wanted to be with one another. They hustled through the throng to their dressing room. With fans pounding on the doors and windows of the facility, the men whooped and hollered among themselves. Then, after being urged to do so by a coach, the naked, bloody, sweaty, and mud-caked players sang the school's doxology.

"This may strike some as a very sacrilegious performance," Davis observed later. "But the spirit in which it was done has a great deal to do with the question, and anyone who has seen a defeated team lying on the benches of their dressing room, sobbing like schoolgirls, can understand how great and how serious is the joy of victory to the men who conquer."

The team was driven to its headquarters at the Murray Hill Hotel, where the celebration went long into the night. The Princeton players were modest and gracious in victory. "It wasn't an afternoon tea by a long shot," said right guard Knox Taylor, "but it's all the better to think over because the Yale men did play so well." As for the Elis, the battered Hinkey "preserved his reputation for wisdom by saying, 'I have nothing to say.'"

Broadway was jammed with delirious Princeton fans, waving flags and twirling their hats on their canes, all while screaming Tiger yells. By early evening the sidewalk was so clogged with revelers that they spilled out onto the street, making it impossible for carriages to pass. Many celebrants descended upon the area's theaters, disrupting the shows with their shouts and catcalls. By the end of the evening, the 30th Street jail was populated with between forty-five and fifty fans, most of them booked for disturbing the peace. Interestingly enough, the majority of the fans were not students—a telling gauge of the widespread nature of the game's impact.

In New Jersey, the few Princeton students who remained on campus during the Thanksgiving break made a racket of their own—ringing the college bell for four straight hours. As the townspeople joined in the celebration, exuberant students paraded to the homes of school professors and administrators demanding speeches. The academics cooperated. "Gentlemen," said one, "I congratulate you that Yale is nowhere and Princeton is everywhere."

Back at the Hoffman House, bookie Billy Edwards had plenty of work to do that night, collecting betting slips from the victorious Princeton fans and passing along their winnings. In all, an estimated $100,000 changed hands, with the biggest losses coming from Wall Street, where several Yale men lost thousands in bets with colleagues at the New York Stock Exchange.

In all, rules and technology aside, it was a day that felt much more like a modern college game than like that first intercollegiate contest between Rutgers and Princeton. What had begun as an informal, gentlemanly pursuit between students of rival universities was well on its way to becoming a thrilling nationwide spectacle.

CHAPTER TWO

THE KANGAROO KICKER

WISCONSIN'S PAT O'DEA STOOD ALONE, 12 YARDS BEHIND HIS CENTER, Roy Chamberlain, and 60 yards away from the goal post. He awaited the snap. It was a seemingly ordinary moment very early in a seemingly ordinary football game—Thanksgiving Day, 1898. O'Dea's Badgers were at Sheppard Field in Evanston, Illinois, taking on Northwestern.

The Wisconsin captain called out the signals. "Nine, ten," the lanky Australian yelled. "Nine, ten." His teammates looked at him incredulously. Unbeknownst to the Northwestern players and the 3,000 or so fans looking on, Pat O'Dea was attempting to make history.

Five years after he had helped lead Princeton to its shocking victory over Yale, former Tiger quarterback Phil King had a new Thanksgiving challenge on his hands. King was in his third year as the football coach at Wisconsin. His initial seasons had been remarkable successes, as the Badgers had captured the first two championships of the newly formed Western Conference, the precursor of the modern-day Big Ten.

In O'Dea, Wisconsin boasted one of the Midwest's first true superstars. He didn't necessarily look the part of a rugged football player. Though unusually tall for the time at nearly 6'2", he weighed just 170 pounds. He was strikingly handsome. His pleasant and expressive face was topped by a generous helping of seemingly never ruffled light brown hair that swooped dramatically across his forehead in a right-handed part. It was O'Dea's legs that really stood out, though, described by one contemporary as "abnormally long and wonderfully developed." Those legs were his weapon of choice. In a short period of time, they had earned him remarkable fame. He drew headlines everywhere he went—the most celebrated kicker in the country at a time when, due to the nature of the rules, the kicker could literally take over the game. With O'Dea booting and the Badgers winning, Wisconsin games were always a big deal. Always, that is, until this one.

The Badgers were coming off a devastating defeat—having fallen 6–0 twelve days before to the University of Chicago. The game was played in miserable field conditions. The mud-caked ball and the inability to plant his feet solidly had neutralized O'Dea's effectiveness. Wisconsin's typical offensive strategy revolved almost exclusively around the Aussie's kicks. With their primary weapon severely limited, the Badgers had fallen apart.

Losing to a conference foe for the first time in more than two seasons had been bad enough, but that the defeat had come at the hands of the Maroons was particularly galling for King. The Wisconsin–Chicago rivalry had quickly become a bitter one—pitting the Badgers' coach against his Chicago counterpart, Amos Alonzo Stagg, whom he viewed as a poor sport.

The antipathy was fueled by debates over a couple of the hot-button issues of the day: player eligibility and the division of gate receipts. It had gotten so bad that the two schools had briefly ceased athletic relations the previous spring before agreeing to an uneasy truce over the course of the summer.

While their mutual boycott was behind them, the acerbic feeling remained. O'Dea had said before the battle with Chicago that it "meant more to Wisconsin than any game of football we ever have played." The loss had been a difficult one to swallow.

The problem now was that it was almost impossible to put the defeat out of their minds. The Badgers were just minutes away from kicking off their game against Northwestern. Yet it was Stagg's Maroons who had stolen the headlines during the course of the week, as Thanksgiving Day had drawn nearer. They were scheduled to host Michigan at Marshall Field on their Hyde Park campus at exactly the same time the Badgers and Purple were squaring off in Evanston. Since neither team had lost to another Western Conference foe all season, the Michigan–Chicago game was now the battle for the championship. The contest between the Badgers and a middling Northwestern team was, in many ways, meaningless. "The game at Marshall Field is undoubtedly the star attraction of the day," the *Chicago Tribune* had commented that morning. Even King and his players would have been hard-pressed to disagree.

Now, as he stood before the team in the cramped dressing room wedged under the grandstand at Sheppard Field, King couldn't help but notice the ambivalence. His players simply weren't used to being in this position. The coach sensed they needed some inspiration. So, just moments before the Badgers were to take the field for the final pregame warm-ups, King delivered a short, unconventional speech. "Gentlemen," he told the players, "score in the first two minutes, and tonight, we'll celebrate with all the champagne you can drink."

The cheer that went up from the players was quickly replaced by mild panic. Two minutes? As powerful as the Badgers were, two minutes wasn't a whole lot of time—particularly in an era when the forward pass was still illegal and results like that 6–0 final against Chicago twelve days before were commonplace. Still, the team charged onto the field with a new-found sense of purpose.

They were greeted by a surprisingly energized crowd. Though Northwestern had endured a difficult season, the lure of a Thanksgiving Day game and a battle with O'Dea and the Badgers was strong enough to fill the grandstand, a covered wood-and-brick structure that stood at one end of the playing field, behind the north goalpost. These were the most exclusive seats—packed with many of Evanston and Madison's most prominent citizens.

Fans lined the sidelines as well, cramming the ten or so rows of bleachers, one side made up predominantly of rooters wearing Wisconsin cardinal, in sharp contrast with the Northwestern purple on the other. The many women in the crowd were particularly resplendent. Enormous feathers flowed from their hats and long pieces of colored ribbons cascaded from their jackets. Alongside the bleachers, horses munched idly on hay as they stood in front of the carriages that had carried many of the fans to the game. Some of the larger coaches were occupied by members of Northwestern's boat club, as well as some fraternities and sororities.

Those students were ready for O'Dea. In its most recent edition, the Northwestern student newspaper had chastised them for their sub-par singing several weeks earlier in a narrow one-point loss to a superior Michigan team. "Song is the most potent thing to awaken spirit and spontaneity in college gatherings," the editors of *The Northwestern* had reminded their readers. In response, the Evanston undergraduates had redoubled their efforts, belting out the university songs each day at chapel. In addition, they had prepared a special tune for the Thanksgiving Day game, sung to the melody of "The Grand Old Duke of York" and aimed squarely at Wisconsin's superstar. The students sang along, as the Northwestern band blasted the tune from its spot in the bleachers:

> The poor old Pat O'Dea,
> He had a wooden leg,
> He shot it up on Sheppard Field,
> Then shot it down again.

Seemingly unfazed, O'Dea went through his warm-ups, which in and of themselves were worth the price of admission. He boomed jaw-dropping punts and converted remarkable dropkicks, routinely splitting the uprights from distances others could only dream of. In a time when field goals were worth five points, one more than touchdowns, and teams often punted on first down, kicker was the single most glamorous position on the field, and the handsome, exotic, and talented O'Dea was redefining the position. He was the best kicker in the West, and fans in that part of the country believed he was superior to any player in football.

Of course, they couldn't say for sure. Games between Eastern and Western teams were virtually unheard of, so most of them had never seen the players from the traditional powerhouses like Yale, Harvard, and Princeton—the schools that had invented the game about thirty years earlier. Those colleges were the gold standard. The West was an afterthought. A total of 187 players had been named "All-Americans" since the first selections were made back in 1889. All 187 had been from the East. In an era when travel was difficult, the Eastern writers never journeyed West to watch games, confident there was nothing to see out in the hinterlands.

When warm-ups were over, O'Dea and Northwestern captain Clarence Thorne met at midfield. Wisconsin won the opening coin toss, which automatically gave a team the ball as well as the choice of which goal to head toward. O'Dea chose the north goal, though the difference was negligible. After an unseasonably warm week, which had seen the temperatures peak in the mid-sixties just three days earlier, the weather in the Chicago area had turned bitterly cold over the past couple of days, with lows in the single digits and highs well below freezing. Still, Sheppard Field was bathed in sunshine, and the day was almost completely devoid of any wind, a bit of a rarity given that the playing surface lay only a few hundred yards from the typically blustery shores of Lake Michigan.

The Purple kicked off to O'Dea, who caught the ball at his own ten-yard line and ran it back to the twenty. Then, in an effort to improve their field position, O'Dea and the Badgers chose to punt the ball right back to Northwestern, hoping to pin their opponents deep in their own territory.

O'Dea's kicking style was an unusual one. When he made contact with the ball, he did so with both feet off of the ground—appearing almost to jump at the pigskin. He did this on both punts and dropkicks, that now-obsolete form of kicking in which a player would bounce the ball off the grass and kick it on its way back up. Though placekicks played a minor role in the game, dropkicks were the typical way to convert a goal.

What O'Dea's approach lacked in convention, it more than made up for in effectiveness. He unleashed a phenomenal punt, one that spun high in the air before landing 50 yards down the 110-yard field, at

Northwestern's 35-yard line. Northwestern kicked it right back, but the punt was a poor one, giving the Badgers the ball near midfield. In light of the improved field position, Wisconsin chose to hang onto the ball and try to move it toward the Purple goal, hoping to gain the requisite five yards in three downs.

O'Dea was far and away the best athlete on the Wisconsin team. In fact, a little more than a year earlier, he had briefly held the world record in the 300-yard hurdles. But, due to the violent nature of the game, King was reticent to use him as a primary ball carrier, out of fear of losing his most valuable weapon. Instead, the Badgers tried two halfback runs, neither of which netted any yardage. The game was nearly two minutes old. O'Dea dropped a dozen yards behind the line and barked out the shocking "nine, ten" signal.

"Slam" Anderson didn't believe what he had heard. As one of the two ends for the Badgers, his duties changed significantly depending on O'Dea's signal call. On a punt, Anderson's job was to race down the field as fast as he could in an effort to tackle the opponent's return man. On a dropkick, Anderson would stay in, blocking the opponent's rusher in order to give O'Dea time to get his boot off. Yes, he knew that O'Dea had called out a signal for a dropkick—but he also knew that it was a preposterous notion. The Aussie was 60 yards from the goal. No one in the history of the game had ever converted a dropkick from farther than 55 yards out.

Convinced that O'Dea had simply misspoken, Anderson sprinted down the gridiron at the snap. That decision nearly doomed the play to failure. When the Aussie caught the ball, he almost immediately had a Northwestern rusher in his face, in prime position to block the kick. It was the man Anderson had neglected to block. O'Dea avoided him with a quick sidestep move, let the ball bounce, and simultaneous with it hitting the ground made perfect contact with his right foot, resulting in a mighty dropkick. The ball flew more than half the length of the field on an awe-inspiring arc, seemingly on a collision course with the grandstand behind the north goalpost. It sailed squarely between the posts and over a fence that lined the field, landing easily 10 yards beyond the goal line, just in front of the stands. O'Dea had booted it at least 210 feet. In a game where lengthy kicks were celebrated the way long runs or passes are today, this was the single most remarkable football play anyone in attendance had ever witnessed.

The initial reaction was one of stunned silence. That bewilderment soon turned to an orgy of sound. Wisconsin fans hugged one another and threw their hats into the air. The game umpire, Everts Wrenn, himself somewhat astonished, signaled a goal. The only person in Evanston who didn't seem fazed by the achievement was O'Dea himself, who, perhaps eager to get on with the now-assured champagne feast, called on his team to assemble at midfield for the ensuing kickoff.

The early 5–0 lead quickly ballooned, as the Badgers went on to win 47–0. O'Dea's record-breaking kick was the story. The *Milwaukee Sentinel* led its entire paper with a bold front-page headline in the left-most column blaring: O'DEA KICKS A 60-YARD GOAL. Just to the right was the story deemed the second most important of the day, announcing that the Spanish cabinet had authorized the signing of the peace treaty that would end the Spanish-American War.

The *Sentinel* praised not just O'Dea's foot, but his all-around game, declaring in another headline that O'DEA PLAYED THE GAME OF HIS LIFE. "The tall young man from Australia shone brilliantly in every play," the paper reported. "He repeatedly saved his men from the exhausting work of line bucking by his famous long punts. He mixed in every scrimmage as he has never done before. He sprinted around the ends for several long runs of 40 yards or less. He tackled low and hard and interfered well for his running mates. O'Dea was preeminently the star of the big Thanksgiving game."

The *Chicago Tribune* described O'Dea's performance as "miraculous," continuing: "Everyone figured O'Dea would work havoc with the chances of the home team, but that he would do such phenomenal punting and drop-kicking as that which electrified the crowd was beyond the wildest dreams of his most ardent supporters." The *Duluth News Tribune* put it more succinctly, saying simply, "Pat O'Dea is king."

And it wasn't just the newspapermen who left in awe of O'Dea's performance. Umpire Wrenn told the *Chicago Times-Herald* afterward that he knew "of no performance on the gridiron to equal O'Dea's wonderful drop kick and goal from the sixty-yard line." King added, "It almost took my breath away to see him try it. I never heard of the goal being made from any distance within ten yards of this new record."

O'Dea's postgame comments were consistent with his on-field demeanor. "I was not surprised at all at making the goal," the Aussie said later. Though there was certainly plenty of newspaper ink spilled regarding Michigan's 12–11 win over Stagg's Maroons, O'Dea's kick made headlines nationwide and gained the attention of the Eastern establishment. At the end of the 1898 season, the Aussie was one of the first Westerners ever named to the All-American team. The legend of "The Kangaroo Kicker" was born.

CHAPTER THREE

FROM SCRUMMAGE TO SCRIMMAGE

PEOPLE HAVE BEEN CONGREGATING TO KICK ROUND OBJECTS FOR centuries—like the craniums of dead people, for instance. Legend has it that the residents of Chester, England, began a tradition of Shrove Tuesday football matches during the Middle Ages, when townspeople amused themselves by booting the skull of a Danish pirate, who, presumably, would have been less amused, had he been around to see it.

By the 1400s, inflated swine bladders had somewhat mercifully replaced skulls. Games were prevalent enough and, apparently, seen as enough of a nuisance, that King James I of Scotland was moved to ban "all rough and violent exercises, as the foot-ball" in 1424. The decree evidently had little impact, as history is littered with descriptions of similar games. A match in the village of Scone, Scotland, for instance, pitted the married men against the bachelors, with one group shooting the bladder into a hole in a field while the other looked to kick it into the river.

Related games made their way to the United States and onto college campuses. In the mid-1800s, Harvard students began each new term with interclass football matches. The sophomores used the violent kicking sport as a means of initiating the freshmen into college life, a tradition known as "Bloody Monday." Those games grew so heated that the faculty banned them in 1860, threatening those who failed to heed the prohibition with expulsion.

Up until the latter half of the nineteenth century, the games that were permitted had a tenor of informality. Classmates or friends would simply gather and play for nothing beyond the sake of playing. It was fun. It was something to do. So, what changed? How did it go from a leisurely activity to an organized sport contested in front of tens of thousands of paid spectators?

The game took off on college campuses due, in part, to a national mentality shift, as intense physical activity became more acceptable. In the eighteenth and early nineteenth century, leisure time at a university was spent in intellectual pursuits. Speech making and oration were the most popular pastimes. Not only was physical prowess deemed unimportant, it was looked down upon. "A man who was known to be gifted in this way, was thereby disparaged in public estimation; if he were known to make much of it, he was more likely to be despised," observed the *Harvard Graduates' Magazine.* "The only things to be admired were mind and soul."

Interestingly, the battle for that soul was experiencing a similar change. Men, in particular, were finding the Protestant movement to be unappealing. In 1832 English writer Frances Trollope observed of the United States that she had never seen a nation "where religion had such a strong hold upon the women or a slighter hold upon the men." That divide intensified over the course of the nineteenth century, as religion grew more and more feminized. As historian Michael Kimmel observes, this passive message even showed up in depictions of Jesus: "a thin, reedy man with long, bony fingers and a lean face with soft, doelike eyes." It led one observer to ask rhetorically, "Have we a Religion for Men?"

Muscular Christianity, a mid-nineteenth-century movement that coupled Christian evangelism with unabashed virility, helped change that mind-set. Physical strength, once seen as antithetical with religious piety, was gradually recognized as a mechanism for bringing men back to the church and thus spreading God's word. Images depicting Jesus "at his carpenter's bench, with sleeves rolled up, leather apron around his torso, and his strong set eyes gazing heavenward, fused the sacred and the muscular."

Influential ministers such as Josiah Strong warned that a faith "which ignores the physical life becomes more or less mystical or effeminate, loses its virility and has little influence over men or affairs." The impact of this shift in thinking was widespread. Elmer Johnson, who wrote a history of the YMCA, observed of the late 1800s that "almost every sport, program feature, training institution, and operational principle of any consequence or enduring value had its origin in this period."

While changing belief systems made the football-like games more palatable, it was the dramatic shifts in education and population that made them practical. More young men were attending college than ever before, thanks to what can only be termed as a nineteenth-century college-starting frenzy. As one historian put it, "Americans founded colleges, then searched for students to serve." By 1870 there were roughly five hundred degree-granting universities in the United States, more than in all of Europe combined.

The growth of universities was accompanied by a lifestyle shift, as Americans increasingly left their agrarian past behind in favor of the city life. The Industrial Revolution crowded people closer together, and their shorter workdays left them with time on their hands—time that could be spent playing or watching sports. As one university history noted, "Given a large number of healthy young men, the talent for organization always present in such a group, relatively easy transportation of players and newspapers eager to dramatize the events, the stage was set for the rise of intercollegiate athletics."

What was new on that fall day in 1869 when the men from Princeton journeyed to New Brunswick wasn't the game itself. The breakthrough was the concept of one school playing against another. Football wasn't born that day; intercollegiate football was.

That being said, there was no real uniform code for what the game would be. Those informal contests that were played between students on campus all had the same overriding idea—that of kicking a ball through goalposts. But there were many variations on the theme and subtle nuances in the rules that had to be agreed upon.

At the time, no American schools were playing rugby, a game that, legend had it, began at the Rugby School in England in the 1820s when a young student picked up the soccer ball and began to run with it. But many weren't playing pure soccer, either. For instance, some schools permitted the ball to be batted with the hands. Others allowed players to catch it and, if they did, to get an unencumbered free kick at the goal. Princeton students generally played by the latter rule, while Rutgers did not permit catching. So, the two teams agreed to play without free kicks in New Brunswick but to allow them in the second of the two games, which was to be played in Princeton the following week. In the end, the game that was played that November day in 1869 would appear to a modern spectator to be an amalgam of soccer and rugby, though any resemblances to the latter were coincidental.

About fifty "rooters" made the 20-mile journey with the Princeton players to New Brunswick. The students spent the early afternoon hours with their hosts—walking around town and passing time playing billiards. Then, in the mid-afternoon, they assembled on an open field near campus for the game.

Each team was made up of twenty-five players. The Rutgers men wore red shirts to distinguish themselves. Some wrapped scarlet turbans around their heads. A group of several hundred spectators lounged on the grass alongside the field to watch, while others sat on a nearby fence. Rutgers took an early 4–2 lead, before Princeton battled back to tie the match at four. The men in scarlet scored the final two goals, though, and prevailed 6–4.

The result, however, was truly secondary. The aim of the day was to have fun, which both sides clearly did. "After the match the players had an amicable 'feed' together," the *Rutgers Targum* reported, "and at eight o'clock our guests went home in high spirits, but trusting to beat us next time, if they can."

And they did. Princeton won the rematch 8–0, but, again, the social component of the day was the story. The Princeton men prepared lunch for the Rutgers team beforehand, then hosted a banquet after the game.

"Speeches and songs, accompanied, of course, by the study of practical gastronomy, passed the time pleasantly until the evening train bore us Brunswickward," read the *Targum* account. "We thank them for their hospitality. If we must be beaten we are glad to have such conquerors." That general attitude prevailed in the early years of the game. Schools only played a few matches each year and little emphasis was placed on the results.

But that tenor changed fairly dramatically in 1876. That year Yale elected a new captain, Eugene V. Baker. Baker instilled in his men a will to win and aimed to do so through far more strenuous training methods than football players had ever seen before. The student body quickly rallied behind the cause. "All in college who can play at all," the *Yale Courant* urged in the autumn of 1876, "especially the larger and heavier men, should be out every afternoon for practice. Let there be no holding back on the part of any."

That same fall, representatives from Yale, Harvard, Princeton, and Columbia met in Springfield, Massachusetts, to codify a uniform set of rules. They also decided to crown a champion at the end of the season. It was a seemingly minor step, but it had far-reaching consequences. The game was no longer simply about playing. It was now about winning.

No school won quite like Yale. Fueled by the "Yale Spirit" that Baker had infused, the men from New Haven lost just once between 1876 and 1884. The team became a source of pride on campus, to the point where, by 1878, students were congregating to watch practice. "The interest which the university feels in the game even surpasses that of last year, and the number and strength of the players who have been brought to light are most encouraging," the *Courant* reported, adding, "all should make a common effort by doing what lies in his power to put in the field the strongest possible team to represent us." The faculty did its part, as, in that same year, players were first allowed to miss class for games.

In that 1878 season, Yale had a new captain, a New Haven native named Walter Chauncey Camp. The son of a schoolteacher, Camp had grown up near the university, and, inspired by the Yale football team, the gawky young man undertook a Spartan training regimen. He swore off sweets, ran through the countryside on his own to build endurance, and began each morning with a set of secret calisthenics in his bedroom. Though he weighed only 156 pounds when he enrolled at Yale in 1876, Camp had evolved into a well-conditioned, impressive athlete. He made an immediate impact on the football field and quickly earned the respect of his teammates.

"When [Camp] was elected captain in his junior year, his quarters in Durfee Hall became the campus shrine, and his word the law," one biographer noted. "If disputes within the team arose, he would gravely state his position and leave the room with a solemn promise to resign if the vote went against him. He always won." Camp's close association with the operations of the Yale football team continued up until the day of his death in 1925 at the age of sixty-six. If Yale was the first football factory, Walter Camp was its foreman.

Though Camp was a fine player, his greatest contributions came off the field, as the single most influential member of the football rules committee. His playing days coincided with a series of dramatic changes in the game.

In the spring of 1874, McGill University of Montreal came to Cambridge to play Harvard. The Canadian school played rugby rather than the soccer-type game favored by the American colleges. Harvard was quickly converted. "The Rugby game is much better favor than the somewhat sleepy game now played by our men," the *Harvard Advocate* declared afterward.

The next year Harvard challenged Yale to a rugby match. Though Yale insisted on a few concessions, the men from New Haven essentially agreed to abandon soccer and play by Harvard's rugby rules. The match was a huge hit—not only with the students who played in it, but also with the spectators, including a couple of Princeton men, who went back home and convinced their schoolmates to essentially switch sports. "The 1875 meeting of Harvard and Yale," football historian Alexander Weyand wrote, "was the game that sold Rugby to the American colleges."

At the same 1876 Springfield meeting that brought about the concept of a championship, the schools agreed to play rugby, rather than soccer, going forward.

As Yale's captain, Camp first attended the rules meeting in 1878, and he quickly began to advocate for change. His most passionate crusade was for the elimination of the "scrummage," which was the manner in which a play started in rugby. When the ball was downed, the men from each side joined together and, arms interlocked, tried to kick it free.

"The original scrummage was a weird and unscientific institution. The ball belonged to neither side," observed Amos Alonzo Stagg. "It was dull business for the backs and the onlookers. For long periods the ball could not be seen and nothing happened. All the spectators could distinguish was a ton and a half of heavyweights leaning pantingly against one another. Eventually the ball would pop out by accident or surrender, a back would seize it for a run, be tackled and downed, and back went the ball into scrummage."

Camp's solution was what came to be known as the scrimmage. Instead of reestablishing possession each time the ball was downed, Camp believed that the downed team ought to retain possession and simply start the play anew. This rule passed at the 1880 convention, along with the reduction to eleven players. American football was born.

There were some stops and starts along the way over the next few years. In the early days, a team that had been declared the champion the previous season had to lose in order to be dethroned. They could retain the championship with a tie. This led to so-called "block" games, where the past season's champion would intentionally play for a scoreless draw, repeatedly snapping and downing the ball.

Again, Camp had the solution—the concept of downs. In order to retain the ball, Camp suggested, why not mandate that a team had to gain a certain amount of yardage? His recommendation passed in 1882, with the committee deciding on three downs to make five yards.

Camp next tackled the game's byzantine scoring system. The method for determining a winner in the early days of football was complicated, focusing on accomplishments rather than points and weighing the accomplishments relatively against one another. By means of example, a goal (a successful kick through the uprights) equaled four touchdowns. Goals could be kicked in one of two ways—either from the field in the run of play or after a team scored a touchdown. So, for instance, one team could hypothetically score three touchdowns and miss all of the kicks afterward and lose to a team that scored just one touchdown but converted the kick.

At the 1883 rules convention, Camp pushed through a plan that assigned numerical values to the scoring plays. Beginning with the 1884 campaign, goals from the field counted for five points, goals after touchdowns counted for four points, and touchdowns themselves were valued at two points. The following year, the value of the touchdown and the goal after touchdown was reversed, and by 1898 the touchdown was worth five points and the goal afterward counted for just one.

So, in eight short years, intercollegiate football had changed quite dramatically. Soccer had been replaced by rugby, the scrummage had given way to the scrimmage, the concept of downs had been introduced, and, finally, a scoring system had been devised. And, though historians debate whether all of these ideas were Camp's alone, he was clearly the driving force that pushed them through.

While the students and recent graduates on the rules committee felt better and better about the game they were creating, football almost immediately met resistance from the various university faculties. In 1873 Michigan challenged Cornell to a game in Buffalo, an invitation that was quickly rebuffed by the university president in Ithaca, Andrew White, who said dismissively, "I will not permit thirty men to travel four hundred miles merely to agitate a bag of wind."

While early objections were due primarily to a sense that the game conflicted with the broader mission of universities, violence was also a concern—and justifiably so. Accounts of early games are chock-full of sentences like this one, describing the 1884 meeting between Yale and Princeton: "There came a crush on one of the edges of the field about midway between the goals. All of the maddened giants of both the teams were in it and they lay heaped, kicking, choking, hitting, gouging and howling." Any modern-day football fans yearning for a return to a simpler, halcyon time when the game was enjoyed by well-mannered and cultured Ivy Leaguers should quickly disabuse themselves of that notion. There was no such time.

The rules exacerbated the issue. For instance, a player wasn't technically down until he stopped moving, meaning a tackled player would often try to squirm forward on the ground, as members of the opposing team jumped on his back or head trying to stop his progress. Additionally, touchdowns didn't count until the ball had actually been touched to the ground, leading to brutal battles called the "maul-in-goal" where members of the defensive team would wrestle with an offensive player who had crossed the goal line to prevent him from placing the ball to the turf. Stagg described a battle in a practice game that lasted "for fifteen minutes—and I do not exaggerate." The maul was restricted to players who had their hands on the ball when the runner crossed the goal line. If a player lost contact with the ball, he could not rejoin the melee, "and if he attempts to do so, [he] may be dragged out by the opposite side."

By early 1885, influenced primarily by the violence in the game, Harvard decided it had seen enough. Declaring football to be "brutal, demoralizing to the players and to the spectators, and extremely dangerous," the school banned the game. The banishment was short-lived, though. Within a year, Harvard was back in the football association.

Other schools embraced the game more enthusiastically. Princeton's president-elect, Francis L. Patton, spoke glowingly of the sport when he addressed the school's alumni at a dinner in New York City in the spring of 1888. "I can well believe," Patton declared, "that out of these brawny contests, some of the very best elements of manhood may emerge." But Patton didn't just support the game with his words, he also did so with his actions, as, during the course of his administration, "intercollegiate athletics rose to an absorbing prestige, with a shocking apathy of conscience."

The absence of scruples likely had something to do with a benefit of the game that outweighed its manhood-building qualities—its ability to generate cash. "I am pretty sure," Patton noted, "that there are friends enough who will see to it that Princeton shall come behind Yale in no gift."

Indeed, money was rapidly becoming a major part of the football story. In the short period between 1885 and 1893, Yale's football-related revenues increased more than thirteen-fold. And, while the direct benefits of the game were enormous, schools quickly came to recognize that it had ancillary benefits. In 1891 a writer for the University of Kansas' student newspaper observed that the "influence and result of our football victories can hardly be estimated. . . . It has advertised the University more than an outlay of a thousand dollars could have done in any other way."

The expansion of the game to schools like Kansas was a major part of the football story, as the sport inspired a manifest destiny of sorts, quickly spreading west. In 1888 about sixty colleges had teams. Within a handful of years, that number had more than doubled. Many of the new adopters were west of the Alleghenies, schools such as Minnesota, Chicago, and Wisconsin. The proliferation was fueled by graduates of the "Big Three" who fanned out across the country like preachers, carrying the gospel of the game in a full-fledged diaspora. Football historian Parke Davis asserted that "at one time in this period there might have been counted no less than 45 former players of Yale, 35 of Princeton and 24 of Harvard actively engaged in teaching the science of the game." Football may have been objectionable to some, but it had too many forces working in its favor. Its rise coincided perfectly with the opening of new colleges desperate for attention and money.

Back east, schools began to recruit actively, often offering inducements to promising athletes. In the fall of 1889, former Yale captain Bill "Pa" Corbin telegraphed Camp, who was serving as Yale's football advisor. The subject was a prospect named Highland Stickney, who, it seems, was in search of a handout. "Stickney wrote," Corbin reported, "Have received good offers from Harvard and Princeton to play football. What will you give[?]" Apparently, not enough. Stickney landed in Cambridge.

By October of 1894, the *Galveston Daily News* declared the nation to be officially FOOTBALL MAD [WITH] THE WHOLE AMERICAN COUNTRY CRAZILY CHASING THE OVAL PIGSKIN ON THE GRIDIRON. After spending a day on campus with the Yale team for an article in the popular publication *Harper's Weekly*, Richard Harding Davis best summarized the growing football fervor when he quipped, "There is only one man in New Haven of more importance than Walter Camp, and I have forgotten his name. I think he is the president of the university."

In newspaper and magazine columns like that one, football had found its greatest ally and another mechanism to help expand the game's reach. The combination of cheap paper, evolving printing technology, enhanced distribution, and skyrocketing literacy rates coalesced to form an era of unprecedented power for newspapers and periodicals. They seized on sports in general and football in particular as a topic to help increase readership, through the newly created sports section of the paper.

Much of the coverage didn't even focus on the action on the field, as in many respects, the game was less important than the event. Football games—particularly the annual Thanksgiving Day contests in New York—were a place to see and be seen. The *New York Herald*'s coverage of the 1892 Thanksgiving Day game was typical. "Mrs. William C. Whitney had a conspicuous box, trimmed profusely in Yale colors and beautifully decorated with a bevy of young girls," the paper reported. "The silvery frost of the wintry atmosphere which settled upon the box framework was strangely similar to the glistening shades of her hair, and her café au lait broadcloth, with garnet and sable trimmings, made a' la Russian and royally fitted, enhanced her appearance.

"His Luminous Magnificence the Sun was patted pleasantly on the back by Mrs. Elliot Shepard when she stepped into the Shepard-Vanderbilt box and remarked, 'what a perfect day; what glorious sunshine!,'" the report continued. "And; indeed, the sun reciprocated thankfully to the compliment and smiled full and bright in her lovely face. Mrs. Shepard wore a burr brown broadcloth tailor made suit, with a soft Scotch turban of velvet and a spotted veil. . . ." And so it went for paragraph after nauseating paragraph.

So, it had all reached a confluence by the mid-1890s. Schools wanted more students, prestige, and money. Players wanted to win. Papers wanted to increase their circulation. Society people wanted to see their names in print. Meanwhile, half a world away, a young Australian was beginning to get restless.

CHAPTER FOUR

MASS PLAYS AND MASS POPULARITY

THE FUNERAL PROCESSION MOVED SLOWLY THROUGH THE STREETS OF Kilmore, Australia. Though it was the middle of the day, the bustling village was virtually shut down. The bankers, blacksmiths, tobacconists, and tailors had all closed their businesses so they could mourn one of Kilmore's most well-liked citizens, a man who one friend observed, "had not an enemy in the world."

Until just a few weeks before, Patrick Flannery O'Dea had been a vibrant and important part of the community. A successful proprietor, he operated the town's flour mill, living with his wife and family in a small cottage next to his business. Though he often remained on the sidelines when it came to public affairs, O'Dea was always quick to participate in charitable causes. Now, it was his bereaved family, shaken by the unexpected loss of its patriarch, that needed help. O'Dea's eight-year-old son, Patrick, shuffled along in the sad march to the cemetery, his life forever altered.

It was a family that had arrived in Australia like many others did—on a ship full of convicts. Patrick Flannery O'Dea's father-in-law, James Crossley, came from England in 1830 after being jailed for stealing caps. He served out his time in the new land as an indentured servant before taking a job as an "overlander," moving sheep and cattle through the unsettled countryside in search of verdant grazing lands. In 1838 he and a group of coworkers were attacked by Aborigines, a horrifying raid that killed eight of the eighteen men. Crossley was among the survivors. Perhaps scarred by the experience, he entered a different profession in the animal trade, opening a butcher shop in the new village of Kilmore.

Kilmore was permanently settled in 1843, generally regarded as the first inland town in the Port Phillip District, an area that is now known as Victoria. Located a bit less than 40 miles from Melbourne, Kilmore lay in the midst of a lightly timbered, undulating region, with fertile land that was ideal for farming and grazing.

While much of Australia's early population was made up of former English convicts like Crossley, a significant number of Irish helped settle the country as well. Patrick Flannery (P. F.) O'Dea was a native of County Clare, having arrived with his family in the 1840s at age eleven. His father, Patrick, went into business in the Victorian countryside, raising horses, cattle, and sheep. P. F. O'Dea and his brothers inherited the business when Patrick died. Though it was successful, it was also isolating. Wanting to move a little closer to civilization, P. F. O'Dea took a job operating the flour mill in Kilmore.

In 1863 P. F. O'Dea and Mary Johanna Crossley, James Crossley's eldest daughter, were married at St. Patrick's Cathedral in Kilmore. Over the next sixteen years, they had ten children, seven of whom survived infancy. Pat was the third-oldest surviving boy. He was born on March 16, 1872—though throughout his life he would claim to have arrived a day later. What Irishman wouldn't want a birthday on St. Patrick's Day? O'Dea was never one to let the truth get in the way of a good story.

By the time of Pat's birth, Kilmore was fairly well-populated, a town of about 1,500 people scattered among nearly 300 dwellings. It had a hospital, two newspapers, and a number of churches. A recently completed train line ran nearby, though the tracks were not extended into the town proper until 1888. A new state school, providing compulsory education up until the age of twelve, was completed in 1875. It was the pride of Kilmore, "well-ventilated to guard against any epidemic." Still, the village was a rather unremarkable place, with one visitor in the late nineteenth century observing that there wasn't anything "particularly worth stopping for."

Not long after her husband's death, Johanna, as O'Dea's mother was known, decided there wasn't anything particularly worth staying for, either. She moved the family closer to Melbourne. It was here that Pat O'Dea first entered the public eye.

Over the holiday break from school in 1888, the fifteen-year-old O'Dea accompanied classmate Robert Crooke to the Crooke family home in Mordialloc, a seaside town south of Melbourne. Their relaxation took a tragic turn on the afternoon of January 3.

Mrs. Crooke, whose name was Annie, took Pat, Robert, and Robert's younger brother Bertie to a beach on the shores of Port Phillip Bay. As was her custom, Annie, an adept swimmer, made her way out into the water. Suddenly, a huge wave struck her, carrying her over a sandbar, which separated the swimming area from the deeper waters.

The woman struggled mightily as she tried to make it back toward land. The boys quickly recognized her predicament. Bertie ran home to get his father, while Pat and Robert attempted to swim out to save Mrs. Crooke. Robert had to abandon his effort, but, as described by a local newspaper, Pat "pluckily swam out in the face of the breakers and he succeeded in obtaining a hold of the lady and in bringing her to shore." When they arrived on dry land, Annie Crooke was lifeless, and despite the best efforts of several onlookers, she could not be revived.

For his brave attempt to save Annie's life, O'Dea was awarded a bronze medal by the Royal Humane Society of Australia. Like his birthday and many other accomplishments to follow, the drowning incident would take on a life of its own.

In an early profile piece written on O'Dea in 1897, a *Milwaukee Journal* reporter described the Humane Society medal that "graces the wall of his room" in Madison—a medal the reporter had presumably seen while interviewing O'Dea. The story mentioned that the commendation was for "saving a woman from drowning," which, as heroic as O'Dea's efforts may have been on that day, is obviously not true. While it's certainly possible that the reporter altered the story on his own, it is clear that the source for the rest of his information was O'Dea himself, and it doesn't seem like too big a leap to conclude that the football star might have embellished the incident to make himself look better.

By 1934 the story had a new, even more heroic, dimension. A newspaper writer reported that not only had O'Dea saved Annie Crooke, but that he had narrowly avoided getting eaten by sharks in the process. O'Dea spent plenty of time with the reporter of that story before it was published, so it seems reasonable to think that the sharks were his creation.

The *Herald Sun* of Australia ran a feature on O'Dea in 2007 that reported the story this way: "On January 3, 1888, while he was swimming at Mordialloc beach, he heard a woman scream and looked up to see a shark's fin. Young O'Dea, churning the water with his arms and legs, got between the shark and the woman. Although he finally got her safely ashore, the woman collapsed and died of a heart attack." It was a story that would have made O'Dea proud.

O'Dea completed his studies at Xavier, a Catholic boys high school in Melbourne, in 1889. In that same year, the seventeen-year-old applied to and was rejected by Melbourne University . . . three times. So, not by choice, O'Dea put his academic life on hold and focused on sports.

While he excelled in many athletic pursuits, Pat had his most success in Australian Rules Football, or "footy." He began to play the game at age eight, when his brother Andrew pieced together a homemade ball made of a bull bladder and a leather cover and inflated with a goose quill. By the time he arrived at Xavier, he had matured into an outstanding player, and he continued to compete locally after graduation.

Footy is a kicking game. Though players can run with the ball provided they bounce it periodically (in O'Dea's time, the rule was every seven yards), the only way to score is by booting the ball through the posts at either end of the field. Hence, in order to excel in footy, a player has to be an accomplished kicker—particularly on the run.

And O'Dea did excel. He played for teams in North Melbourne and Melbourne in the early 1890s and was named as an alternate to the

All-Victorian team in 1894. In 1895 he made the move to Essendon, just north of Melbourne, and his first appearance for that side received favorable reviews in the Melbourne *Argus,* which reported that he played with "more resolution than usual . . . and quite satisfied Essendon with his debut." Though many newspaper articles in the United States would later report that O'Dea held "the distance kicking record" in Australia, there is no evidence to support this assertion.

While Pat was pursuing his footy career, his older brother Andrew left home for the United States. Andy, an accomplished athlete himself, departed in the retinue of a boxer named Frank "Paddy" Slavin, the Australian heavyweight champion, who hoped to get a shot at the famed John L. Sullivan. It never happened, and Andy eventually broke off from Slavin. Andy had been a rower of some renown in Australia, competing for the Yarra Yarra Rowing Club, which took its name from the Yarra River on which it was located. He turned his attention back to that sport and accepted a job coaching a local rowing club in Minneapolis before being offered a position as the University of Wisconsin's crew coach in 1895.

Andy arrived on Wisconsin's campus right when football was beginning to take hold in the Midwest. The game had evolved significantly since the scrimmage was adopted fifteen years earlier, but it was still quite dissimilar from the one we're familiar with now. The ball was rounder, and therefore far easier to kick. At 110 yards from goal line to goal line, the field was 10 yards longer than it is in the modern game.

The scoring, as described with the lofty value of the field goal and the two-point goal after a touchdown, placed a huge premium on the kicking game. Due to the rules of the time, these kicks were far trickier propositions than they are today. That scoring system, combined with the frequent punts, many executed on first or second down, meant that kickers were the unquestioned stars of 1890s football. A good kicker could turn a mediocre team into a great one. An outstanding kicker could become a national celebrity.

Substitutions were legal, but if a player was replaced, he could not return. This meant, obviously, that all of the players were involved in both offense and defense. It also meant that the kicker was a position player, often playing fullback. The defensive fullback position was what would be referred to today as safety. With no legal forward passing, there were just two ways to advance the ball—running and kicking. The first player who received the snap (generally the quarterback) was prohibited from running with the ball unless it had first been in another player's hands. Thus, the plays were not only limited but also a bit slow to develop.

Given the narrow options for moving the ball, gaining the requisite five yards in three plays was a difficult proposition. The problem was exacerbated in 1887 when the football association, led by Camp, legalized tackling below the waist. That decision cut down severely on the effectiveness of open-field running and led to the rise of so-called "mass plays." The concept was a simple one: Since the highly restrictive rules didn't necessarily favor the speedier or more athletic side, teams turned to brute force in their efforts to advance the ball.

Penn's legendary coach George Woodruff devised an attack called "guards back." In this formation both guards lined up a couple of yards behind the line of scrimmage, one in front of the other. About four yards behind them were three more players—the fullback and both halfbacks. There were several variations of the play, but the most common one involved a handoff to one of the backs. The players in front of him would all plow forward, providing "interference" or blocking for the runner. They would focus their efforts on one opponent on the defensive line, meaning the would-be tackler might have to take on four or five blockers on the same play. The results were often devastating.

Other plays took on forms that would be only marginally recognizable as football today. The "turtle back" is a case in point. In this play the offensive team would organize itself in a tightly packed oval, with the farthest forward players on the line. After the snap the ball was handed to the designated runner, who would disappear into the mass. The players around him then began to revolve around the perimeter attempting to hold their formation, thus preventing defenders from getting at the ball carrier. All the while the oval moved forward, eventually opening up and launching the runner around end.

The rules at the time also allowed blockers to attach straps to the back of their jerseys, which ball carriers could hold onto during their plunge into the line. This was a strategy favored by Yale and its revolutionary guard, William "Pudge" Heffelfinger. Heffelfinger, a Minneapolis native, was a freakish athlete. At 6'3" and just over 200 pounds, he was considered enormous for the time, but he was also faster than most backs. A three-time All-American, Heffelfinger became the most feared player of the late 1880s and early 1890s. As football historian Alexander Weyand noted, "The sight of this swarthy giant, a white bandage around his head to protect his ears, stampeding through the opposing line like a bull elephant, with a halfback clinging to a strap sewed to the back of his canvas jacket, was something once seen, never forgotten."

With players like Heffelfinger out front, the advancing wedges greatly increased the violence in the sport, exposing both sides to potential brutality. The effects on the defense are obvious, but the offense was often beaten up as well. The preferred method for breaking up the wedge, after all, was for a defender to strike the man at the front in the jaw with an open hand. Heffelfinger had a different strategy, though. He kicked his opponent in the face. During Yale's game with Princeton in his freshman year of 1889, "Heffelfinger took a running leap and, with his knees drawn up in front of him, struck the apex man. That halted the wedge."

In 1892 the mass play gave birth to the "momentum play," which combined the mass formations with the added element of a running start. The most famous of these, the "flying wedge," was the brainchild of Lorin Deland, a military historian who not only never played football, but also never even attended a game until he was in his thirties.

Deland believed that Napoleon's concept of increasing force by "multiplying mass by rapidity" could be applied to the football field. He envisioned a play where an entire team full of blockers would gain momentum by starting well behind the line of scrimmage, arriving at the line to plow over their opponents at the precise moment that the ball was snapped. He discussed the idea with Harvard's captain, Bernie Trafford, who encouraged him to design a play. The original flying wedge was a kickoff play, as the rules at the time allowed teams to begin by simply kicking the ball an inch forward, picking it up, and tossing it back to a teammate to run it.

The play was first used in the 1892 game between Harvard and Yale. "Trafford remained in the middle of the field with the ball, while the other ten men separated in squads of five each, each squad taking a position about fifteen yards behind Trafford and toward the sides of the field," the *New York Times* reported the next day. "Then the ten men started to run toward Trafford, and as they came near him he put the ball in play, passed it back and joined in the general rush toward the Yale players. By this trick the Harvard men were able to get additional momentum, and they carried the ball fifteen yards into Yale's territory before they were downed."

The possibilities of the momentum play were immediately evident, and teams spent much of the time leading into the 1893 season developing similar plays of their own, adapting them to involve not just kickoffs but also snaps from the line of scrimmage. The flying wedge as a kickoff play was eliminated in 1894, when it was mandated that kickoffs travel at least ten yards before the kicking team could recover. That same year the committee declared that, "No momentum mass play shall be allowed," with "momentum mass plays" defined as ones where more than three men start moving before the snap or group together more than five yards behind the play. Unfortunately, this rule didn't go nearly far enough. If anything, the game seemed to get more brutal.

In November 1894, in front of an overflow crowd of 25,000 fans in Springfield, Massachusetts, Harvard and Yale played one of the most violent games in the history of the sport. The newspaper accounts were vivid in their descriptions:

"Hayes gained two yards around right end, and Hinkey, in attempting to stop him, hit him a blow right in the face with his fist."

"It seemed to be Hinkey's main object to disable the best players of Harvard."

"In one of the quick line ups Murphy gave Hallowell a quick smash in the eye that escaped the notice of both umpire and referee."

"Butterworth had grown worse and was staggering about the field weak and useless."

"In one of the fierce rushes [Murphy] was knocked senseless. It was five minutes before he got up and rubbed his head with a 'Mamma, where am I?' look on his face."

"After a wait to two minutes [Murphy] staggered to his feet, but was plainly in no condition to play football. He did not even know which was his goal, and between each two plays had to have the situation explained to him."

Yale won the game 12–4, but the result was clearly secondary to the violence. Toward the end of the game, Murphy was taken off the field on a stretcher and transported to the local hospital. Word began to circulate that he had died. While those rumors proved unfounded, there were some who believed the game itself had been dealt a fatal blow.

"An ordinary rebellion in the South American or Central American States is as child's play compared with the destructiveness of [to]day's game," the *New York Times* proclaimed, while the *Boston Globe* asserted, "It is inevitable that what took place today should create no end of discussion as to whether the game should be continued or not."

Dr. William A. Brooks, a former Harvard captain, announced that he would not officiate the following week's Princeton–Yale game due to his disgust over the state of the sport. "No more serious blow has ever been delivered against the American game of football than the manner in which the Harvard–Yale game was played today," Brooks declared. "I am . . . convinced that unless representatives of both universities learn to play the game free from objectionable features, the game must stop."

Harvard's president, Charles Eliot, an outspoken opponent of the sport, said of football in his President's Report the following spring, "It has become perfectly clear that the game as now played is unfit for college use." Though Harvard refused to play Yale for the next two seasons, the sport did go on. And more than a thousand miles away from Springfield, in the small isthmus city of Madison, Wisconsin, it soon spawned a new superstar.

CHAPTER FIVE

TO MADISON

ANDY O'DEA AND FOUR OTHER YOUNG MEN STOOD ON THE SHORES OF
Lake Mendota in Madison, Wisconsin, gazing at the choppy water. It
was early on a Monday morning—April 6, 1896. Just two days earlier,
they had been out on the lake, beginning their training for the upcoming
season in the two newly purchased shells that now rested on the shore
beside them.

Andy and three of the other men had eagerly anticipated moments
like this one all winter, training in the gymnasium on a stationary rowing
machine, urging one another on. Though they wanted nothing more than
to take the boats back out, it became clear that this was not a morning
for crew practice. The northwest wind was howling, chilling them to the
bone, and more importantly, the waves were high. While the boats were
sleek, they were also fragile and easily swamped. Heading out at this hour
would be too risky, and disappointed as they were, they all knew it.

Andy was preparing for his second season as the coach of the Wisconsin rowers. Among those alongside him were three of the students
who had helped him build a competitive team in 1895—sophomores
L. C. Street, Curran McConville, and John Day.

Andy hadn't anticipated standing beside the other man, but he was
certainly pleased to be in his company. Pat O'Dea had arrived in Madison only weeks earlier. Bored with his life in Australia and in search of a

new adventure, he had come to North America at least in part to find his brother. He was aware that Andy was on the vast continent, though he didn't know exactly where.

Pat had arrived in Vancouver and, knowing of Andy's interest in boxing and rowing, began to inquire in gyms and at boathouses about his brother. One of the oarsmen told him that an Andy O'Dea, practitioner of the unusual Yarra-Yarra stroke, had recently taken a job as the crew coach at Wisconsin. Pleased to get the tip, Pat shook the man's hand in thanks. "There are maybe a thousand Andy O'Dea's in the world," he told him, "but only one who could be teaching the Australian stroke 'Yarra-Yarra' at Wisconsin." So Pat hopped on a train and made the long journey to Madison.

He stepped off into a thriving small city. Electric streetcars, which had replaced the wildly unpopular mule-driven models four years earlier, whirred busily through the town's streets. Of Madison's roughly 16,000 residents, about 650 had telephone service, a number that would more than double during the next four years. Electric lights, introduced to the city just eight years earlier, now illuminated its streets and homes. Still, the town's leaders were wrestling with the perplexing issue of disposing with Madison's raw sewage. The decision to dump it into the lakes that surrounded the isthmus city had proven to be a bad one, with the shorelines now "covered with fecal matter in varying stages of decay."

Human excrement aside, the lakes did provide a lovely backdrop for the university town, which doubled as the center of the state's government. A gorgeous white-domed capital building dominated the downtown square, a hub of urban activity. A new city boathouse, designed by a little known native son named Frank Lloyd Wright, highlighted the Lake Mendota shoreline, just a few hundred yards from the university campus. The school itself was growing rapidly, with a total enrollment of nearly 1,300 students, a number that had increased more than 50 percent over the previous four years.

When he arrived on campus, Pat quickly happened upon John "Ikey" Karel, who told the Aussie that he knew where to find his brother and ushered him down to the boathouse. Though the siblings hadn't seen each other for years, their exchange was unsentimental and matter-of-fact.

"Hello," said Pat to Andy.

"Hello," said Andy to Pat, "what brought you here?"

"I got tired of Australia."

"Well this is a good place."

That was apparently all the convincing Pat needed. He decided to stay. Ikey helped him find a place to live, and Pat O'Dea began to assimilate into campus life.

Andy's crew team had seemed like the perfect place to start, which was how Pat found himself on the shore that blustery early spring day. The five men stood in silence for a while, trying to will the winds to stop, but it was clear that conditions weren't going to improve any time soon. The students among them agreed to head to class and to give it a shot again in the afternoon.

They reconvened hours later. The weather was marginally better. Yes, the wind was still blowing, but it had died down a bit during the course of the day. The water wasn't exactly placid, but it was an improvement over the morning. Thoughts of the long winter cooped up inside flashed through their heads. They decided to give it a whirl.

The first boat hit the water at about 3:30 in the afternoon. Andy was seated closer to the bow, and Street sat behind him in the stroke position. They headed northwest, directly into the wind, aiming for a popular spot called Picnic Point, a peninsula that jutted out into the lake about a mile from campus.

A few moments later, the other three men set out in the second boat. As the newcomer, Pat rode in the back, serving as the coxswain. McConville sat toward the front, with Day behind him.

As great an athlete as Pat was, he might have met his match in John Day. In addition to being a gifted rower, Day had recently won both the high jump and the pole vault at the university's mid-winter athletic meet. He was one of the most popular students at Wisconsin, as well, serving as president of the sophomore class. He was also a gifted orator. Day had been trained on that front by his mother, Janette, a well-known elocution-ist. In fact, she had made the 40-mile journey from her home in Janesville, Wisconsin, to Madison over the weekend. Though she always enjoyed spending time with her only son, there was a professional component to her visit. On Wednesday evening, John was slated to compete in an oratorical contest, the winner of which would represent Wisconsin in the Northern competition later in the school year. Janette was in town to help her son perfect his speech.

Andy and Street had made it about three-quarters of the way to Picnic Point when the weather quickly began to deteriorate. The winds picked up dramatically. The two men forged on, hoping that the squall would pass. It did not. The tiny scull began rocking precariously as waves washed over it. Since they were closer to Picnic Point than they were to campus, they made the decision to keep rowing. The boat was filling up. They needed to turn it over to avoid sinking. The two rowers jumped over-board, and in the chaos, a stray oar hit Andy in the head. Street swam over to help his severely dazed coach. After much wrestling, they managed to position themselves over the underside of the boat. Clinging desperately to the hull, they shouted for help.

About a quarter of a mile away and out of sight from the other boat, Pat and his fellow oarsmen were having similar problems. O'Dea's hands were free, and he used them in an effort to bail out the boat. For a moment, it seemed that might work, but the winds picked up again and the waves crashed over them. It was clear to Pat that he was fighting a losing battle. He told Day and McConville that they would need to get out and turn the boat over. John's eyes widened in panic as he revealed the secret he had never shared with his fellow oarsmen. John Day, regarded by some as the best athlete in the state of Wisconsin, didn't know how to swim.

Pat O'Dea sprang into action. As soon as they hit the water, he grabbed the flailing Day and pulled him up onto the underside of the boat, urging Day to hold on. The craft bobbed and swayed repeatedly in the turbulent waters. Their hands went numb from the bitter cold. They screamed for help.

Back on dry land, a man named Stanley Wheeler was watching the rowers through the window of the engineering building, which afforded a beautiful view of the lake. His relaxation quickly turned to shock as he saw the men struggling. He scrambled down the stairs and out to the boathouse, yelling for help as he went. Several men came running, one of whom—Hereward Peele—would be a future football teammate of O'Dea. Wheeler quickly took charge. He helped Peele and another man get into a rowboat and launched them out toward the distressed crew members. Then, he and another responder got into boats of their own and followed closely behind.

Exhausted, Andy and Street clung to their scull. The wind and waves tossed them off on a couple of occasions, but they managed to regain their grip. The situation on top of Pat's boat was even more critical. Each time their group was tossed, they had to struggle mightily to get John Day back on board—a challenge exacerbated by the bitterly cold water.

Pat gripped the boat with one hand and Day with the other. In the chaos, he saw Wheeler coming to rescue them, perhaps a hundred yards away. At that instant, a huge wave hit the boat, throwing the three men off, and Pat lost his hold on Day. By the time the Aussie got his bearings, Day had drifted a good distance away. Seeing that Curran McConville had regained his hold on the boat, Pat tried desperately to make his way over to John. But he had gone under. He never resurfaced.

Devastated, Pat made his way back to the overturned shell just as Wheeler's boat arrived. "Come on," Wheeler screamed through the chaos. Pat looked at McConville. "You go first," he shouted. "I'll hold on here. Have them send someone for me once you get to shore." He didn't have to wait for long. Peele rowed up mere moments later and took Pat back to dry land with him.

The third rescue boat reached Andy and Street a few minutes later. They had been in the frigid water for half an hour. Both men were sprawled across the now-overturned bottom of the boat, nearly unconscious. Andy was rushed to a local residence and Street was taken inside the gymnasium. Though the situation initially appeared dire, both survived.

As his visiting mother cried uncontrollably on the shore and his father, alerted by telegraph, rushed to Madison from Janesville, a search party was dispatched in an effort to locate John Day. His body was recovered at just after nine o'clock that evening.

A somber mood engulfed the university. An enormous group gathered the next morning at Fitch's undertaking room, not far from the Wisconsin campus. Some mustered the courage to go take one last look at their friend. Others simply milled about in shock. Day's body was placed in a hearse, and hundreds of students trailed behind as the procession made its way to the depot. From there, the coffin was taken by train to Janesville.

John Day was laid to rest on Wednesday in a moving ceremony that included the reading of his contest speech. Pat and Andy O'Dea were among the many from the university in attendance. Perhaps due to that incident, Pat never competed for the Wisconsin crew team. He settled in as a law student, and the following fall, his athletic talents took him in a decidedly different direction.

On a late September day in 1896, Pat was strolling through campus when he stumbled upon the football team going through its preseason practice. The Aussie was struck by the oddness of the sport. There were a few similarities to the Australian Rules game that was his specialty—lots of running and kicking. But this sport was played in fits and starts. For the life of him, he couldn't figure out what was going on.

The next few moments border on the apocryphal—though Pat told and retold the story quite consistently throughout his life. A stray ball rolled in his direction. As he had so many times in Australia, O'Dea picked up the ball and booted it back toward the players. It flew far over their heads and landed perhaps 75 yards from where he was standing. The players looked at one another and started to shout at the unfamiliar figure. Thinking he had somehow made a breach of etiquette, Pat turned to walk away. But he was quickly intercepted by a short, curly-haired fellow who introduced himself as Phil King, head football coach.

"Where did you learn to kick the ball like that?" King asked, sizing up the man who he instantly recognized as a potentially valuable weapon. O'Dea explained that he was Andy's brother, and he had played footy in Australia.

"How would you like to join our football team?" King asked. "We could really use you."

"That's a Chinese game, not football," O'Dea responded hesitantly.

But the coach was apparently persuasive, as, by the next day, Pat O'Dea was a member of the Wisconsin football team.

O'Dea joined at a time when the sport was beginning to pick up momentum on the Madison campus. Football had taken a little longer to gain a foothold at Wisconsin than it had at some other Midwestern universities. This was largely due to the resistance of John Bascom, the president of the school from 1874 to 1887, who, in the words of one university historian, "deplored college athletics." His successor, Thomas Chamberlain, was only incrementally more enthusiastic, though he did allow the school to start competing in intercollegiate football in 1889.

It was during the presidency of Charles Kendall Adams, who took over the university leadership in 1892, that football truly began to flourish in Madison. By the next year, the student newspaper, the *Daily Cardinal,* emphasized the need for all able-bodied students to participate. "Perhaps it is not morally wrong for a person who has athletic ability to keep out of competitive events," the paper stated. "However there is no question but that it is very decidedly athletically wrong."

Within a few years, campus life in the fall began to revolve around the sport. "Football news filled the pages of the *Daily Cardinal* during the season to the exclusion of almost everything else," a university history notes. "Victories were announced in bright red colors, defeats in funereal-black borders." Passion for the game occasionally got out of hand. A fight broke out at one off-campus boardinghouse after a Wisconsin student refused to pledge support for the team. By the time the scuffle ended, one young man had been shot in the foot.

Adams initially hired Parke Davis, a former Princeton star, to coach the Badgers football team. He stayed for just one year and was succeeded by Stickney, the onetime Harvard player who had written Yale captain "Pa" Corbin a number of years earlier in search of a handout from Walter Camp. Stickney's departure after two seasons paved the way for King to take over in 1896. When the former Princeton quarterback arrived on campus that fall, he became the seventh coach in the first eight years of the program's existence.

After King stumbled upon O'Dea, the Aussie had only a few days to acclimate himself before the Badgers' season opener in Madison against Lake Forest College, a school located on the shores of Lake Michigan north of Chicago. Of that first game, O'Dea recalled many years later, "I didn't even know the rules. I spent half the game watching it, and the second half playing."

Not much was expected of Lake Forest. The Badgers had won four of the five previous meetings between the schools, including a 26–5 victory in 1895. The general lack of enthusiasm was reflected in the crowd. A relatively small group of fans packed into the wooden covered grandstand that stood along one side of Randall Field, a former military base and fairgrounds that had been the site of Wisconsin sporting events for the past several seasons. In vintage student-journalist fashion, the *Daily Cardinal* reporter put his own (presumably nonpaying) job on the line when he wrote, "the present scribe will go out of business if the Varsity doesn't win by 20 or 24 points to nothing."

As it turns out, his position was secure. Pat was forced into action just after halftime with the Badgers already up 34–0, as starting fullback and team captain John Richards was sent to the sidelines with a knee injury. O'Dea made an immediate impression: "He punted clear over Lake Forest's backs on the first attempt," the *Cardinal* reported, "and the ball was 85 yards from where O'Dea stood when they fell on it." That 85-yard punt is in the Wisconsin record books to this day as the sixth-longest in Badgers history and the third-longest of O'Dea's career.

O'Dea also tried to drop-kick a goal from the field late in the game. "He stood exactly 60 yards from Lake Forest's goal when he kicked the ball, and probably had it not been for the wind the ball would have gone between the posts." As it was, the "beautiful kick . . . missed by barely three feet." Moments later, time was called, and the Badgers walked off the field with a 34–0 victory.

Though O'Dea had played only briefly, word of his performance spread. In fact, it initially caused some confusion. Pat was such an unknown commodity that some wire reports initially indicated that Andy had suited up for the Badgers. Under the headline 'Twas Not Andy O'Dea, the *Minneapolis Journal* ran a clarification, informing its readers the man who came in for Richards was actually "Patrick O'Dea, a brother of the trainer and a student at the university." King quickly promoted the talented newcomer to the "first eleven."

Two days later O'Dea was in the news for another reason. As the Badgers practiced for a midweek game with Madison High School, their newest player lined up for a punt. Suddenly, one of the "second eleven" players broke through the line and blocked it. "I ran for the ball intending to fall upon it," O'Dea told a reporter from the *Daily Cardinal* later that evening, "but on account of the closeness of the crowd fell short of it and with my arm reached for it across the plank bordering the track. Somebody in trying to fall on the ball then fell on my arm." The prognosis was not a good one. O'Dea's arm was broken.

While the *Cardinal* reported that Pat would "not be able to play for a month or more," the *Eau Claire Leader* was even more pessimistic, saying that O'Dea was "done up for the season." The *Leader* saw this as a significant blow for the Badgers, noting that O'Dea (who, to this point, had played one football game in his life) was "famous as a great punter." The promise the newcomer had shown was quickly put on hold.

CHAPTER SIX

THE CHALLENGE OF AMATEURISM

THE 1896 SEASON THAT SAW PAT O'DEA MAKE HIS DEBUT FOR Wisconsin was a monumental one in Midwest football. It was the first year of competition in the recently christened and awkwardly named "Intercollegiate Conference of Faculty Representatives," which would come to be referred to as the Western Conference and, eventually, the Big Ten. The conference was formed as a reaction to the most perplexing problem of college football's early years—that of player eligibility.

As the stakes involved in the games got larger, schools began to wrangle with the issue of who should actually be allowed to play on their teams. There had been some attempts at legislation in the early 1880s, with movements both to limit the number of years in which a player could participate and to ban professional athletes from intercollegiate contests. The enforcement was left to individual schools, whose teams were essentially run by students and graduates. Not surprisingly, many of them chose simply to ignore the rules.

The first true eligibility controversy had arisen between Harvard and Princeton in 1889. The Tigers had a team full of questionable characters. Among them was a twenty-six-year-old named Elwood Wagenhurst, who had graduated from the school the year before, played professional baseball, and was now attempting to play football at Princeton while simultaneously coaching at Penn. Princeton captain Edgar Allan Poe said of Wagenhurst: "We do not deny that the reason of his returning for a post-graduate course is to play football."

He was joined on the team by Walter "Monte" Cash, who had played for Penn the year before but left as soon as the season ended, heading back to his home in Wyoming. He was invited back east by Princeton and arrived on campus with two pistols and a deck of playing cards, which would explain the nickname. He entered school as a special student just weeks before the Harvard game.

Harvard objected and released a number of letters that they believed highlighted the indiscretions at Princeton. For instance, one Harvard man produced a note from a former Tigers captain that read, "I can get your board, tuition, etc., free. The athletic men in Princeton get, by all odds, the best treatment of any of the colleges." The Princeton folks said it was all just a big misunderstanding. "[H]e refers simply to the fact that, as a democratic spirit prevails at Princeton, athletic students can win a certain social position which they could not at some other colleges," Princeton's advisors and graduate managers wrote in a statement. "Nothing else is implied in this passage." Besides, the Princeton men argued, their school left the decision of who should and shouldn't play up to the students, and they did not want to take from that group "the power of initiative in the development of independence of character and action."

Meanwhile, others accused Harvard of similar behavior. A Penn player named R. R. Ammerman released a letter that was published in a Philadelphia newspaper in which he claimed "a scholarship and pecuniary compensation, a ticket to Boston, etc., were extended to me by a Harvard man in early November, to enter the Law School at Harvard and become a member of the . . . Football Eleven." Not surprisingly, Harvard denied the claim.

That kind of back-and-forth squabbling was typical of the controversies at the time, which, on reexamination, essentially boil down to "he said, she said" disputes. In the big picture, the game's leaders repeatedly expressed an interest in creating a fair system that would work. On a game-to-game basis, though, schools seemed more focused on doing whatever they could to get their questionable players on the field and their opponents' questionable ones ruled out. In the 1889 case, the two sides eventually withdrew their claims of ineligibility, and Princeton whipped the Crimson 41–15. Harvard refused to play the New Jersey school for the next five years.

The problems weren't limited to the Harvards, Yales, and Princetons of the world. As the game spread in the late 1880s and early 1890s, abuses materialized throughout the country. As one history of the University of Illinois notes, "There were no codes of (eligibility) rules and no organizations to enforce any." Charles Baird, who managed Michigan's football team in 1893 and later became the school's athletic director, recalled that seven of the eleven players on that 1893 team were not actually enrolled in school. Few involved really saw this as much of a problem. "No one thought of inquiring about their standing," Baird said.

The situation was similar at Notre Dame. The South Bend school's 1896 team included a tackle named Frank Hanley, who made no secret of his lack of academic ambition. An article in *Harper's Weekly* noted several years later of Hanley: "Asked what he took at the college, he naively replied, 'Baths!' Not an undesirable course, especially for a football player," the writer quipped, "but hardly sufficient to maintain class-room standing."

Equally troubling was the phenomenon of the "tramp" athlete—students who might show up just before a big game, play, and then wander off, or, in some cases, might switch schools in the middle of the season. Perhaps the most prominent example of a tramp was future Michigan coach Fielding Yost. Yost began the 1896 season as a tackle at West Virginia. He then "transferred" to Lafayette just in time to play in a shocking upset win against Penn. And almost as soon as that game ended, he made his way back to Morgantown and proceeded to finish off his career at West Virginia.

The problems weren't limited to the college game. In 1893 *Harper's* accused the famed prep school at Exeter of importing three men in their twenties to play against rival Andover. Noted writer Caspar Whitney

blew the charade open, complete with details about each of the merce-
naries and their backgrounds. Among them were two professional athletes, one of whom, according to Whitney, was also a well-known circus
performer. As soon as the game was over, Whitney alleged, the three men
disappeared, never to be seen on campus again. As you might expect, the
writer was outraged: "As the boy is at school," Whitney wrote, "so will
he be at college; as at college, so in after-life. If he begins on dishonest
principles, where will he end? If the seeds of professionalism are sown at
schools, how shall we ever keep them from taking root at colleges?"

Professionalism bothered Whitney, and many others, immeasur-
ably. It is impossible to talk about the eligibility issues of the day without
touching upon professionalism, as the two were inextricably linked. In
much the same way, it is impossible to talk about professionalism without
discussing class and (obvious race and gender issues aside) the American
movement toward a more egalitarian society.

Amateur sport as we think of it today began in England, and that
country's sharp class divisions were reflected on the playing fields. Professional athletics were looked down upon—the domain of those who
lacked the wealth and leisure time to participate in sport for sport's sake.
In some pursuits, such as golf and tennis, this attitude persisted well into
the twentieth century. Amateurism and social elitism went hand in hand.

That class divide was reflected in the university system in England as
well, a system dominated by the two elite institutions in the country—
Oxford and Cambridge. Those two schools began to compete in cricket
and rowing in the late 1820s, viewing the games as friendly, collegial student matches, a mind-set that still held sway as the turn of the century
approached.

Many of the most powerful early boosters of American collegiate
sports wanted to see a similar attitude here. Perhaps none had a bigger
platform than Whitney, who wrote about amateur athletics for *Harper's
Weekly* throughout the pivotal decade of the 1890s.

Whitney constantly discussed the threat professionalism posed to
the college games, warning that "continuously aggressive vigilance is the

price of purity in college sport." In his view, it was quite simple: Men were either amateurs or pros, and pros had to be kept out of the college games at all cost. "Semi-professionalism is a paradoxical and a meaningless term," Whitney wrote. "There are no degrees of amateurism."

What Whitney viewed as professionalism differed greatly from today's definition. Not only did he fulminate against obvious issues—using players who had been paid, illegal recruitment, and tramp athletes—but he also denounced practices such as, well, practices. Whitney believed strongly that teams should only work out during the college term. In the fall of 1896, for instance, he took the University of Pennsylvania to task for what amounted to a preseason training camp, charging that the school spent a month in an off-campus hotel preparing its men for the season ahead. "This is not the spirit of sportsmanship that thrills under the glory of honorably contesting for victory," Whitney wrote of Penn's practices. "It is the spirit of the professional, to whom victory is everything, and the game mere means to that end."

Along the same lines, Whitney protested high ticket prices, off-campus games, and the Thanksgiving Day battles. He was also deeply troubled by a new career path that developed around the game in the 1890s—that of the professional coach.

The earliest college football teams were coached by the students themselves or, as the game became more sophisticated, by recent graduates who worked in an unofficial, uncompensated capacity. Yale, in particular, had this system down to a science, as the previous year's captain often remained in New Haven the year after his graduation to oversee the team. Those coaches were relegated to mere spectators on game day, though, as, in a concept borrowed from rugby, all on-field decisions were to be the domain of the captain. Coaching from the sidelines was seen as a violation of the amateur ideal. "Now the good name of the sport demands that this offensive feature be recognized and penalized," Whitney wrote in 1899. "I suggest taking the ball away from the side receiving coaching."

Walter Camp, while generally referred to today as Yale's "coach," technically only served in that capacity for five years right after his graduation, though some dispute whether he was even the coach in those years. He held a full-time job with the New Haven Clock Company and often missed practices, depending on his wife, Alice, to go watch the day's training and then huddling with her and the captains at night to plot strategy. As historian Ronald Smith notes, "Whether or not Camp was officially a head coach, it is clear that he was the individual who most Yale captains went to for coaching advice and direction for the team." Camp's role was so significant that one professor began a letter to him with the greeting, "Dear Oligarch."

The movement against professional coaching was tenable in the East, where many recent graduates, well-versed in the nuances of the game, lived in close proximity to their alma maters. It was a far bigger challenge in the West, though, where the game was new and experienced men were harder to find. This was the dilemma facing University of Chicago president William Rainey Harper in the early 1890s, and the decision he made to address it changed the direction of the game forever.

A linguistic prodigy who entered college at age ten and graduate school at Yale at age seventeen, Harper seemed an unlikely candidate to alter the college athletic landscape. After all, this is a man whose doctoral thesis boasted the scintillating title, "A Comparative Study of the Prepositions in Latin, Greek, Sanskrit and Gothic." That specialty led him to a position teaching Hebrew at the Baptist Union Theological Seminary of Chicago. It was there that he first met oil baron John D. Rockefeller, a trustee of the seminary.

Rockefeller originally dreamed of using a portion of his fortune to start a major Baptist university in New York, but eventually he was persuaded to look to Chicago instead. Plans were made to open the doors of the university in the fall of 1892, and finding a president was Rockefeller's first step. He immediately thought of his friend Harper and offered him the spot in September 1890.

The task put in front of Harper was a difficult one: not simply to create a university from scratch, but also to create one that would rise from nothing to instantly compete with the likes of Harvard, Yale, and Princeton. It is a measure of just how far football had come in the twenty-one years since that first game in New Brunswick that Harper made the sport part of his plan. As historian Robin Lester notes, "Harper saw football as an important means to elbow his way into the select circle of higher education." He didn't know much about the game himself, but he knew who he needed to get in touch with. Harper quickly wrote to one of his former students—a young man named Amos Alonzo Stagg.

Stagg was born in 1862 in West Orange, New Jersey, the poor son of a local shoemaker. The stocky youth gravitated toward sports, excelling particularly in baseball. Like Walter Camp, he built up his endurance running to and from school. He worked harvesting grain and cutting hay, which helped build his physique. Young "Lonnie," as he was known, performed reasonably well scholastically, but he hit a dead end after grade school. West Orange had no high school. If he wanted to attend the one in Orange, he would have to pay tuition. So, Stagg went to work "tending furnaces, lawns and gardens, cutting wood, [and] beating carpets." He paid his own way through Orange High School in three years.

Stagg decided to become a minister, setting his sights on attendance at Yale. Unable to pass the school's entrance exam, he followed a childhood friend to Phillips-Exeter Academy in New Hampshire, where he again worked his way through school. Life in New Hampshire was rough. Stagg was so strapped for cash that he didn't even have enough money to afford underwear. He subsisted on a diet of crackers, stale bread, and milk—cuisine that cost him a grand total of sixteen cents a day—and lived off-campus in an unheated attic.

After spending the 1883–1884 school year at Exeter, the now twenty-two-year-old Stagg gained admittance to Yale. He matriculated in the fall of 1884 and spent the next four years dazzling batters as a pitcher for Yale's baseball team. In 1887, in an exhibition game against the Boston Nationals professional team, Stagg struck out future Hall of Famer "King" Kelly, perhaps the greatest player of his time. Upon returning to the bench, Kelly was heard to mutter, "Think of a son of a gun who can pitch like that going to be a minister." The next season, Camp struck out twenty players in a game against Princeton, prompting one writer to observe, "The greatest man in America today undoubtedly is Pitcher Stagg."

As his fame as a hurler grew, Stagg was offered numerous professional contracts, but he turned them all down, citing the sordid lifestyle of a pro athlete. It was a rationale that seemed appropriate for an aspiring minister. "There was a bar in every ball park," Stagg observed, "and the whole tone of the game was smelly."

After making a name for himself on the diamond, Stagg turned his attention to the gridiron in the fall of 1888, his first year as a divinity graduate student in New Haven. He went out for the football team, earning a spot as a starting end on one of the most dominant teams in the history of the sport. Yale went 13–0 that season, outscoring its opponents by an incredible 698–0. The next year, Stagg was named a first-team All-American.

His athletic career was going better than his academic one. He spent two years at the divinity school taking a wide range of courses, including a biblical literature class taught by a young professor named William Rainey Harper, before deciding he was not cut out to be a minister. Stagg later attributed the decision to "an inability to talk easily on my feet," though his ultimate career choice also involved a great deal of public speaking.

He left Yale in 1890 and eventually made his way to the International Young Men's Christian Association Training School in Springfield, Massachusetts, joining a staff that included James Naismith, who would invent basketball there a year later. Stagg took over as the school's football coach. He did more than just lead the team, though. Capitalizing on his fame as both an athlete and an advocate of Muscular Christianity, Stagg went on tour to promote the school, speaking of the virtues of a life that combined athletics and religion. He was serving in that capacity when Harper, his former professor, contacted him with the invitation to come to Chicago.

Harper's proposal was unprecedented. He was not simply offering Stagg a part-time position as the school's coach. Instead, he was offering him a tenured professorship, heading up his own academic area—the Department of Physical Culture and Athletics. The football team would be the centerpiece of the department, and Harper made it clear he wanted to win. "I want to develop teams which we can send around the country and knock out all the colleges," he wrote to Stagg. "We will give them a palace car and a vacation too."

After some deliberation and negotiation, Stagg accepted the job at a yearly salary of $2,500, nearly twice that of the average professor. The new coach was on the job simultaneous with the opening of the university, which was barely ready to go when he arrived on campus in September 1892. "The carpenters still were at work in Cobb Hall, the one structure nearing completion," Stagg recalled many years later. "We entered the building over bare planks, and, in lieu of knobs on the doors, the teachers carried square pieces of wood to insert in the doors to turn the latches." The University of Chicago hadn't quite gotten around to doorknobs, but it did have a football team, and one of the nation's most famous stars leading it.

Within a week of its first classes, the new university played its first game, topping a local high school. Just three weeks later, they were on the field against Northwestern, playing the Evanston school to a scoreless tie. Stagg not only coached the team that first year, he also played on it due to a dearth of students. As an early university song put it, "Then Stagg was catcher, pitcher, coach, shortstop and halfback too: For in those days of 'Auld land syne' our good athletes were few."

By the next season, the team was on its way, knocking off Michigan without Stagg in the lineup—a victory that led one of the school's professors to remark, "We will have a college here soon if this keeps up." The editors of the school's weekly newspaper agreed, asserting that the win gave Chicago "what we most need—a reputation." They reminded their readers that "the best colleges are, as a rule, the leaders in athletic games."

Stagg's early participation was not seen as unusual in the Midwest, where nonstudents continued to infiltrate the top teams. In 1895 an indignant Whitney wrote of the situation at schools like Michigan, Chicago, Minnesota, Illinois, and Northwestern, "Men offer and sell themselves for an afternoon for from twenty-five to two hundred and fifty dollars, and apparently there is something like a scale of prices just as there is for horses and cows and grain."

Whitney cited numerous examples: a Chicago lawyer who was paid $500 to play for Minnesota, a former Princeton player who earned $250 to compete for Michigan against Chicago, and a player on what amounted to a Chicago professional team who was plucked off a city cable car on his way to a game by Michigan's manager, agreeing to play the rest of the season in Ann Arbor for $600. The student newspaper at Illinois, the *Daily Illini,* described one of Stagg's players as the school's "professional star," saying that the man "has been in athletics there since the institution opened," and joked that he would still be enrolled at Chicago at the end "of modern civilization."

Steps were being taken to curb the abuses. In the winter of 1895, seven Midwestern schools met in Chicago to formulate a series of rules to govern intercollegiate athletics. Eight of those twelve original regulations focused on the issues of eligibility and professionalism. Among the mandates: players had to be bona fide students, athletes could not be paid, and coaches could not play. The rules went into effect in 1896 with the formation of the Intercollegiate Conference, consisting of Purdue, Minnesota, Wisconsin, Illinois, Northwestern, Michigan, and Chicago. Whitney roundly approved: "The meeting last winter in Chicago marked the beginning of a new and clarified era in Western college sport," he wrote.

Yet, as important a step as the formation of the Western Conference was, plenty of problems still remained.

CHAPTER SEVEN

"THE MOST MISCHIEVOUS OFFENDER OF THE YEAR"

As Pat O'Dea's broken arm healed in Madison, controversy swirled over eligibility issues. Five days before Wisconsin's opener against Lake Forest, the faculty had met to discuss a football concern. Several of the men who had been practicing with the team were ineligible under the rules agreed upon in Chicago. The belief among those gathered was that Wisconsin had adopted the new code the previous spring, though that assumption was about to be put to the test.

The clause referred to as the "six-month residence rule" was the most contentious component of the agreement among the seven schools in the new conference. It required students who had played previously for another school to spend six months on their new campus before participating in athletics. The idea was to eliminate the problem of the "tramp" athlete. Though the rule had seemed like a great idea in theory, the practical application had proven to be a challenge. Already, Chicago, Northwestern, and Michigan had made it clear that they would not abide by it. All of those universities had significant graduate schools and claimed the regulation unfairly hampered them from using grad students, who had, for years, been integral to their success. Why they approved the rule in the first place is anybody's guess.

Against this backdrop, the Madison faculty was faced with a difficult choice. Wisconsin, too, had a number of strong football players who would not be eligible under the residency requirement. Still, the professors held firm, refusing to rescind the rule. An editorial in the *Chicago Times-Herald* voiced its support of the decision. "The action may weaken the team, but it puts Wisconsin in a desirable position," the paper opined. "Football never was so near shipwreck as it was last year when the undeniable facts about the hiring of players came out." Caspar Whitney, the staunch defender of amateurism, wired his approval, telling the *Daily Cardinal*: "All friends of honest college sport applaud and support Wisconsin."

In the complicated university structure, though, it turns out that the faculty did not have the final say. That distinction belonged to the university regents. Though everyone had been operating under the belief that the regents had approved the rules, university president Charles Kendall Adams now revealed that they had not and would not—at least for now. Just four days after the faculty meeting, on the eve of the Lake Forest game, the regents decided to postpone a decision regarding the enforceability of the residency requirement until January, which, not so coincidentally, was after the end of the football season. "This will allow all the new men to play," the *Cardinal* reported, "and leaves Wisconsin's chances of becoming champion of the west very bright."

It was certainly not the first time Adams had sacrificed academic integrity for athletic success. One of the players on the team, a guard named "Sunny" Pyre, was a Wisconsin graduate who had continued to play for the Badgers even after earning his degree. In 1895 he started at tackle for Wisconsin while working on his PhD in English. As was required of a doctoral candidate, he also taught at the university. On November 16, 1895, Pyre was scheduled to give a Saturday lecture at the university extension in Chippewa Falls, about 200 miles northwest of Madison. On that same day, the football team was to be in Minneapolis for a game against Minnesota. Pyre appealed to his supervisor for help. He was told it was "absurd to ask for the postponement of a lecture for a football game."

The team felt it needed Pyre, though, and asked President Adams whether anything could be done. He quickly replied in the affirmative and sent a telegram to Pyre, who was at a different lecture stop, informing him that he would be able to play. He added: "Now go in and win." As for his supervisor, who had been operating under the misguided notion that academics were more important than the football team—he was put on a 3:30 a.m. train to Chippewa Falls to help reschedule the lecture.

Given that recent history, it was no surprise that Adams had decided not to enforce the new eligibility rules. But the regents' delay did nothing to quell the controversy surrounding the decision. In fact, it dominated the headlines of the *Cardinal* during the course of the fall, as hardly a day went by where there wasn't some sort of coverage of the issue. To their credit, the student editors of the paper took a strong stand against the university's decision. "The considerations involved in the question are numerous, but . . . if the rules were wholesome at the time of their adoption, they are now," the paper editorialized on the day of the Lake Forest game. "If they were good rules when considered in the abstract . . . they are just as good now, when the first real test comes. If they are right, they should be enforced."

A few weeks later, Whitney echoed those sentiments in *Harper's* in a scalding repudiation of the school's decision, declaring, "Wisconsin stands disgraced before the college world." He outlined the series of events for his readers: Wisconsin's acceptance of the rules the prior spring in Chicago, the decision of the faculty to uphold them, and Adams's instruction to the regents to ignore the faculty's recommendation.

"There are two sides to most stories, but this has only one. And that one is thoroughly noxious from the beginning to the ending of its recital," Whitney wrote. "From being a leader in the reform making for healthful college sport, Wisconsin has become the most mischievous offender of the year. Compared with this disregard of ethics by Wisconsin, the 'inducing' of athletes last year by other Western universities was of no consequence. In the latter case the offenders were enthusiastic, oftentimes ethically ignorant, alumni, who deluded the faculties. In Wisconsin's case, the men who trample upon the very spirit of amateurism are the highest officials of the university!"

Whitney went on to list the names of five men who had played against Lake Forest who should have been ineligible under the rules. Pat O'Dea was among those he singled out. Though Whitney didn't specify the reason for O'Dea's ineligibility, it became clear as the controversy played out that it was a function of his status as an "adult special" student—a category that included those who were admitted to the school despite deficient academic backgrounds. Under the proposed rules, adult specials—like everyone else—had a six-month residency requirement for athletic eligibility. Though nobody had the time or resources to investigate it, O'Dea might also have been ineligible as a result of his participation in Australian Rules Football. While he was technically an amateur, the world of Aussie Rules in the 1890s operated much like American college football, with teams and wealthy patrons often finding ways to make under-the-table payments to top players. The Chicago rules banned anyone who had ever made money for their participation in athletics.

Whitney's attack was published in its entirety in the *Cardinal,* and the next day Adams responded. His defense essentially amounted to: "Everybody else is doing it."

"To suppose that by enforcing the rule we could compel others to enforce it," Adams wrote, "is too much like supposing that by going to war with mere recruits we could induce our enemies to discharge their veterans."

The team's captain, John Richards, expressed a similar opinion. "Everybody here is anxious to put out winning teams and all lament the existence of a weak one," he said. "The institution—including faculty—sends out its best team and tells them to win from Minnesota, Chicago and Northwestern. But if it places restrictions upon it and fetters it in such a manner that it will lose there is certainly an injustice. Of course, it can be claimed that we would be heading a reform, that would reflect great credit to our college. Even here we can accomplish little without the cooperation of other colleges, and Wisconsin must not think that it is big enough to rule the west."

With their questionable men on the field, the Badgers went on to have the best season in their brief football-playing history. They beat Madison High School, Rush Medical College, Grinnell, and Beloit in October; then, in their first big game of the season, they knocked off Stagg's Chicago team 24–0 on November 7 in Madison. The Maroons played without their injured star, Clarence Herschberger, and their performance was subpar. In the opinion of one reporter, they "tackled around the neck, ran slow and were not stout-hearted."

The only disappointment for Badgers fans was the lackadaisical effort given by the operator of the new "bulletin board," which was rushed into service for the game. The board, which carried a price tag of $50, was to give ongoing updates of the Minnesota–Michigan game being played at the same time in Minneapolis. The *Cardinal* had eagerly described the marvel of modern technology in the days leading up to the game. "Every three minutes," it reported, "reports will be hung, showing who has the ball, the number of downs and the number of yards to gain." In order to help defray the costs of the installation and operation of the device, the price of admission was raised from 50 to 75 cents.

The board was put in place, but the updates were never posted. Team management stated afterward that, though it had received periodic telegrams, the decision was made not to "shift the movable bag" since no touchdowns had been scored. "It goes without saying that the crowd would have been vastly interested in watching the exciting struggle . . . at Minneapolis if indicated on the bulletin board and the neglect of the men in charge is lamentable," the *Cardinal* opined.

No bulletin board was necessary to watch the Gophers two weeks later. They came to Wisconsin for a much-anticipated showdown. A school-record crowd of nearly 5,000 watched a battle that went right down to the wire, with John Richards plunging over the goal line for the game-winning touchdown in the final minute.

Wisconsin fell short in its quest for a perfect season, though, tying Northwestern on a sloppy field in Evanston on Thanksgiving Day. The mere four days off in between games was too much to overcome for the banged-up Badgers, with Richards saying afterward, "the Minnesota game knocked us to pieces."

Chicago beat Michigan on the same day—the Wolverines' first loss of the year—meaning no Western team had an unblemished record or the clear claim to the "championship" that would have gone along with it. Wisconsin's case seemed strongest, though, as they were the only Western team that hadn't lost to any of the other conference schools. Still, the unbalanced schedules left that fact open for debate, at least for the time being.

The day after the Northwestern game, the seven conference schools met again in Chicago to revisit the rules issue. They emerged with a renewed pledge to enforce what were essentially the same guidelines they had adopted and ignored the year before.

Just four days after the season-ending contest, Wisconsin's faculty representative brought the new rules up for a vote at a meeting. Adams was in attendance, and the implication was that decisions made would be upheld by the regents. Not only did the faculty vote in favor of the regulations, it also added a local addendum strengthening the language of the rule pertaining to adult special students like O'Dea. Whereas the Chicago meeting stipulated that adult specials would be subject to a six-month waiting period to play, Wisconsin voted to extend that waiting period to a year. If there had ever been any doubt, it was now clear that Pat O'Dea was ineligible for athletics until the spring. It seemed like a safe route to take. After all, the season was over.

Except, as it turned out, it wasn't. A group called the Chicago Press Association had been trying to get the Carlisle Indian School from Pennsylvania to the city for a game. The Indians refused the initial propositions, eventually saying they would come only if they could play the "champions of the West." During the first week of December, the Press Association wired Wisconsin with the challenge, a move that, it was pointed out, "finally settles the question of the western championship." The Badgers quickly accepted. Phil King had left after the Northwestern game but was reached by telegram and pledged to return to Madison. The team resumed practicing. In blatant disregard of the rules agreed to only days before, a now healthy O'Dea practiced with them, with the intention of playing in the game.

The match was to be played December 19 at the fabulous Chicago Coliseum, a new arena on the south side of the city, which had seen William Jennings Bryan give his famed "Cross of Gold" speech while accepting the Democratic nomination for the presidency the previous summer. The novelty of the indoor game created plenty of buzz. "The scene on the field lighted by electricity will be something quite out of the ordinary," the *Daily Cardinal* predicted.

In Carlisle, the Badgers would face a team that had played a brutal schedule without a whole lot to show for it. While they had wins over four lesser opponents, the Indians had dropped all of their games against the East's most powerful teams—losing to Princeton, Yale, Harvard, and Penn by a combined 59–12. Though, as the *Cardinal* pointed out, "When it is considered there are only about 100 students from which to select the material for the team, the record this season is nothing short of marvelous." It was to be the first major game between an Eastern and Western team in the 1896 season.

Both teams arrived in town on Friday. The Carlisle players got a tour of the city's top attractions, including the Stock Exchange, the Board of Trade, and the Art Institute. They stayed at the swanky Palmer House hotel, where they were "the objects of much curiosity." The Badgers, meanwhile, took in a performance of *Rip Van Winkle* that evening. They rested on Saturday before heading over to check out the Coliseum late that afternoon.

The arena was a sight to behold—"unlike anything ever witnessed before," the *Chicago Tribune* observed. "Under the glare of scores of arc lights, in a temperature like that of a sunny October afternoon, the game was played with all the conditions ideal to secure the comfort of spectators and the best work on the part of the players." With an enormous crowd of 8,000 looking on, the Badgers took the field first and one player immediately grabbed the spotlight. "Patsy O'Dea, their champion drop-kicker, a recent acquisition, won plaudits by kicking a half-dozen drop-kick goals from well out toward the center of the field, just for practice." After the "pale faces had the field to themselves for nearly half an hour," the Carlisle players finally came out and warmed up for a few minutes before the game got under way.

Depending on which account you believe, Wisconsin was either thoroughly outplayed or was a victim of circumstance. The *Tribune* described the Indians as "quick on the line-up, sharp at dodging, hard to tackle, alert and indefatigable." The same paper saw the Badgers as "easily winded."

The *Cardinal*, meanwhile, lashed out at the "unfairness" of the crowd, complaining, "It is generally presumable that a team battling for western honors on a western field would receive the encouragement of an audience whose honor and reputation they were fighting for." Instead, it noted that the Badgers were "greeted with hisses, while every move of the 'clean protégés of the east' evoked the wildest applause." This, the report claimed, influenced the umpire, who "was not stout-hearted enough to give decisions contrary to the wishes of a rabble crowd."

The most memorable incident of the game came courtesy of O'Dea's right foot, as one of his punts got stuck in the metal girders that held the Coliseum's massive roof "and there it remained until a boy in the gallery climbed out and dropped it to the ground." Many years later, in a letter to the *New York Times*, a reader who had been in attendance that night recalled seeing the "Indians standing open-mouthed, waiting for the pigskin to return to earth" while the crowd stood in "awe-stricken silence" until the "foolhardy boy" knocked the ball back down.

Carlisle won the game 18–8. While there was at least one person in attendance who claimed that "[h]ad the game been outdoors and with a square umpire, Wisconsin would have won easily," that was clearly not the prevailing opinion on the Illinois Central train afterward, where the Indians were surrounded by "an admiring group of young women anxious to gaze at the descendants of the natives, who had beaten the sons of their fathers' conquerors at their own game."

The Badgers, meanwhile, headed back to Madison the next day, their "championship" season having ended on a bit of a sour note. As for O'Dea, the faculty met again to discuss his situation in the spring and issued the following ruling: "Resolved: That Mr. P O'Dea, being registered as an adult special, not having resided at the university for one year and being deficient in scholarship is not eligible for any athletic team."

It was a meaningless edict. Within just a few months, O'Dea represented Wisconsin in the Western track meet—justifiable, perhaps, because his year of residence had now passed. He'd be back on the field for the football team the following fall.

CHAPTER EIGHT

THE RISE OF THE FOOTBALL MEDIA

THE CAPACITY CROWD OF 20,000 PEOPLE SHOEHORNED THEMSELVES into Yale's football stadium on a late fall day in 1900 for the annual showdown with Harvard. The conditions were perfect for football: not a cloud in the sky; brisk, but certainly not cold, though the occasional wind gusts reminded the throng that the bitter chill of winter was just around the corner. Still, in the words of one chronicler, it was "one of those clear, crisp New England days which make life worth living."

The minutes until the scheduled 2:00 kickoff ticked away. As fans of both schools cheered lustily, Yale's mascot, a bulldog dressed in a blue sweater, raced out onto the field and, seemingly without any prompting, barked menacingly at the Harvard faithful. The Yale fans, their blue pennants flapping in the breeze, gave an even louder yell. Their feelings for their rival were tough to explain—an interesting mix of respect and disdain. "No other athletic contests are just like those between Harvard and Yale," the scribe noted. "In athletics, the highest ambition of either is to defeat the other."

Unbeknownst to many of the Yale rooters, however, their chances of topping the men from Cambridge were far slimmer than they had been less than a week before. Yale's captain, Frank Merriwell, known to all football fans for both his remarkable skill and his impeccable character, had spent the last several days suffering from a frightening illness—one that, just two nights earlier, had caused him to lapse into delirium.

"Now men, all together, once more for old Yale!" Merriwell had shouted from his bed, clapping his hands, while his teammates, a number of whom were keeping an around-the-clock vigil in his room, shook their heads sadly. Several had tears welling up in their eyes. Merriwell was both the greatest athlete and the greatest leader they had ever known. As his fever raged unabated, they had even begun to consider the possibility that he might not survive.

Thankfully, Merriwell had pulled through. By Saturday morning, he was well enough to summon the team for a meeting in his study. "The doctors have forbidden me to go to the field," he told his teammates. "So I will have to sit here as well contented as may be, watching the dispatches that come from the field, anxiously waiting one that says, 'Yale wins!'"

He concluded with some words of inspiration. "Fight as Yale fights in the last ditches," he told them. "Never say die! Never let up!" His teammates gave out a cheer so loud it could be heard in the courtyard outside. Merriwell's speech had an incredible impact on the men, who had been so dispirited by his illness and impending absence from the biggest game of their lives.

But the Elis couldn't win on emotion alone. Harvard dominated the first half. All but a handful of plays were run in Yale territory. Still, the men from New Haven almost miraculously prevented Harvard from scoring—forcing both a fumble and a turnover on downs inside their own 15-yard line. All the while, they shouted "Merriwell!" using their ailing captain for inspiration. Soon the crowd picked up on the battle cry, "and the name of 'Merriwell!' rolled skyward in a thunderous outburst." The battle was scoreless at halftime.

The second half started much like the first had ended. The Harvard men moved the ball steadily, dominating the line, though they were unable to convert that dominance into points. Yale's offense was completely ineffective without Merriwell, and the Elis eventually resorted simply to punting back to Harvard each time they gained possession. One of those punts was returned into Yale territory. Harvard drove the ball down to the Elis' 20-yard line and, rather than risk another mistake, decided to attempt a goal. The kick was a beauty. Harvard had a 5–0 lead.

The news of Harvard's score was quickly carried to Merriwell. He had sensed from the previous dispatches that things weren't going well but kept hoping for some sort of fluke occurrence that might give his team a shot. The slip of paper that the young messenger boy handed him confirmed that one wasn't in the offing. The Yale captain could stand it no longer. He raced into his room, pulled on his uniform, and, cleats pounding on the stone stairs, raced to the courtyard.

In a stroke of good fortune, Morris, a trusted local cab driver, happened to be standing outside. "Ten dollars to drive me to the field in ten minutes!" Merriwell yelled.

Merriwell leaped into the cab, while Morris grabbed the reins and urged his horse forward, his whip whooshing through the air. The houses of New Haven raced by them in a blur. Merriwell sat anxiously, hoping against hope that his arrival would not come too late. There was not a moment to spare.

As they reached the stadium, Merriwell sprang out of the cab and charged inside. There were five minutes left in the game. Harvard was driving. As his astonished teammates looked on, their captain went directly to Yale's coaches and demanded to be put in the game. They tried to dissuade him, arguing that he was putting his life in jeopardy. Merriwell would not be denied. "Take out Haggard!" he said of the man who had replaced him at halfback. Realizing who they were up against, the coaches acquiesced. Merriwell entered the fray.

The Crimson had the ball at Yale's 48-yard line. They ran two plays. The defense they had been carving up just moments before stiffened— inspired by the appearance of its captain. The game was nearly over. Harvard decided to punt.

Merriwell fielded the kick at his own 10-yard line. He dodged the first tackler and made his way upfield. His teammates blocked perfectly— Harvard men fell left and right. One Yale hit was so ferocious that the man who delivered it, Frank's teammate and close friend Dade Morgan, fell to the ground on contact, having lost consciousness. As the crowd roared, Merriwell raced on. Finally, there was just one man between him and the goal line. That man was Harvard's captain and surest tackler, Fulton. He dived to hit Frank low. Merriwell leaped into the air. "High and fair like a flying bird over Fulton he sprang, then struck the ground, stumbled, fell to his knees, staggered up, fell again and, rising with a last effort, literally shot himself across the line for a touchdown just as the whistle blew to end the game."

The rules allowed Yale a chance to kick the goal after the touchdown. As the crowd yelled deliriously, Merriwell defied the suddenly strong wind, drilling a perfect goal to give the Elis the 6–5 victory. They had won the championship.

The campus celebrated long into the night. Merriwell was unable to participate. He blacked out just seconds after his game-winning kick. When he awoke two hours later, he was back in his room. Cheers echoed outside his window. One of his teammates was sitting by Frank's bedside. He noticed the star's eyes were open. "They're cheering for you, Merry," he said, "for you, because you won the game!" Merriwell asked his friend to open the window. He leaned out, waving his handkerchief, as the crowd that had gathered below cheered. His lips shook and his eyes filled with tears. Would his heroism never cease?

Across America, satisfied readers closed their copies of *Tip Top Weekly*. Burt Standish had done it again. Merriwell was one of the most famous characters ever created in a literary subgenre known as the dime novel. During a span of twenty years, Standish, whose real name was Gilbert Patten, churned out a 20,000-word Merriwell adventure every week. And although publisher Street and Smith didn't keep exact circulation numbers, conservative estimates put that figure at about 135,000 copies a week, meaning the company sent out roughly seven million Merriwell books every year.

Merriwell wasn't just a football star—he excelled in every sport he tried. As a pitcher, for instance, he was known far and wide for his double-shoot, a curveball that started off straight but then curved in one direction before amazingly changing course midway to the plate and bending the opposite way. On top of that, he was a model citizen, standing for all that was virtuous, despite spending his life surrounded by any number of scoundrels who were trying to steer him off course. In a scene that typified his character, Merriwell told one ne'er-do-well, "I do not use liquor, and I will thank you to put away that flask."

That Street and Smith chose Merriwell as a means of reaching America's youth is evidence of the power not just of college sports, and football in particular, but also of the power of the written word in spreading the game. The popular press, which had scarcely existed sixty years before, was the sport's greatest ally. Merriwell was simply a culmination of a process that had actually begun even before that famed first game between Rutgers and Princeton.

In the early portion of the nineteenth century, readership of magazines, books, and newspapers was largely restricted to the privileged classes. The reason was simple—these were the people who could both read and afford to make purchases. At the time, "newspaper" was almost a misnomer. The papers didn't report news in the way we think of it today. They were much more focused on dissemination of editorial opinion than on the description of everyday events. And, given the hefty price of six cents per copy, those papers' editorials tended to be highly partisan, catering their opinions toward the upper classes.

But in 1833, a New York City printer named Benjamin H. Day stumbled upon a different business model. Day was looking for a way to advertise the services of his printing shop and decided to do so on what amounted to a handbill that would contain a summary of the day's news. He sold it for a penny, a fraction of the cost of a daily newspaper. He called it the *New York Sun*. The public snapped it up nearly as quickly as Day could churn it out. And with that, the news business was forever changed. "In short," historian Will Irwin observed many years later, "here was a *news*paper, the first on our soil."

What Day had started, James Gordon Bennett quickly refined. In 1835 Bennett, a Scotsman who had been working in the US newspaper business for a decade or so, started a penny paper of his own—the *New York Herald*. As he announced the endeavor, he made no bones about his methods, saying simply, "I renounce all so-called principles." Give the man credit. He lived up to that manifesto. "Bennett, ruthless, short in the conscience, expressing in his own person all the atrocious bad taste of his age, was yet a genius with a genius power of creation. And he, through two stormy, dirty decades, set an idea of news upon which we have proceeded ever since," Irwin wrote. "He set out to find the news, and to print it first."

Bennett tried every imaginable method to beat his opponents to print—utilizing everything from flag-signaling systems to hot-air balloons. He had vast networks of couriers—some as far away as Europe—who worked tirelessly to get the latest dispatches to the *Herald*. They were so successful that during the Mexican-American war of the 1840s, officials in Washington complained that they were getting information from Bennett's *Herald* more quickly than from their own official government transmissions.

Bennett changed more than just the method of news gathering, though. He changed the nature of news itself. Bennett's stories often weren't about the most significant issues of the day. "He, first of all Americans," Irwin wrote, "violated the sanctity of the home; he made private scandals, personal troubles, the business of a newspaper." The 1836 murder of a New York prostitute named Ellen Jewett, for instance, dominated the *Herald*'s front page, trumping even information about the ongoing Texas War of Independence. "News was received from Texas, highly disastrous to the colonists," the *Herald* reported, "but the private tragedy of Ellen Jewett almost absorbed all public attention." Though it seems like an obvious move in hindsight, the decision to broaden the newspapers' appeal was a revolutionary one.

The addition of sports coverage was simply a means to add to that breadth—to expand into a new domain. It certainly wasn't a huge priority. Bennett, for instance, initially used his delivery room superintendent, Joe Elliott, to cover the sporting world for him. In 1847 Elliott was dispatched to Harper's Ferry, Virginia, to report on a bare-knuckle prize fight between "Yankee" Sullivan and Englishman Robert Caunt. The bout itself is a reasonably insignificant one in the history of the sport. Caunt was horribly overmatched and was defeated in a mere twelve minutes. What was important about the proceeding was how quickly the news was dispatched back to New York for publication. Thanks to the speed of horse-riding couriers, Bennett's *Herald* ran Eliott's full two-column, front-page story with a blow-by-blow description of the fight just days later.

Technology quickly made efforts like that one unnecessary. By the 1850s, telegraph wires dotted the country. The increased efficiency in the news-gathering operation was matched by improvements in the dissemination process. Day had begun the *Sun* with an old handpress, not much different than the one Ben Franklin had used more than a half century before. That press could, at best, produce 300 sheets per hour. Within fifteen years, the cylinder press increased that rate to 8,000 copies per hour. By the 1890s, the technology had advanced to the point where a single press could produce 72,000 eight-page papers in sixty minutes—or 576,000 sheets per hour—nearly 2,000 times more than had been possible just sixty years earlier.

And those presses were churning out more newspapers than ever before. In 1870 there were 3,500 papers in the United States. A mere twenty years later, that number had more than tripled to 12,000. By the mid-1890s, it was fair to conclude, as writer J. W. Keller did, that "the modern newspaper is the greatest power on earth. In comparison with it every other individual influence sinks into insignificance."

That explosive growth and influence changed the nature of the industry. Competition now reigned. Papers became an entertainment vehicle—aimed at appealing to as broad a swath of the population as possible as they battled to survive in a suddenly glutted field. Their business model changed as well, as the focus shifted from subscriptions to advertising. In the mid-1870s, ads accounted for about 35 percent of the industry's revenue. By the turn of the century, that number had swelled to 90 percent.

Writer and publisher Frank Munsey observed that newspapers had become "a business enterprise, pure and simple, conducted with business instincts and business energy."

The advent of the sports section was an offshoot of that competition for circulation and advertising dollars. Sports coverage had gradually increased since the days of the Sullivan–Caunt fight, to the point where it had become a newspaper staple by the early 1880s. It was during the next twenty years, though, that sports writing really took off. It's impossible to credit one single person for that change, given the gradual nature of the process, but Charles Dana of the *Sun*, Joseph Pulitzer of the *New York World*, and William Randoph Hearst of the *New York Journal* all played significant roles. Between 1881 and 1893, the *World*'s sports coverage increased six-fold, while the *Sun*'s expanded fifteen-fold. Hearst got into the game a little late, as he didn't purchase the *Journal* until 1895, but he quickly upped the ante. "Finding his rivals running from three to seven columns of sport news daily," historian William Nugent noted, "he doubled, trebled and quadrupled the space." Once readers got a taste of the sports coverage, they wanted more. As historian Michael Oriard put it, "Sport both benefitted from and contributed to the newspaper revolution of the era: sports coverage attracted readers, who in turn looked to daily newspapers to satisfy their growing desire for more and more sport. College football, initially, was simply a beneficiary."

The implication is that there was no real decision to cover football. The decision was to cover sports, and on a number of levels, football was simply in the right place at the right time. On a week-to-week basis, the fact that the games were largely played on Saturday gave the sport an instant leg up. The Sunday paper was the biggest one of the week, and editors needed something to fill the pages. "The daily newspaper was not redesigned to accommodate football," said Oriard, "football was simply available for promotion."

On a broader level, though, the association with the nation's elite colleges, and the respectability that went along with it, was also critical to the increase in newspaper coverage. "College football," Oriard writes, "benefitted from the desire of the non-college-educated, 'respectable' middle class to emulate the social elite." Hence, the focus that we've already seen on the activities surrounding the game—the carriages, the decorated houses, and the printed detail regarding the occupants of the boxes at the stadium. It all helped separate football from sports like boxing, which were less socially acceptable.

It's important to note that, for the vast majority of fans, the press wasn't simply their entree into the game. It was the entirety of their football experience. Not only was this a time long before television and radio, but it was also a time during which long-distance travel remained a bit of a challenge for most people. Even if fans were able to make it to the game, there wasn't a whole lot of room for them, as most of the stadiums of the day were still relatively small. For no other reason than mathematics alone, then, the importance of newspapers becomes clear.

In 1889, for instance, the Yale–Princeton Thanksgiving Day game in New York City drew 25,000 fans from a city population of 2.4 million, meaning only 1 in 100 New Yorkers could have attended the contest. As Oriard points out, though, given the location of the schools that were playing in the game, it's reasonable to assume that many of the fans came in from Connecticut and New Jersey. So it's safe to conclude that the actual number of New Yorkers in attendance was far less than 25,000.

Yet, at the time, the city had fifty-five daily papers, with a total circulation of nearly 1.8 million. So, even by the most conservative estimates, New Yorkers were roughly ninety times more likely to read about the game than actually see it. "The daily press in New York," Oriard concludes, "had an impact on college football in the 1880s and 1890s greater than television on professional football in the 1950s and 1960s."

That meant that the writers did more than just report on the game; they served as the sole eyes and ears for many who considered themselves fans of the sport. Given this fact, the papers did everything they could to provide the best and most extensive coverage. Hearst, for instance, paid celebrity journalist Richard Harding Davis $500 to write about the Yale–Princeton game in 1895, a sum that Davis wrote to his brother "was quoted as the highest ever paid for a single piece of reporting." The edition sold out. In the words of Davis, "The *Journal* people were greatly pleased."

The magazine industry flourished right along with the newspapers, aided by many of the same factors. Favorable postal laws also played a role in the rise of periodicals, which could be mailed at a second-class rate. As a result, the number of monthly magazines skyrocketed from 280 in 1860 to more than 1,800 by 1900. In the decade of the 1880s alone, magazine advertising grew at a rate of nearly 300 percent.

As with the newspapers, much of the early magazine coverage focused on glorification of the game. For example, after Harvard beat Yale in 1890 for the first time in fifteen years, Davis wrote a laudatory piece in *Harper's Weekly,* singing the praises of Harvard's captain and star, Arthur Cumnock, a real-life precursor to Standish's fictional Frank Merriwell. Davis credited Cumnock not simply with leading Harvard to football victories, but with changing the entire tenor on the Cambridge campus.

When Cumnock arrived at Harvard, Davis wrote, "The prevailing tone was Harvard pessimism, and the manly thing, so the incoming Freshmen were told, and the chief end of man was to drink, and gamble politely . . . and cut recitations." But in his four years, by Davis's account, the football captain "threw all of his influence on the side of temperance in all things, fair play at either play or work, and showed at all times, whether on or off the field, the courtesy and modesty and strength of a gentleman."

The characterization didn't seem like a stretch to the readers of the time. "The larger-than-life football hero," Oriard notes, "lived in the popular imagination beyond conventional standards of vice and virtue. The hero-worship and contempt that football players continue to evoke today, the conflicts that routinely arise in college football between social, ethical, and moral and education values on one hand and popular heroism on the other, originated in football's narratives of the 1890s."

Among those heroes was Pat O'Dea, who became a favorite of Midwestern writers starting in 1897. As the newspapers across the region chronicled his remarkable exploits, the Australian ascended from near anonymity to superstardom.

CHAPTER NINE

"BIGGER THAN ANY OF PILLSBURY'S GREAT MILLS"

THOUGH PAT O'DEA HAD BRIEFLY MADE AN IMPRESSION ON THOSE WHO had been following the Badgers closely in 1896, those ubiquitous newspapers expected little of him or the Wisconsin team as a whole heading into the 1897 season. That being said, newspaper predictions at that time were even more of an inexact science than they are today. One of the biggest challenges for prognosticators of the day was simply knowing who would actually enroll in school. In the days before scholarships, players came and went and new candidates might roll into town on the first day of classes and find themselves at practice that afternoon.

The *Milwaukee Sentinel*'s season-preview piece on the Wisconsin team didn't mention O'Dea and had a rather tepid take on the Badgers' prospects. Another Milwaukee paper felt the same way, describing various Badgers as "fat," "slow," "unnecessarily rough," and having "much to learn about the game." Of O'Dea, the paper mentioned that he was "perhaps the most phenomenal punter in the country," but saw him as essentially a one-trick pony, adding that "his value as a football player remains somewhat problematical."

Less than a week later, though, on the day of the season opener, the *Minneapolis Journal* painted a much rosier picture for the Badgers, indicating that, over a two-day span, Wisconsin had gone from looking like a group "that would find it difficult to hold its own with first class high school teams" to one that now appeared "strong."

The improvement was due to the new talent that had arrived on campus for the opening of classes. Coach King now had thirty candidates to choose from, though only four had been in the previous year's first eleven. Fullback Pat O'Dea, "the kangaroo kicker," was singled out among the most promising players. The paper mentioned that O'Dea did not have the "line-smashing" abilities of his predecessor, John Richards, but that he was superior as both a punter and sprinter. It concluded noncommittedly, "it is possible that O'Dea has solved the fullback problem for Wisconsin."

There wasn't much time to work out the kinks. The Badgers began preseason practice just a week before the season opener, scheduled for October 2 at home against Lake Forest. King spent the first few days focusing on the most rudimentary of skills—things like falling on loose footballs and basic tackling techniques. The latter was aided by the advent of the tackling dummy, a wooden apparatus that players used to hone their skills.

Coaches were always on the lookout for the next great advancement, and the dummy is a prime example. During the 1897 season, Penn's coach, George Woodruff, eschewed the wooden version for "the live dummy," and volunteered himself for the position. Disgusted with his team's tackling struggles, Woodruff appeared at practice "in great wads and rolls of padding and invited his charges to throw him." The *Minneapolis Journal* raved about the brilliance of Woodruff's plan, noting, "it is impossible to hurt the live dummy in any tackle with the armor used." Reinforcing its reputation for institutional ingenuity, rival Harvard took things a step further, sending a heavily padded ball carrier into the line for forty-five straight minutes during its practice. The *Journal* scribe was clearly impressed, reporting that the Harvard "plan worked admirably."

Teams also spent a significant portion of the preseason coordinating signals, which, in the days before the huddle, were the method of communicating which play would be run. The need for signals became apparent when football moved from the scrummage to the scrimmage. Teams had to have some sort of coordinated plan when the ball was snapped. In the early days, most squads called their plays with the use of gestures, but over time, opponents became adept at deciphering those movements.

Coded audible signals were the next logical step. Captains would yell out sentences with certain key words embedded within them. For instance, Yale's signals from 1882 included such utterances as "Look out quick, Deac!" and "Play up sharp, Charley!" Eventually, teams happened upon the idea of using numbers instead of words. There is some debate as to where and when precisely the numerical signals were invented. Historian Alexander Weyand credited a player at the Pennsylvania Military College in 1887, who he said came up with the idea of using cadets' serial numbers as a means of communicating who would carry the ball. Amos Alonzo Stagg claimed that the numerical signals were invented by Yale in 1889, when he was a part of the varsity team.

Regardless of their origins, the signals quickly evolved into an integral part of the game. "They became more and more complex in the later '90s," Stagg recalled, "running into problems in addition, multiplications, subtraction, even division, until football threatened to become an advanced course in mental arithmetic." The challenge was compounded by the rapid-fire nature of the game. After a ball carrier was brought down in the early days, players scrambled back to their feet and lined up right away. The snap came just ten seconds or so after the prior play had ended—making many of today's no-huddle offenses, where a play is signaled in from the sidelines after which the quarterback might spend fifteen seconds relaying blocking assignments, look slow by comparison. So, it was imperative that everyone was on the same page. "Signal practice" was a critical part of every team's pregame routine.

That complexity, and the limited preparation time at the outset of the season, led most of the major teams to schedule what amounted to practice games to get them ready for their higher profile opponents. Wisconsin's 1897 schedule was a case in point. The Badgers rolled through their first five games against an assortment of small college and high school teams by a combined total of 115 to nothing. While it was tough to glean too much about the team given the level of the competition, the *Chicago Tribune* quickly recognized O'Dea's individual talent. After the Badgers' season-opening 30–0 win over Lake Forest, the paper concluded simply, "Pat O'Dea is a wonderful kicker." But how wonderful was his team? That wouldn't be known until the Badgers' October 30 showdown with Minnesota, a matchup that generated enormous enthusiasm on the Wisconsin campus.

News of the impending game dominated the pages of the *Daily Cardinal* all week, as the paper reminded the students that "the Varsity must win this game and that all possible support is necessary to achieve this end." The editors excerpted an article from the *Minneapolis Journal* with a less-than-flattering scouting report on the Gophers. Minnesota was coming off a loss in one of its build-up games to Iowa State, which, at the time, was considered to be a second-tier opponent. "The University outfit," it said of Minnesota, "which had been touted a world beater all season, is showing up in poorer form as far as playing the game is concerned than it did a week ago."

Still, the *Cardinal* did all it could to avoid generating overconfidence, reminding Wisconsin rooters of Minnesota's recent dominance in the series, particularly when playing at home. The paper implored the students to do their part—detailing train schedules, ticket availability, and hotel space for those who were planning on making the journey to Minneapolis. It also helped publicize a pep rally, referred to as a "mass meeting," scheduled for the Wednesday night prior to the game—an event that would give the students who would not be making the trip one final chance "to show [their] feelings towards the Varsity eleven."

In anticipation of the rally, the *Cardinal* held a contest, encouraging students to submit songs and yells to be performed both at the meeting and in Minneapolis on Saturday. The top entries were published in the paper, which students were instructed to bring along with them that evening so they would have access to the lyrics. Among the winners was a song submitted by Phillip Allen, class of 1899, meant to be sung to the melody of the popular ragtime tune "There'll Be a Hot Time in the Old

Town Tonight." This adaptation proved so popular that it briefly became the school's fight song and remains a constant at Badgers sporting events to this day, perhaps most prominently at football games, where the band plays it after every Wisconsin touchdown.

Some of the other winning entries proved to be less enduring, however. For instance, it's been a while since any Wisconsin fan taunted Minnesota by cheering "Go-pher, Go-pher, Go-pher Go; Can't play football—No! No!! No!!!" or supported the locals by shouting "WIS-CON-SIN! WIS-CON-SIN! Will we win? Well I should grin; We'll win the tin; If it is a sin; and blow it in; on WISCONSIN." It's hard to believe those didn't catch on.

Newspapers in hand, five hundred students, nearly half of the undergraduate population, heeded the call, jamming into Library Hall, a spired stone structure that was one of the largest public buildings on campus. After a few introductory speeches, which were barely audible above the din, the team marched in single file. The ensuing pandemonium was nearly deafening. The students cheered lustily—"Varsity! Varsity! U! Rah! Rah! Wisconsin!" The commotion lasted for several minutes, finally dying down a bit when "Sunny" Pyre, the professor who had eschewed his lecture duties to play against the Gophers two years earlier, took the podium.

"That's the kind of cheering we're going to need on Saturday!" he told the audience. "Good hard cheering is vitally important in the midst of any football contest!" He then introduced the players one by one, culminating with O'Dea. "It will not be necessary for Wisconsin to make any touchdowns on Saturday," Pyre proclaimed, "for O'Dea alone could kick enough goals from the field to win the game!"

This elicited even more cheers. Coach King and several of the players, including his Australian star, then addressed the audience, each greeted by roars and wild applause. After everyone took some time to rehearse the new yells in unison, the meeting disbanded.

The anticipation was growing in Minnesota as well. Thursday's *Journal* went into great detail regarding each team's preparations, assuring its readers that, after the previous week's embarrassing defeat, the Gophers were "working harder than at any time this season." They certainly knew they'd be in for a challenge against Wisconsin, and O'Dea was the player who had them most concerned. "He is not highly rated for his other work," the paper said, "but when his leg swings, Wisconsin rooters are willing to forgive all his shortcomings."

The next evening, two horse-drawn omnibuses left Wisconsin's campus just before 6:30 p.m., packed to the gills with fifteen players apiece. When they arrived at the train depot, another huge crowd was there to greet them. Again, the cheers resonated: "U Rah! Rah! Wisconsin!"

An interloper had the nerve to yell out Minnesota's university cheer, one that still endures: "Ski-u-mah, Minnesota!" he shouted.

"Hang 'em, kill 'em!" the Wisconsin fans responded. Thinking it best to keep a lower profile, the lone Gopher supporter wasn't heard from again.

The scene became so chaotic that the players hunched close to one another to avoid getting trampled by their own fans. They were more than a bit relieved when the train rolled into the station "to whirl them away to Minneapolis for their great battle." They were followed by several more trainloads of supporters. As game day dawned, estimates were that as many as 1,000 Badger fans had invaded Minneapolis.

Hours before kickoff, both teams' cheering contingents jammed into the stands at the Old Athletic Park, a tiny baseball stadium wedged up against the West Hotel in downtown Minneapolis. The Minnesota crowd filled the south bleachers, with the Badgers fans across from them. The bands arrived an hour before game time, and from that point on, both sides exchanged yells, the "Ski-u-mahs" and "U Rah! Rahs" volleying back and forth in what amounted to an auditory tennis match. At 2:45, fifteen minutes after the scheduled kickoff time, the Badgers finally took the field. They gathered in a circle and passed the ball between one another while the north bleachers exploded in cheers. The Gophers emerged moments later. Fully 6,000 people were on hand by the time the game finally began—with the bleachers, the boxes, and the carriage stands all completely packed.

The Badgers won the toss and elected to take the ball and the wind. And then, in the words of the *Milwaukee Sentinel*, "the supreme moment of higher education in the West had come"—a sentence that reinforces the point that the loss of perspective in the world of collegiate sports is not a recent phenomenon.

On the first possession of the game, the Badgers' strategy immediately became evident: They wanted to turn it into a kicking game. Captain Jeremiah Riordan "called out," in the words of the *Sentinel*, "a conglomerate mass of figures as puzzling as a Chinese rebus and which would make a mathematics professor feel like a deaf and dumb man at a singing school." While it might have sounded complex, the upshot of the plan was simple—the Badgers snapped the ball to O'Dea, who immediately punted it away.

O'Dea's kicks allowed the Badgers to control the field position throughout the first half. The Gophers were unable to move the ball effectively, as, digging deeper into his bag of ethnic and generally politically incorrect metaphors, the *Sentinel* reporter observed that a Minnesota runner on this day "stood about as much chance for his life as a belligerent German at an Irish picnic."

The Badgers won the ongoing war of attrition, with O'Dea generally outkicking his counterpart, H. C. Loomis, by about 25 yards. Wisconsin eventually converted this field-position advantage brought on by its superiority in the kicking game into three first-half touchdowns, each worth four points. Those scores combined with three successful two-point goals after the touchdowns gave them an 18–0 lead just before the half ended.

It was then that O'Dea came through with the kick that may have launched the legend. The *Sentinel* reporter described it as "the really great spectacular event of the contest."

"Thirty-five yards away were the signals of victory, the goal posts. Before him, eleven men, with teeth clenched in determination that he should not do it. Back shot the leathern egg to his arms. Quicker than a wink, he dropped it. As it struck the ground, his right foot struck it clean and square. Away it soared into the air, straight and true between the posts, as if it had been shot by rule and line." The fantastic boot set off a celebration on the Wisconsin sideline. Unable to contain his joy and amazement, Pat's brother Andy, who was serving as the team's trainer, leaped into the air and twirled himself completely around. The goal was good for five points and gave the Badgers a commanding 23–0 halftime advantage.

The kick was recounted quite differently by *Los Angeles Times* columnist Dick Hyland fifty-two years later. Hyland's source for the description was Edward "Dad" Moulton, Minnesota's trainer that day, who went on to a long and successful career as a track coach at Stanford.

Moulton's account, said Hyland, went like this: "Pat started to run the ball wide, got trapped and proceeded to drop-kick the ball over the Gopher goal from 40 yards out on the dead run."

But that, according to Moulton, wasn't even the most noteworthy of O'Dea's accomplishments on that day. "A moment later, he stood on his own goal line and punted the ball over the Minnesota goal, 110 yards away! Dad Moulton . . . said he dropped the water bucket in amazement when O'Dea got it off."

While the record book backs Moulton's account, as Wisconsin credits O'Dea with a school-record 110-yard punt in the game, there are a couple of problems with this story. First, though highly complimentary of O'Dea's punting work, the various newspaper accounts carry no mention of the Australian star actually booting the ball the length of the field. Second, the *Daily Cardinal* had reported earlier in the week that there were special ground rules in effect for the game, as the field at the bandbox of a stadium was only 105 yards long, though this too was not mentioned in the game stories, so it is possible that it had been rectified by game time.

Regardless of whether or not it actually happened, the 110-yard punt against the Gophers became part of the O'Dea legend, perpetuated by none other than O'Dea himself. When discussing the kick many years later, a reporter joked that there "must have been a hurricane at your back, eh, Pat?" O'Dea replied, "No. There wasn't enough wind to rustle the maples that day."

The second half was a carbon copy of the first, with the Badgers continuing to dominate. Many of the Minnesota fans began to file out dejectedly in the middle of the second half, taunted by a Badgers supporter who yelled, "What are you leaving for? Ain't this a good enough game?"

The Badgers walked off the field with a 39–0 win. The 39 points were more than Wisconsin had scored in its seven prior meetings with Minnesota combined, and the newspaper accounts left no doubt who was responsible.

Under the headline O'DEA's GREAT KICK, the *Sentinel* reported, "Pat O'Dea did it. . . . Tonight the name of O'Dea is on the lips of everybody. He is bigger than any of Pillsbury's great mills." O'Dea's heroics weren't limited to kicking either, as he also "made the two longest runs of the day" on punt returns, showing that "his legs could do other things than punt."

The *Chicago Tribune* echoed that praise, saying of O'Dea's punting and kicking, "Nothing prettier has been seen on this field for a long time," adding, "O'Dea . . . not only kicked well but ran with the ball and tackled in a manner that pleased the watching thousands."

While Pat got the bulk of the credit, it was clear that this was a total team effort. "Never in history has a Wisconsin team played with the form displayed to-day. Every man played as though his life depended on it," the *Sentinel* raved. "Men who were thought to be weaklings and faint of heart were the foremost in the fray and they did not let up even for a single minute."

It was the Badgers' first-ever win in Minneapolis, and it was particularly sweet given the nature of the rivalry and the fact that the Gophers had won five of the prior seven meetings. After all, "it is an admitted fact that some men continued their university course for no other reason than to get a chance again to line up against Minnesota in a football game."

The victory set off a huge celebration amongst the Badger faithful who had made the journey northwest to Minneapolis. The Wisconsin fans gathered at the adjacent West Hotel, where they cheered, shouted, and held a two-hour-long "war dance," amid the band's repeated blaring of "Hot Town" and other popular tunes. The players were there, and each received thunderous ovations from the crowd. The party continued long into the night, with the university musicians marching from street to street in downtown Minneapolis, leading the enormous throng of red-clad revelers.

Back in Madison, many of those who had not made the trip had gathered at Library Hall. Thanks to a long-distance telephone setup, the action was continuously updated from Minneapolis, with announcements of the results of every play being made to the crowd. When the contest was over, an estimated 1,500 Badgers supporters took to the streets in celebration. The procession was led by a band, which provided an incessant, if somewhat less than musical, din. One of the revelers held a large banner decorated on one side with a picture of an enormous leg and the caption Pat's. The other side bore the inscription Chicago next. 40–0—a warning of sorts for Wisconsin's upcoming opponent. Residents and shopkeepers joined in the revelry, decorating their homes and stores with signs that read 39 to nit and other references to the Badgers' dominance. Bonfires, artillery fire, and nonstop shouting and chanting proceeded well into the evening.

The ride home was equally celebratory for the Badgers. As was typical of the day, the train made stops at virtually every crossroad. Each time it halted, the triumphant Badgers were greeted by excited throngs "waiting to glimpse the kicking kangaroo." Teammate Walter Alexander remembered that the team had fun with the fans that day, bringing out other players one by one—each of whom was initially greeted by cheers, which quickly turned to boos when it became apparent they weren't O'Dea.

The team finally rolled into Madison on Sunday afternoon—their arrival setting off additional jubilation, with more than 2,000 fans in attendance. After much cheering and reveling, the team was hustled onto a waiting bus, presumably to be hauled back to campus, but due to an apparent miscommunication, there were no horses to pull the vehicle. Undaunted, the Wisconsin fans literally took matters into their own hands. Two ropes were attached to the bus, "and in less than a minute the heroes of Saturday's game were being whirled up the hill by good Wisconsin muscles, accompanied by lusty Wisconsin yells."

When the procession finally reached campus, King and O'Dea both briefly thanked the students for their enthusiasm and their contribution to the team's victory. The satisfied crowd slowly began to drift home. The Badgers, meanwhile, turned their focus back to the gridiron. Another game was just six days away.

CHAPTER TEN

"THERE'S MURDER IN THAT GAME"

ON THE SAME LATE OCTOBER DAY THAT O'DEA AND THE BADGERS vanquished their great rival, the University of Georgia had a showdown of its own scheduled in Atlanta against the University of Virginia. Though Southern football was still not as highly regarded as the Eastern or even the Midwestern game, the anticipation on campus mirrored that which surrounded the more established powers. The Georgia student newspaper, *The Red and Black*, covered its pages with previews of the game, calling it "without a doubt the greatest athletic event that has ever occurred in the South." Though the paper acknowledged that the team from Charlottesville was a stronger unit, it refused to back down. "Every man on both teams realizes the fact that there is much at stake," the student scribe wrote, "and each one will enter the game with a determination to win or die."

Virginia dominated the game from the outset, with its strong line repeatedly battering Georgia's smaller, weaker unit with plays aimed right at the tackles. The men from Charlottesville were running exactly that type of play early in the second half when tragedy struck. Virginia halfback Julien Hill took a handoff and followed his blockers into the line.

Georgia fullback Richard Vonalbade Gammon rushed forward in an effort to tackle Hill. "Gammon missed his mark," the *Atlanta Journal* reported, "and fell heavily on his head, his chin striking the ground first.

The two teams tripped and fell on him." Players from both sides quickly popped back up for the next snap. Gammon didn't move.

"Von" Gammon, as his friends knew him, was the archetype of the Southern gentleman. "Von was of such heroic build and nature," an acquaintance recalled many years later, "that many held it the highest privilege to stand in his presence, that they might do his bidding, or simply be free to admire his noble qualities. He never smoked, drank, cursed or got out of humor."

Gammon also excelled at sports. He had grown up in an athletic household in Rome, Georgia, about 65 miles northwest of Atlanta. His family's two-story wooden home was an epicenter of sorts for kids in the neighborhood. The sprawling property on the banks of the Etowah River doubled as a recreation area: two tennis courts, parallel bars and a punching bag on the back porch, trapeze in the barn, and a locker in the cellar with every imaginable piece of sporting equipment kids could ever want—from skates, to baseballs, to mitts and football equipment.

Von's father, J. A. Gammon, was a local clothing merchant and a city councilman. His mother, Rosalind, was a member of the Daughters of the Confederacy. A tall, auburn-haired woman, she delighted in the constant presence of Rome's youth, often interrupting their play to hand out some freshly prepared sweets.

In addition to her kindness, Rosalind was known for her determination and strong convictions. Many years later, when a telephone lineman came by to inspect the family's property for an installation, Mrs. Gammon insisted that he do the job without damaging her favorite tree. After a short discussion, during which the workman implied that it might not be possible, he went on his way to continue his survey. When he reappeared later that day, saw in hand, he found Rosalind sitting under the tree waiting for him . . . wielding a double-barrel shotgun. Not surprisingly, the tree was spared.

As Gammon lay motionless on the field, many in the crowd immediately jumped to his aid. He was covered in sweaters and blankets and surrounded by a brigade of doctors, who quickly injected opiates to relieve the eighteen-year-old's obvious pain. Their diagnosis was a grave one. Von had a fractured skull. He lay on the field for nearly an hour, lapsing in and out of consciousness, before an ambulance arrived to take him to a nearby hospital. Gammon lingered for eleven agonizing hours. He died just before 4:00 a.m. on October 31, 1897, with his father at his side.

Reaction in Georgia was swift and severe. The day after Gammon's death, his teammates met and decided to disband the University of Georgia football team. That same day, the Georgia Senate proposed a bill that would make organized football games illegal in the state—punishable by fine. The state's House of Representatives offered up similar legislation just three days later. Within weeks both bills had passed by a combined tally of 122 to 7. They needed only the governor's signature to become law.

The statewide press, by and large, supported the measure. The *Athens Banner* called football "inhuman," while the *Columbus Enquirer* wrote that the banishment of the game would be "hailed with delight by thousands in Georgia." In a banner headline, Gammon's hometown paper, the *Rome Tribune,* proclaimed, Football Must Go; Stop The Deadly Game. The *Atlanta Journal* took a similar stand. In an editorial that ran the day after the bill's passage in the Senate, the paper concluded that the state had seen enough football "to force the conclusion that it is not a game that should be encouraged." It continued, "Governor Atkinson will, of course, sign the bill . . . and football matches may be considered a thing of the past." The article concluded that "Football will never become a great American game."

As Atkinson pondered his next move, he met resistance from an unlikely source—Rosalind Gammon. Just two days after her son's death, she penned a letter to Rome's representative in the Georgia house, James B. Nevin, urging him to help prevent the game's banishment, writing, "Grant me the right to request that my boy's death should not be used to defeat the most cherished object of his life."

Moved by Rosalind's pleas, and genuinely conflicted about the role of government in such a matter, Atkinson vetoed the bill. The measure, Atkinson declared, would go "beyond the proper limits of legislation, ignore the rights of parents, violate a sound legislative policy and oppose a fundamental principle of our government." Atkinson concluded by saying the game should be reformed rather than banished. The sport resumed at the University of Georgia in the fall of 1898, and Rosalind Gammon went down in history as "The Woman Who Saved Southern Football." A plaque detailing Gammon's death and his mother's pleas to continue the game is displayed prominently in Georgia's football complex to this day.

At the time, though, it seemed the stay of execution for the sport might be only temporary. Debates about the future of football raged throughout the 1890s—a difficult decade for the game. Those participating in the more rational disputes essentially fell into two camps. On one side were those who believed the sport was out of control. They cited the conflict with the mission of universities, the disproportionate focus on the game, the fawning media, and, most persuasively, the game's violence, as a means to further their argument. On the other side, boosters of the game, while generally admitting that it could and should be reformed, argued that the positive impact in areas such as character building and school spirit outweighed the potential drawbacks.

Much of the resistance came from inside the universities. Harvard, the nation's oldest and most prestigious college, was a case in point. The *Harvard Graduates' Magazine* carried frequent articles criticizing the role of the game in Cambridge. In an 1893 piece entitled "The Abuses of Training," graduate J. Ralph Finlay outlined a typical schedule for the Harvard eleven, contending that, "in November, the practice takes up nearly the whole day." Finlay ran through a litany of evils associated with the overemphasis on the game—everything from declining academic performance, to battered and bruised bodies, to a dependence on sleeping medications. His disdainful and moderately ironic conclusion captured the conundrum that surrounded college football in the 1890s and continues to challenge it today: "[W]hen their mental condition was such that study of any kind was useless; when their pale and haggard faces, dull eyes, and languid manner were constantly commiserated by classmates and professors; one might reasonably suppose that these men were having at least a fair amount of football. But it seems they were not, for they did not beat Yale."

Though not quite as focused on Harvard's struggles against its rival, many of the university's instructors were equally unimpressed with the emphasis placed on the sport. "During the autumn a veritable craze seizes the community on the subject of football," economics professor Frank William Taussig wrote, "and for weeks the most important question before the public (at least of the seaboard States) seems to be whether eleven youths dressed in red, or in black and yellow, will show themselves more expert in rushing a football than eleven other youths dressed in blue."

Harvard president William Eliot never missed an opportunity to criticize football, observing in his President's Report of 1895 that the game "grows worse and worse as regards foul and violent play, and the number and gravity of the injuries which the players suffer," while pointing out "the ever present liability to death on the field." In Eliot's mind, there was plenty of blame to go around for the game's evils, as he pointed a finger at virtually everyone associated with the sport, excepting, interestingly enough, the players themselves. "They are swayed by a tyrannical public opinion—partly ignorant and partly barbarous—to the formation of which graduates and undergraduates fathers, mothers, and sisters, leaders of society, and the veriest gamblers and rowdies all contribute."

But it wasn't just the ivory-tower academics who found football appalling. After witnessing a particularly brutal Harvard–Yale match in the 1890s, boxing champ John L. Sullivan boarded a train for New York City. In the washroom, he encountered noted football official Paul Dashiell, who asked the prizefighter what he had thought of the match. Sullivan lowered his voice to a whisper before observing, "There's murder in that game."

Many at Harvard agreed. After the bloody debacle against Yale in Springfield in 1894 that ultimately led to a brief cancellation of the series between the two schools, the Cambridge university took up the broader question of football's future. In February of 1895, the faculty voted by a margin of 24 to 12 to ask the committee on athletics to ban the game.

In response, the committee proposed a number of changes covering areas as disparate as rules alterations and ticket sales, designed to make the sport both safer and saner. The committee stated that they "have no illusions as to the evils of intercollegiate football in its present condition: but they are reluctant to believe that Yale and Harvard teams cannot compete with each other in the spirit of gentlemen, or that it is impossible to bring the sport into a proper relation with the main purpose of college life."

Another back-and-forth exchange ensued, with the faculty issuing a statement declaring that it remained "of the opinion that no student under their charge should be permitted to take part in intercollegiate football contests," only to be overruled by the athletic committee, which said the game should and would continue.

Despite the internal resistance, the decision to continue playing the sport had the strong support of several prominent Harvard alums. As early as 1893, Theodore Roosevelt, then serving on the Civil Service Commission, advocated in favor of the game, contending that sports in general, and football in particular, helped create well-rounded men. In an article in *Harper's Weekly*, Roosevelt, the advocate of Muscular Christianity, acknowledged some inherent risk in football, but concluded, "it is mere unmanly folly to try to do away with the sport because the risk exists." The future president expressed a similar opinion in an 1895 letter to Walter Camp, saying that he was "utterly disgusted" with the efforts by Eliot and the Harvard faculty to banish the game, adding that he "would a hundred fold rather keep the game as it is now, with the brutality, than give it up."

Just a year later, addressing the Harvard graduating class of 1896, Senator Henry Cabot Lodge echoed those sentiments. "I happen to be one of those," Lodge proclaimed proudly, "who believes profoundly in athletic contests. The time given to athletic contests and the injuries incurred on the playing-field are part of the price which the English-speaking race has paid for being world-conquerors."

Given the aggressive efforts to reduce risk and injury in our time, attitudes like those of Roosevelt, Lodge, and many other defenders of late nineteenth- and early twentieth-century football seem almost impossible to fathom. What were they thinking? What kind of person would view injury, or even death, on the football field as some sort of grand, collective "character builder?"

The context of the time is crucial here. Fewer and fewer men were engaged in professions that focused on traditionally male characteristics, such as physical strength, bravery, or vitality. This shift brought the entire concept of what it meant to be a man into question. No one would impugn the ruggedness of early or mid-nineteenth-century farmers, artisans, Wild West settlers, or Civil War soldiers. But, as the workplace evolved, the number of men engaged in such virile occupations decreased. "Where would a sense of maleness come from for the worker who sat at a desk all day?" Elliott Gorn asked in a study of the rise of bare-knuckle boxing.

Many believed that something was needed to fill that void, to prevent an entire generation of males from deteriorating into a bunch of effete sissies. "The whole generation is womanized," a character in Henry James's 1885 novel *The Bostonians* complained. "The masculine character, the ability to dare and endure, to know and yet not fear reality, to look the world in the face and take it for what it is . . . that is what I want to preserve."

Organized sports, particularly violent ones, were part of the answer. They weren't simply contests unto themselves, but part of a broader metaphor, a chance to simulate the physical struggles that developed manly men. In 1896 Walter Camp noted the "remarkable and interesting likeness between theories which underlie great battles and the miniature conquests on the gridiron." For Roosevelt, who had tirelessly developed his body after a sickly childhood, the message was simple: "In short, in life, as in a foot-ball game, the principle to follow is: Hit the line hard; don't foul and don't shirk, but hit the line hard!"

University of Chicago president William Rainey Harper put it all in starker, more shocking terms. "If the world can afford to sacrifice the lives of men for commercial gain, it can much more easily afford to make similar sacrifice on the altar of vigorous and unsullied manhood," Harper said in 1895. "The question of a life or a score of lives is nothing compared with that of moral purity, human self-restraint, in the interests of which, among college men, outdoor athletic sports contribute more than all other agencies combined."

While some football advocates defended the game with statements like Harper's, others contended that the injury problem wasn't nearly as bad as the sport's opponents were making it out to be. In 1894 Walter Camp posited just that argument in a book entitled *Football Facts and Figures*. Camp sent out questionnaires to current and former players, as well as coaches and administrators. He then published them, claiming, "in order to have a fair showing of both sides, all the letters received . . . are printed." That assertion was cast into doubt many years later, with one historian claiming that as many as 20 percent of the responses were omitted.

Even still, Camp did quote some former players who had their hesitations about the sport. "The game as played today is much too rough," said one, while another discussed an injury that had kept him out of school for six months and that had "cooled my ardor for the game personally." But even those notes were couched in language that spoke positively of the football experience.

Some repeated the arguments of Roosevelt, Lodge, and Harper, claiming that the nation's prospects depended on the game's survival. "[T]he man of the future must be able to elbow his way among rough men in the foul air of primary elections; he may need courage enough to take his part in vigilant and safety committees and the like; he may need to 'tackle' an anarchist now and then and perhaps oftener. Where shall he develop his courage?" one respondent asked. "Can he do it where there is no physical danger? If the game of football has a moral and mental side to it, if it furnishes good ideals of courageous manhood and of physical excellence to those who play it and to those who look on, if it can rescue the dude from his nambypambyism, then play football."

More typical were such testimonials as the one from Pudge Hef-felfinger, the most feared player in the game just a few years before, who said of football, "During all the years I have played, I have known no one personally who has been seriously injured."

Camp's book certainly had a place in the debate, but the strongest arguments about football took place in the popular press, many of which emulated the Yale advisor's approach, soliciting and publishing a wide range of opinions. One popular tactic among the game's supporters was a tendency to, in essence, blame the victim. Within a couple of weeks of Gammon's death, for instance, the *Chicago Tribune* surveyed a number of national football captains about the issue of violence in the sport. Cornell's captain asserted that most of the injuries had taken place in smaller schools, "where the men have a crude knowledge of the game." Princeton's Garrett Cochran concurred, saying, "Of course the game is rough, but the majority of those who are injured throughout the country . . . are men or boys who are not in condition to play the game." Penn's captain, John Minds, went so far as to suggest that players were faking injuries in order to get fresh men into the game.

But, gradually, more and more newspapers began to campaign for reform. The *Chicago Tribune* railed against the sport, saying "it is ridiculous to apply the term 'game' to the rush of bruisers carried on for gate money in the presence of thirty thousand spectators." The *New York Tribune* assumed a similar stance, contending, "The chief objection to football . . . is that a football player enters every game with a reasonable expectation of being more or less completely crippled in the course of it." Throughout the 1890s, the same newspapers and magazines that had helped build up the game now became its harshest critics. This was particularly true in New York, as a byproduct of a trend that came to be known as "yellow journalism."

Yellow journalism got its name from a comic strip called *Hogan's Alley,* which originally was published in Pulitzer's *World.* The strip's main character was a child in a yellow nightshirt, known as the "Yellow Kid." The cartoon proved so popular that Hearst paid its creator to move it to the *Journal* as well, and it came to symbolize the battle between the two newspaper magnates—hence, the term "yellow."

Yellow journalism encompassed much more than the tussle over a comic strip, though. It was a movement that took the gradual shift toward human-interest stories and expanded it in a sensationalistic manner. It was a natural offshoot of the circulation wars of the late nineteenth century—a means for increasing distribution, which, in turn, paved the way for higher advertising rates. It was characterized by enormous headlines, frequent use of large pictures, and, often, flat-out fabrications. The articles themselves contained, in the words of author Will Irwin, "reading matter so easy, with the startling points so often emphasized that the weariest mechanic sitting in his socks on Sunday morning, could not fail to get a thrill of interest."

Joseph Pulitzer is generally credited with originating what came to be known as the "yellow" movement. By the end of the 1880s, his *World,* in Will Irwin's opinion, "was altogether the most reckless, the most sensational and the most widely discussed newspaper in New York." It was also the most successful. In 1890 Pulitzer moved his operation into the new Pulitzer Building on Park Row in Lower Manhattan. It was a spectacular edifice—the tallest in the world upon its completion—topped off by a stunningly ornate dome, visible well into New York Harbor. "The first sight of the New World for immigrants entering New York," Pulitzer biographer James McGrath Morris notes, "was not a building of commerce, banking, or industry. Rather, it was a temple of America's new mass media."

One glance at Pulitzer's shrine reinforced the power of sensationalism. Thus, "When William Randolph Hearst purchased the *Journal* in 1895," Irwin noted, "he copied and even amplified Pulitzer's approach." As Irwin put it succinctly, "Life, as it percolated through the *World* and *Journal* became melodrama."

Football's troubles happened to coincide with the peak of the "yellow" battles in the mid-1890s, and through the combination of its violence and popularity, the sport became easy and frequent fodder for the "yellow" press. On November 7, 1897, just a week after Gammon's death, Hearst's *Journal* devoted its entire front page to football violence, under the headline, A LAW TO MAKE FOOTBALL A CRIME. It included three vivid illustrations of players with broken spines and fractured skulls, each purporting to show the exact injuries that had killed players on the gridiron that fall. One of the drawings included the caption, "How Von Gammon Was Killed by Concussion of the Brain." The accompanying article included the text of Georgia's antifootball bill.

Not to be outdone, Pulitzer's *World* published a front-page story on football violence on the following Sunday. The centerpiece was an enormous drawing of a skeleton wearing only a sheet emblazoned with the word DEATH. The figure was snapping a football. Behind it was a field strewn with fallen players. The caption read, "The twelfth player in every football game."

Of these articles and others that appeared throughout the next few years, Michael Oriard has observed, "These cannot be considered campaigns to clean up football; they were campaigns for circulation." Indeed, as Oriard points out, the same papers that on their front pages were calling for an end to the sport, also carried evenhanded accounts of the previous day's games, "untouched by any suggestion that elsewhere in the paper football was being exposed as mayhem."

The *New York Herald* on November 13, 1897, was a case in point. Under the headline DEATH ON THE FOOTBALL FIELD, the paper listed the names of nine players who had perished playing the game in the previous year, complete with detailed accounts of their demise. The paper claimed that it was publishing the report in order to arouse public spirit to rescue the sport "from a brutality which is only paralleled by the exhibition in the Coliseum of ancient Rome, where men died to gratify the savage instincts of onlookers." Right next to that story was a glowing preview piece about the renewal of the Harvard–Yale rivalry, which had been on hiatus for two years after the violent 1894 game in Springfield. The article contained not one mention of the brutality that was plaguing the sport.

While the methods of the yellow press might have been extreme, the truth was that the game was in serious trouble. In addition to the near-banishment in Georgia, antifootball bills were introduced in Indiana, Nebraska, Arkansas, Missouri, and Illinois—all of them in 1897 alone. The Illinois bill hit particularly close to home for Pat O'Dea and the Badgers.

CHAPTER ELEVEN

SLUGBALL

As Pat O'Dea stood ready to receive the opening kickoff of Wisconsin's showdown with the University of Chicago, he had to be a bit awed by the scene around him. Chicago's Marshall Field was packed. "The spectators stood on sawhorses, overturned barrels and the covering of the grandstand. They sat astride of fences, peered out of windows and hung on to telegraph poles," the *Chicago Tribune* reported the next day. "Far off in the distance—so far that the individuals in the mass were barely distinguishable—the roofs of overlooking buildings were black with people." The paper estimated that 10,000 fans were on hand on that November day in 1897—the largest crowd in the field's history.

The story wasn't just how many people were there, either. It was who was there. Former Wisconsin governor George Peck, Wisconsin senator John Spooner, and Chicago mayor Carter Harrison Jr. were among the dignitaries packed into the grandstand. They had come to see a game that many thought might determine the championship of the West—as both teams came in boasting undefeated records. Most in the stands were feeling the buzz of eager anticipation. But one notable attendee, Chicago alderman Nathan Plotke, was feeling nothing but dread.

O'Dea caught the kickoff and weaved his way upfield. "Plotke," the *Tribune* reported, "drew in his breath sharply." O'Dea was taken down, sandwiched between two Chicago tacklers just shy of midfield. "There, I knew they'd kill him!" Plotke reportedly exclaimed. His face showed some relief as all three men jumped up and took their places for the first snap of the game. Plotke allegedly "smiled weakly," and "perspiration stood out on his forehead in drops."

Nathan Plotke had hoped this game would never occur. He was the sponsor of a bill that would prohibit the playing of football games within Chicago's city limits. The ordinance was supposed to be brought to a vote in the city council meeting a few days prior to the game, but those proceedings were put on hold out of respect for fellow alderman Henry Ludolph, who was struck by a train and killed on his way to the meeting. Now, a horrified Plotke sat in the stands watching the game he opposed so strongly.

Plotke was a German by birth, having immigrated to Chicago in 1860 at the age of eighteen, settling in a portion of the city's North Side that was heavily populated by natives of his homeland. He was both a practicing attorney and a politician, serving as the assistant state's attorney before his election to the city council. To call Plotke a crusader would be an overstatement. Prior to his campaign against football, his most publicized endeavor had come the previous winter when he led a successful ban against view-obstructing high hats in the city's theaters. For months now, the local papers had been referring to him with terms like "the hat ordinance man."

Plotke's antifootball proposal was straightforward, aiming to ban the playing and watching of the game within the city limits of Chicago. Each offense would be punishable by a fine of between five and fifty dollars. The proposal had the strong backing of the *Tribune*'s editorial staff, which had been merciless in its attacks against football throughout the mid-1890s, derisively referring to the game as "slugball."

"When slugball has been driven out," the *Tribune* opined at the end of the 1896 season, "then, perhaps, the students will enjoy the restoration of that interesting and wholesome game of football which some people will remember as an admirable part of the athletic curriculum of the colleges a few years ago."

The attacks continued at the outset of the 1897 season. "[F]or several weeks to come," the paper editorialized at the end of September, "the various grounds set apart for the killing, wounding, wrenching, bruising and slugging of certain young men who were sent to college to obtain a liberal education will be occupied for this elevating purpose." As debates over football's future raged in its pages throughout the fall, the paper remained consistent in its strongly worded critiques of the game. "THE TRIBUNE's main position remains untouched," the paper remarked in late November, "namely: that slugball as it is now played is not only a brutal, ungentlemanly, and demoralizing game, but the most brutal, ungentlemanly, and demoralizing of all games. . . . As THE TRIBUNE has already said: There are numerous sports and manly exercises which are just as beneficial to mankind as slugball is, and are free from its objectionable features; and there appears no reason, therefore, why it should not be condemned for a disgusting, brutal, degrading, ungentlemanly, dangerous and often fatal practice."

Incidents such as the death of Georgia's Von Gammon gave the paper plenty of fodder, and the *Tribune* kept a running tally of slugball casualties throughout the 1897 season. An article published on November 12, the day before the Wisconsin–Chicago game, read, "Since Oct. 25, when THE TRIBUNE stated the summary to be two killed, three probably fatally injured, and eighty-eight severely injured, two more players have been killed, two have been injured with probably fatal results, and thirty-eight have been severely injured."

As a means of furthering its case, the paper essentially sent a reporter to Marshall Field to watch Plotke watch the game. The result was an article that had the feel of a "yellow" fabrication. ANTI-FOOTBALL CITY FATHER LOOKS ON WITH HORROR, one headline proclaimed. SURE WISCONSIN AND CHICAGO LADS WILL INFLICT DEATH, read another. While it is eminently plausible that Plotke was shocked by the game's brutality, many of the quotations and observations that were attributed to him throughout the story border on the preposterous. For instance, the reporter claimed to have caught the following one-sided conversation between Plotke and his companion: "'See, they have a band,' said the protector of the people's limbs, "'and hundreds of instruments to make a noise. That is just like real war, isn't it? They want to drown the groans and screams of the wounded, I suppose.'"

After Wisconsin's Hereward Peele was knocked out of the game with a wrenched knee, the paper claimed these observations from Plotke: "There is a fine young fellow condemned to live out his life with one leg—a hopeless cripple. If I can prevent one suffering mother's heart from breaking—I shall feel myself well repaid for a year's labor in getting my football ordinance into force. Some day I shall be put in history with Garibaldi and George Washington."

Finally, Plotke had seen his fill. "O, this is terrible! Take me away! Take me away! I can't bear the sight any longer," he purportedly exclaimed. Then "[h]e covered up his face with his hands and did not look out again on the hilarious throng until well on his way to a carriage." As upset as Plotke was after viewing the spectacle, his was the minority opinion.

The buildup to the contest had begun almost immediately after the Badgers' win over Minnesota two weeks before, with the *Daily Cardinal* reporting, "Never has there been so intense an interest in football circles as at present."

Wisconsin had played one game in the interim, an 11–0 win over Beloit, a small in-state college near the Illinois border. Though the score was a bit underwhelming, most Wisconsin rooters quickly dismissed any calls for concern. It seemed reasonable to assume that the team hadn't been properly focused due to its impending showdown with the Maroons. Additionally, O'Dea had battled a sore leg for much of the week, though he managed a goal from the field in the second half and punted marvelously, repeatedly sending the ball "over the heads of the baffled collegiate." His performance once again drew headlines. O'DEA'S DAY AGAIN, proclaimed the *Milwaukee Sentinel,* while the *Daily Cardinal* agreed that O'DEA'S KICKING WAS A FEATURE OF THE GAME.

The Badgers departed for Chicago in the early afternoon of Friday, November 12, accompanied by several coaches and trainers as well as the eighteen-member university band. After a trip of a bit more than five hours, they arrived in the city and headed straight for the Victoria Hotel in the south portion of the Loop, where they checked in and had dinner. After the meal the team enjoyed a variety show from the boxes of the Chicago Opera House.

While the Badgers were relaxing downtown, a little farther south some of the Maroons were, well, acting like college kids. Herschberger and one of his teammates got wrapped up in an egg-eating contest. The Chicago star consumed a startling total of thirteen. Sadly, history does not tell us whether that was enough to win the contest. But that battle had a huge impact on the more important one the next day, as Herschberger had to be held out of the lineup due to a severe stomach ache. He was, Chicago coach Amos Alonzo Stagg recalled many years later, "of no use to us."

After about fifteen minutes of scoreless play, the Badgers struck. Wisconsin blocked a Chicago punt, Harvey Holmes scooped it up, and then raced 45 yards for the touchdown, which gave the Badgers a 4–0 lead. A bit later in the half, O'Dea, in the brilliantly metaphorical words of the *Middleville* (Michigan) *Sun*, "composed as a woman cutting biscuits from soft dough," nailed a dropkick, reported variously at between 40 and 50 yards, though definitely "one of the longest . . . ever made on the Chicago field." That put the Badgers up 9–0. Shortly thereafter, O'Dea showed off his punting prowess, as he boomed a 75 yarder. Just before the half, O'Dea proved he was more than just a great kicker, returning a punt 47 yards, deep into Chicago territory. The Badgers eventually punched in a short touchdown, with Peele carrying it across the goal line. They led 13–0 at halftime.

While O'Dea's exploits had stolen the show, the Badgers also shined on defense. Wisconsin was surprisingly strong at the ends, purported before the game to be one of its weaknesses. The Maroons' speedy backs were unable to get outside and eventually were relegated to simply trying to run straight into the line, where they had their most success. They did manage a late touchdown and safety, due in large part to two Wisconsin fumbles, but the game was never in doubt in the second half.

As for Herschberger, the previous night's feeding frenzy turned him into a spectator. The Chicago students yelled to put him in after halftime, and Stagg nodded his approval. The Maroons' star took off his sweater and began to put on his jersey, but, after a brief consultation with one of Chicago's trainers, he thought better of it. The sweater went back on, and Herschberger spent the rest of the game watching dejectedly from the sidelines.

The November sky began to darken as the game dragged on, until it became virtually impossible to distinguish the players from one another. With Wisconsin leading 23–8 and time still left in the game, the fans began to encroach on the field. Within moments the gridiron was "a jumble of mixed up players and crowding spectators. It was a sight, unique and strange to see from the grand stands, and it stopped the game. The Chicago team left the field. It had enough."

As the Maroons and their fans departed dejectedly, the Wisconsin contingent began its celebration. A young Badger supporter, crimson ribbons flapping in the light breeze, made his way up the flagpole by the bleachers, knife between his teeth, and cut off a University of Chicago flag that had been flying throughout the game. The young man slid down and hid the flag under his overcoat. "Some students in Madison," the *Milwaukee Sentinel* predicted, "will doubtless be richer by a treasure which the Chicago men . . . will regret perhaps almost as much as they do the game."

When the team returned to the Victoria Hotel, it was greeted in the lobby by a huge throng of supporters. Coach Phil King addressed the masses, and then he and Captain Jeremiah Riordan were hoisted on the crowd's shoulders and paraded around as the group howled with delight, singing "Hot Time" and belting out Wisconsin yells. The celebration continued long into the night, with Badger players and fans taking over the third and fourth floors of the Victoria, making "the walls resound with 'U rah-rah Wisconsin' as though there was no one else in the house."

That was mild compared to the scene back in Madison, though, where the sounds of horns and firecrackers pierced the night, while a mass of undergraduates marched through the city performing university yells.

The celebrating students eventually convened on the lower campus, where they built a bonfire fueled by whatever scraps they could find, including "all the loose wood at Ladies' hall." Despite the contributions from the women, the wood supply was depleted quickly. Hoping to keep the conflagration going, a group of revelers attempted to tear down the fencing around the construction site of the new library, before being fought off by a dozen or so night watchmen.

The papers the next day left little doubt as to who was responsible for the Badgers' win. The *Tribune*'s account began with one word, "Outclassed," but quickly turned its focus to O'Dea. "Pat O'Dea did it," the paper stated, adding, "one man's toe settled the struggle." The *Milwaukee Sentinel* agreed, saying, "O'Dea's punting was the most brilliant feature of the day."

King and Riordan both said afterward that they thought the final margin should have been even larger than it was, actually expressing some dissatisfaction with Wisconsin's play. The Badgers' self-critique didn't sit well with Stagg, who challenged Wisconsin to return to Chicago at some point over the next few weekends for a rematch, offering up a massive $5,000 guarantee. Riordan quickly shot down the idea, saying, "Would Princeton play Yale a second game if she defeated her Saturday? Certainly not and there is no precedent for such a move."

Of course, there was also the issue of whether football would remain legal in Chicago. The city council gathered to vote on Plotke's ordinance the Monday after the game, and while the *Tribune*'s coverage might have led one to believe it had a reasonable chance at passage, the truth was quite the opposite. Mayor Harrison was a strong proponent of the game, and he vehemently opposed the measure. All of his cabinet members and several other leading aldermen shared that perspective. Additionally, a coalition of aldermen from predominately Irish wards united against the bill, fearing that it would also prohibit Gaelic football, a favorite of their constituents. Seeing the writing on the wall, and hoping to avoid the embarrassment of an overwhelming defeat, Plotke asked to have the measure moved to a committee, with hopes that it would die there. The opposition blocked that move, demanding that the ordinance be brought to a vote. It was defeated 57 to 5. The local football world turned its attention back to the fight for the Western championship.

Only one intercollegiate contest still remained for the Badgers. They were slated to face Northwestern on Thanksgiving Day in Evanston. To fill the nearly two-week void between games, though, King scheduled a contest against a group of Wisconsin alumni, the first-ever such matchup, but an event that would become a bit of a tradition during the next decade.

In a game that was dismissed as "little more than a farce" by the *Daily Cardinal,* the alumni prevailed 6–0, handing the lackadaisical and disinterested Badgers their first loss of the season. The defeat, though, would have no impact on the Western championship, which focused only on games between conference schools. In fact, speculation ran rampant that King had actually wanted the varsity to lose in order to protect them from overconfidence heading into the Northwestern game. "King suspected letdown," the *Milwaukee Journal* claimed, "so he 'framed' the varsity with the officials in the alumni game and the decrepit old grads won by a touchdown. Then King soundly berated the team as a bunch of quitters." With those words ringing in their ears, the Badgers used the loss as motivation and turned their attention to Northwestern.

By this point, O'Dea, the relative unknown at the outset of the season, had become the clear focus of the Badgers team, and on the day before the game, the *Milwaukee Journal* ran a lengthy piece profiling the Wisconsin star. "The present season in the west will be remembered for one feature more than for any other one thing—the brilliant career of Pat O'Dea of the University of Wisconsin team," the *Journal* asserted. "He has put new life into his team and treated spectators to kicking that is not surpassed in the country for its length and beauty."

The article then gave a bit of O'Dea's background, including the untrue story of his "saving a woman from drowning" during his youth in Australia. It provided details on his Australian Rules Football career, where he was "recognized as a star of the first magnitude," but also focused on other athletic accomplishments. "Just before coming to the United

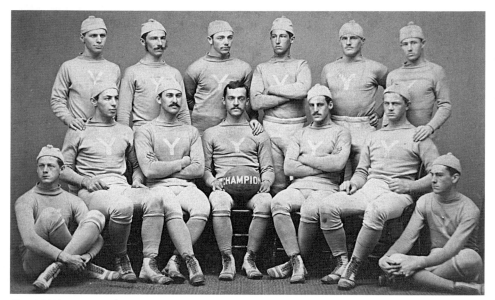

The 1876 Yale football team. Captain Eugene V. Baker (holding the football) emphasized strenuous training methods and instilled in his men a desire not just to compete, but to win. This new focus on victory set intercollegiate athletics on the path it follows to this day. Walter Camp is standing with his arms crossed, over Baker's left shoulder.
COURTESY OF MANUSCRIPTS AND ARCHIVES, YALE UNIVERSITY LIBRARY

An artist's rendering of the first ever intercollegiate football game between Princeton and Rutgers in November 1869.
COURTESY OF MANUSCRIPTS AND ARCHIVES, YALE UNIVERSITY LIBRARY

Walter Camp in his Yale senior class picture.
COURTESY OF MANUSCRIPTS AND ARCHIVES, YALE UNIVERSITY LIBRARY

With 50,000 fans watching, Princeton's Phil King places the ball at midfield to begin the 1893 game against Yale. The Tigers are aligned in a flying wedge.
COURTESY OF MANUSCRIPTS AND ARCHIVES, YALE UNIVERSITY LIBRARY

The Princeton team that upset Yale on Thanksgiving Day, 1893. Captain Phil King stands in the center row with his left hand on his hip. William Ward, who scored the winning touchdown, reclines beside the player with the ball.
AUTHOR'S COLLECTION

THE TWELFTH PLAYER IN EVERY FOOTBALL GAME.

An 1897 cartoon in Joseph Pulitzer's *New York World*—an example of the type of yellow journalism that fueled the debate regarding football violence.
AUTHOR'S COLLECTION

The 1894 Yale football team in a wedge formation.
COURTESY OF MANUSCRIPTS AND ARCHIVES, YALE UNIVERSITY LIBRARY

Pennsylvania, lined up in its revolutionary "guards back" formation in a game against Harvard during the 1897 season. Note the number of men behind the line of scrimmage as well as the absence of a neutral zone between the two teams.
COURTESY OF MANUSCRIPTS AND ARCHIVES, YALE UNIVERSITY LIBRARY

CHICAGO AND WISCONSIN.
NOVEMBER 12, 1898.

The 1898 game between Chicago and Wisconsin at Chicago's Marshall Field. The Maroons prevailed 6–0 in a contest marred by pregame disputes between the two schools.
COURTESY OF SPECIAL COLLECTIONS RESEARCH CENTER, UNIVERSITY OF CHICAGO LIBRARY

The 1899 Wisconsin football team. Pat O'Dea is in the middle row, fourth from the right as you face the photograph. Phil King is standing toward the back in the brimmed hat. Andrew O'Dea is seated in the front row, with the cap and the mustache. Given that the number of men in the photograph matches the number of men in the traveling party, it is possible that this picture was taken en route to the Yale game.

Yale's Howard Richards races 65 yards for a touchdown in the Elis' 1899 game against Wisconsin.

A rare photo of Pat O'Dea in action. O'Dea is seen here punting in Wisconsin's 1899 game against Yale.

University of Chicago coach Amos Alonzo Stagg in 1901.

The University of Chicago's greatest star, Walter Eckersall, being honored at halftime of his final home game in 1906. Less than two months later, Eckersall was expelled from the university.

University of Chicago coach Amos Alonzo Stagg observing the University of Arkansas football team in March 1910. Arkansas was experimenting with possibilities for implementing the forward pass. Stagg is in the dark pants on the far left.

The (Madison) *Capital Times* celebrating Pat O'Dea's return to Wisconsin for the 1934 Homecoming celebration.
COURTESY OF DAVE VITALE

Pat O'Dea on the cover of the 1934 Wisconsin Homecoming program, the day O'Dea made his return to Madison.
AUTHOR'S COLLECTION

Pat O'Dea kicking, Red Grange holding in a 1957 photograph.
COURTESY OF DAVE VITALE

A letter from Pat O'Dea to a fan, written just a few months before O'Dea's death in 1962. In it, O'Dea references a 110-yard punt against Minnesota in 1897—a play that is not supported by contemporaneous accounts. He also discusses his famous running dropkick against the Gophers in 1899.
COURTESY OF DAVE VITALE

Feb 5-1962

Greetings Frank!
  It was in 1897 that I made the 110 yard punt against Minnesota I do not recall if Buzz was in that game but he was captain in 1899. When I made the 60 yard running drop kick over our Dobies Head final score was 19 Minn. 0. 1897 score was 39 Minn. 0 —
Best as always
Pat O'Dea

States," the paper reported, "O'Dea rode the winning horse in the greatest annual steeple chase race in Melbourne. But this sport did not meet with the approval of his parents and he gave it up."

The writer observed that "O'Dea does not look the athlete he is. He is tall, thin and lanky, but there is not an ounce of superfluous flesh on his body." Appearances aside, O'Dea's skill was immediately apparent to anyone entering his room, as the walls were lined "with more ribbons and medals than a prize dog at a bench show."

After outlining the Aussie's accomplishments in the 1897 season, the paper concluded by describing his unusual style. "A feature of O'Dea's punting is his ability to kick the ball while on a dead run fully as far and as true as when standing still. This he does by a peculiar side movement."

As it turned out, though, there were not many opportunities for O'Dea to showcase that style in the game against Northwestern. The conditions were nothing short of brutal. An almost continuous downpour over the previous couple of days relegated the field to a glorified mud pit. The muck prevented the Badgers from executing their normal kicking game, which, as it turned out, they didn't really need. Henry Cochems plowed through the Purple for three rushing touchdowns, and Wisconsin cruised to a 22–0 win. Meanwhile, a bit farther south, Chicago handed Michigan its first loss of the season. Those two results combined to make the Badgers the undisputed Western champs.

The team remained in Chicago for a celebratory Thanksgiving dinner. Not surprisingly, the turkey disappeared quickly. They had plenty to be thankful for. It was a season that had seen the Badgers outscore their opponents 210–14—including an 84–8 margin against their three highest profile opponents: Minnesota, Chicago, and Northwestern. "Wisconsin has a clear and unquestionable title to the western championship," said Everts Wrenn, a well-known official. "In my opinion the Badger team is by all odds the strongest team in the West this season." Northwestern coach Jesse Van Doozer agreed, saying, "if any team can claim the championship, that team is Wisconsin. In general form, they are superior to all the others."

The impact of the Badgers' season was felt throughout the state, with the *Chippewa Falls Herald* seeing it as a bit of a turning point in how the school would be viewed by the youth of Wisconsin. Students who may not have known about the university before, the paper said, might now be inclined to continue their studies in Madison. "Hereafter the game will be stoutly defended by the people of the Badger state and earnest prayers which will be constantly offered up by its numerous admirers will be for a continuance of the development of such formidable football weapons as the wonderful leg of Pat O'Dea."

As O'Dea and his teammates left the Chicago area to head back to Madison, representatives of the seven Western Conference schools gathered the day after Thanksgiving at the Chicago Beach Hotel, near the University of Chicago campus, to discuss football's future. The day ended with a surprising announcement. "Resolved: That this conference unanimously favors such a modification of the rules now governing football as will make the game less rough."

Under the headline No More Slugball, the *Tribune* hailed the decision as "a step which will startle the whole football world." Though light on specifics, which were to be determined by a subcommittee headed by Stagg, the report mentioned that mass plays would be done away with, that linemen would no longer be allowed to move into the backfield to block, and that open-field play would be emphasized. "It is the most spectacular, most exciting and greatest college game we have," said one anonymous member of the committee, "but it cannot be continued as at present."

Particularly noteworthy was the fact that the first steps toward reform had been taken by the Midwestern schools. "It violates all traditions and precedents," the *Tribune* noted, "for the East has owned the game from its beginning." Another committee member, again quoted anonymously, said, "We shall pay no attention to what the East does. We are big enough and strong enough out here to take care of the thing and are glad to take the initiative in a much-needed reform."

While it all sounded good, the reality turned out to be something altogether different. Eastern officials denounced the schools for their "impertinence." With an eye on future games against Eastern teams, Wisconsin withdrew its representative from the subcommittee, so as not to offend the establishment. Looking to placate the Midwest, Yale's Walter Camp reached out to Stagg in the spring of 1898 and invited him to join the Eastern rules committee, though scheduling conflicts prevented him from actually participating for several years. By January 1898, the promised changes had failed to materialize, leading the *Tribune* to ask with exasperation, "What has become of their reform? What are they doing?" The short answer: nothing. The schools were continuing on exactly the same course. One needed only to glance at their balance sheets to understand why.

CHAPTER TWELVE

"THERE'S MONEY IN IT"

"MONEY, MONEY, MONEY SEEMS TO BE THE CRY," CASPAR WHITNEY wrote in his 1894 book, *A Sporting Pilgrimage*, "it will be the curse, if indeed not the downfall, of honest university sport." By the 1890s money had indeed become an integral part of the football story. In 1892 a company called Vitascope, which manufactured an early form of the movie camera, offered $25,000 for the film rights to the Harvard–Yale game. The proposal was turned down, since it would have necessitated playing the game on a 55-yard field due to the limitations of the cameras. Even without the Vitascope money, the 1894 game between the two schools netted $119,000, more than $3 million in today's currency. There was clearly money to be made in college football.

While the revenues tied directly to the game were growing, schools increasingly began to see football as a valuable public-relations tool—a means of publicizing their university and energizing alumni, which, of course, had further financial implications. With more publicity and highly engaged alums came an increase in donations.

No school grasped the PR power of football more than the University of Chicago. Noted economist James Laurence Laughlin, a member of the Chicago faculty, somewhat snidely referred to the school as "The Greatest Show on Earth," with President Harper playing the role of "The P. T. Barnum of education." In that metaphor, it's fair to say that the football team quickly evolved into Harper's circus. And just two years after the school opened its doors, that circus took to the road.

After an 1894 season that had seen the Maroons play a stunning eighteen-game schedule, eight of which came against other four-year colleges, Stagg happened upon the idea of a postseason trip to the Pacific Coast to play a number of games, including at least one against Stanford. The newly founded California school was coached by Stagg's mentor, Yale's Walter Camp, who headed west to work with Stanford's team at the end of the Elis' season. Stagg's justification for the trip: money and publicity.

It was the cash that initially caught Stagg's eye. Stanford and California were drawing significant crowds on the coast—a reported 11,000 for their 1894 game. What's more, the schools had charged up to $1.50 per ticket, three times the face value of a seat at the Chicago–Michigan game.

Stagg quickly went to work trying to arrange a deal, exchanging a series of telegrams with a number of Stanford officials, including a student by the name of Herbert Hoover. The future president was serving as the treasurer of the school's athletic association. Eventually, the two sides came to an agreement: In order to help cover the cost of its travel expenses, Chicago would be guaranteed $1,000 or 75 percent of the gate receipts. Other schools also wanted an opportunity to play the Maroons while they were out west, but Stagg held out for favorable terms. After the University of California offered a 50–50 gate split, Stagg declined, reasoning, "I do not see the justice in receiving 75 per cent of the gate receipts from Leland Stanford and then playing [the] California Varsity for 50 per cent."

While money was a driving force behind the decision to play in California, publicity also played a role. As Stagg stated simply, "we could use the advertising." He got no argument from his boss. "President Harper was entirely agreeable," Stagg remembered later, "as he was toward anything legitimate that put the university's name in print."

Expenses for such a journey were a major concern, but Stagg caught a fortunate transportation break. A Chicago woman named Mary

McMahon, who owned her own buffet sleeper car, offered it to the Chicago team for a nominal fee. Stagg was delighted to accept, sight unseen. The trip out west was doubling as his honeymoon, and the private car, which had a "stateroom" that he and his wife would occupy, only added to the allure of the journey. "I should take my bride to Golden California in a palace on wheels," Stagg thought in anticipation of the trip.

The Chicago papers gave glowing descriptions of the Maroons' accommodations. One raved about the interior of the "white coach," including descriptions of the players' berths. It left out no details, including the locations of the storage departments for the luggage and food. A second paper gushed over the "elegantly equipped car," which had been "fitted up especially for the convenience of the class of people who are to be its occupants." The team hired a chef and a porter, both of whom received plaudits in the local press, with one paper describing the former, C. F. Bishop, as a man "with an unblemished reputation as a culinary artist." McMahon allowed the school to decorate the coach especially for the occasion, painting the words: "The University of Chicago Football Team" in huge maroon-bordered black letters on the side of the train car. As one student observed, the team was a "traveling advertising organization of the University." Stagg's enthusiasm was palpable. "From numerous letters I have received from points along our route," he said, "we are in for royal receptions before we reach the Golden Gate."

Reality turned out to be a little different. Stagg was shocked when, on the day of the team's departure, he actually saw the car for the first time. "The wheels were flat, the paint scabrous, the body humped at one spot and sagged at another," he recalled many years later. Though it had been described in the papers as having "thirty berths," the accommodations were actually bunks, and the upper ones collapsed the first night out from Chicago under the weight of the men, who were then forced to double up in the lower bunks. As bad as that was, things soon got considerably worse. On its way over the Rockies, the train caught on fire.

The coal stove that warmed the car overheated, igniting the woodwork. The team tried in vain to signal the crew, Stagg recalled, but "the train air cord ended with the car ahead of us, [and] the rear flagman was away from his post." The horrified players took matters into their own hands. "While the train toiled upgrade, we fought the fire with axes and water and beat it after a blistering fight," Stagg recounted. "Had the flames ever worked through to the outside, where the wind could have got at them, we either should have had to jump for our lives or have been burnt to a crisp." The team quietly wired ahead for a substitute car, and the mishap was somehow kept out of the papers. Upon their arrival, the players described the journey as "a picnic."

The Maroons split two games with Stanford, winning a Christmas Day game in San Francisco and losing four days later in Los Angeles. They then returned to the Bay Area, where they dropped a New Year's Day game to a local athletic club. As was typical at the time, they had brought their own drinking water with them on the journey, but they had been forced to use a significant portion of it to fight the fire. Their supply exhausted, the Maroons had to consume the local liquid, which Stagg believed upset their stomachs, thus contributing to the defeats. He didn't get much sympathy from the San Francisco press, which quipped that the Chicagoans "were not used to water that [they] did not have to chew." Facing a minor deficit, the team stopped on the way home for a game against the Salt Lake City YMCA, which it won handily. The meager gate receipts in Utah weren't enough to close the small financial gap, which totaled $136.

While technically a money loser, Stagg believed that the western trip had been well worth the hassle. He got no arguments from other midwestern schools such as Wisconsin, Minnesota, and Michigan, which, within months, were rumored to be planning long-distance journeys of their own. As historian Robin Lester notes, "Chicago's extravagant trip heralded the faint beginnings of a national commercial enterprise characterized by inter-regional play." Indeed, just eight years later, Michigan and Stanford played on New Year's Day in Pasadena in the first-ever Rose Bowl game, a grand tradition that remains—more than a century later—one of the highlights of the college football season.

But at Chicago in the 1890s, no one was thinking a hundred years down the line. Harper was focused on raising the new university's profile, and football was simply part of his formula for doing so. As journalist Milton Mayer observed of the early years at Chicago, "Rockefeller gifts were celebrated like football victories, and football victories were celebrated like the Second Coming." Indeed, the two were inextricably linked.

In 1895, the year after the Maroons' West Coast journey, Chicago found itself trailing Wisconsin 12–0 at halftime of the teams' battle at Marshall Field. As a disgusted Stagg addressed his troops, Harper burst into the dressing room and told the team that Rockefeller had just promised the school a three-million-dollar gift. "Our benefactor," he said of Rockefeller, "believes in the greatness of the University. The way you played in the first half," he continued, "leads me to wonder whether we have the spirit of greatness in ambitions. I wish that you would make up your minds to win this game and show that we do have it." The Maroons dominated the second half, winning the game 22–12.

While Chicago's ambition in its early years provides a vivid example, the school was simply part of a large, nationwide movement. "As football's potential for public relations became evident," historian Michael Oriard observed, "presidents often had to reconcile their own moral misgivings to the sport's pragmatic benefits in attracting both students and financial support."

Take Colorado College in Colorado Springs, for example. In the 1890s it was trying to shed a reputation as a mere literary institution and saw football as a ticket to broader acclaim. Before a game against the University of Colorado, university president William F. Slocum entered the locker room to address the team. "Colorado College is a great institution, but it can never gain the recognition that it deserves until it has a winning football team," he told them. "You are Tigers, and a Tiger is the fiercest beast of the jungle; it can whip any other beast on earth. Take that spirit into the game today. Go out and win."

The emphasis on public relations and, ultimately, on money made many in the educational field uncomfortable. "There has grown up around football an unpleasant business atmosphere of profit and loss," one grad wrote in the *Harvard Graduates' Magazine* in 1895. Not surprisingly, President Eliot agreed. He observed that the public's interest in football "has made it easy to collect large sums of gate-money, both on college grounds and on public grounds convenient to New York and other cities. The money thus easily got is often wastefully and ineffectively spent. There is something exquisitely inappropriate in the extravagant expenditure on athletic sports at such institutions as Harvard and Yale."

Criticism came from outside academia as well. Edwin Godkin, founder of the weekly magazine *The Nation,* said of the sport, "we know of no compensating advantage to put over against the distorted conception of life, and particularly of college life, the false standard of individual and college distinction, and the evident retarding of young men in arriving at serious and worthy ideals, all of which have been involved in the increasing glorification of college athletics." The *Chicago Tribune,* meanwhile, said of football's rise, "This monstrous perversion of sport can be seriously defended only on the ground that 'there's money in it,' for the gatekeepers of the battlefield and for the treasury of the university."

Chicago had its system down to a science. Football's place in the university was firmly established. As Professor Phillip Allen noted a few years later, the school had two purposes: "to spread the light of knowledge over the western world and to 'lick' Michigan."

By the late 1890s, the administration was doing everything it could to ensure the proper athletic material for the accomplishment of the latter goal. The university had approved a system for enrolling "unclassified" students, whose primary purpose at the school was to participate in athletics. These students entered Chicago in much the way Pat O'Dea did at Wisconsin—without any examination and without needing to declare themselves candidates for a degree. They spent the summer taking a couple of courses with professors who were in on the academic ruse, a plan that left plenty of time for recreation. "[T]here are few pleasanter places for summer residence than the University of Chicago," Caspar Whitney observed as he exposed the plan in *Harper's Weekly,* "with the lake, Jackson Park, fine roads, and a public golf-links not a half a mile away."

By the time football began in the fall, these players had established residence and, at least by Chicago's reckoning, were eligible to represent the school on the gridiron. That this flew in the face of the Western Conference's standards seemed not to bother the university one bit. Stagg had always seen the eligibility rules as a bit of an unnecessary hindrance anyway, and he would often appeal for exceptions to the conference rules for Chicago athletes. "A university whose regulations are so loose as to permit the practical abandonment of class-room, by its athletes," Whitney complained of Chicago's view of academics, "needs thorough shaking up."

The problem was that Chicago's opponents weren't in much of a position to do anything about it—and that came back to finances. While the West Coast swing had highlighted the PR potential of taking the show on the road, Stagg soon came to realize that the best strategy for Chicago was to play at home, and to do so frequently. The reasoning was simple—due to its location in far and away the largest metropolis in the region, Chicago was uniquely positioned to make money from football gate receipts. Lots of money. Lots more money than could be made in, say, Champaign, Illinois; Madison, Wisconsin; or West Lafayette, Indiana.

Stagg used this advantage to dictate the locations of the Maroons' games and the manner in which the receipts would be divided. He even insisted that University of Chicago opponents help pay for half of the improvements to Marshall Field—generally increases in the seating capacity—in advance of the biggest games. The argument, of course, was that the larger capacity meant more money for both sides. But while the opponents only cashed in once, Chicago could take advantage of the changes in perpetuity. "Michigan is tired of building grand-stands and making other improvements to Chicago's grounds, which are saddled in as part of the legitimate expenses of the games," the Ann Arbor school complained in the late 1890s. "Last year cost us $1100."

And, yet, as the dispute played out over the course of several seasons just before the turn of the century, the opponents kept coming. Though they were frustrated by Stagg's stubbornness, the payday derived from a game in Chicago was too tempting to resist. Between 1897 and 1899, for instance, the Maroons played 47 games, 44 of which were at home. For its part, Chicago insisted that it would be happy to play on the road, but would do so only under favorable economic conditions. The school required either a guarantee for a road game equivalent to what its opponents would get in Chicago or that its visitor accept as its guarantee the same amount that it would pay Chicago if it traveled.

For instance, a home game at Chicago might net each school $3,000, while a game in Madison might clear only $1,000 per side. So, if Chicago were to host Wisconsin twice, it might be able to clear $6,000, whereas if they played one game on each campus, the take would be only $4,000. Chicago proposed two solutions. The first was that Wisconsin accept $1,000 for playing in Chicago. That would mean that Chicago would get the other $5,000 from the home game, which, added to the $1,000 for the return game in Madison, would mean it would still clear $6,000 for the two games. Alternatively, Stagg said Wisconsin could guarantee Chicago the same $3,000 for a game in Madison that the school would get at home. Given that scenario, Wisconsin would actually lose $1,000 in the home game, though it would make $3,000 off the game in Chicago. Either way, in the hypothetical example, Chicago stood to make $6,000 from a home and home series, $4,000 more than Wisconsin.

Stagg saw this athletic Darwinism as the only fair solution, as opposed to the model that the other schools proposed, which was to simply alternate hosting and split the gate receipts equally. "(U)nder the thin guise of a demand for 'perfect equality,' the Universities of Michigan, Wisconsin and Illinois are insisting that it is Chicago's duty to do what the Creator of all the universe himself does not do," Stagg complained. "They assume that persons occupying unfavorable business positions ought to receive as much remuneration as persons enjoying the most exceptional opportunities for trade and profit, and, if they do not receive as much it is the duty of those better off to give of their earnings enough to make all share alike."

Stagg referred to his model as "a matter of self-preservation," an assertion that Caspar Whitney attacked in *Harper's* as further evidence of the manner in which finances were distorting the world of college football. "The self-preservation of what?" Whitney wrote. "Of student athletics for the health of the body and the glory of the sport, or of a big successful business?"

In the spring of 1898, as the financial issues threatened to boil over, Chicago and Wisconsin threw additional fuel on the fire. Just days before the conference's spring track meet, Chicago, in conjunction with Michigan, protested the eligibility of two of Wisconsin's top stars, James Maybury and Henry Cochems. The schools alleged that the pair had competed for cash prizes at track meets under assumed names. As was the protocol in such situations, the protesting universities provided a number of sworn affidavits from witnesses who claimed to have seen the men compete.

The cases were heard in a seven-hour session the day before the meet in Chicago. Both men were acquitted of the charges. Convinced that justice had not been served in the case, Chicago, Michigan, and the University of Illinois all withdrew from the Western Intercollegiate Athletic Association—deciding to hold a separate meet of their own the following day. In a stroke of nomenclatural genius, they dubbed their new league the Western Intercollegiate Amateur Athletic Association. At the same time, Chicago severed all future athletic relations with Wisconsin, including the football game scheduled for the fall of 1898.

The local press was aghast. "The three schools have been criticized and scored roundly by outside athletic circles and by other members of the association," the *Chicago Tribune* reported. "Their conduct has been characterized as unsportsmanlike and childish." The contention was that the rules for trying protests had been followed, and that the three departing schools needed to abide by the group's decision. Stagg, in particular, came under criticism for his comportment. He reportedly had strong evidence against the two men but held it back until the last moment. As this ran counter to the rules for such proceedings, the committee had refused to hear the information.

The larger issue, of course, was the future of the conference. Given that they had Chicago, with its financial strength, on their side, the three withdrawing schools were in a position to succeed without Wisconsin, Northwestern, Minnesota, and Purdue. "They are strong enough to be a law unto themselves," the *Tribune* pointed out, "whether their course is right or wrong." The issue was whether the other four could survive without Illinois, Michigan, and, most important, Chicago.

The situation promised to get worse before it got better. In his frustration, Wisconsin president Adams wrote to Chicago's Harper in the summer of 1898, accusing Stagg of ruining the athletic relations between the two schools. The Chicago coach, Adams contended, had "violated without any justification" the agreements on dealing with eligibility issues. The cancellation of the football game particularly galled Adams. It was a move, he said, that lacked both "comity" and "courtesy." The ongoing dispute threatened to derail the future of Midwestern football.

CHAPTER THIRTEEN

"THEY ALL KNEW STAGG WAS A SHAM"

THE DISAGREEMENT SURROUNDING THE ELIGIBILITY OF WISCONSIN track and football athletes James Maybury and Henry Cochems continued into the summer of 1898, leaving the Badgers in a tough spot. For the past few years, the battle with Chicago had been the most anticipated game on the schedule. It certainly would have been true in the 1898 season, as the teams boasted the two most exciting players in the West—Pat O'Dea and Clarence Herschberger. But as a new school year dawned, Chicago refused to schedule Wisconsin, due to Amos Alonzo Stagg's ongoing insistence that the two Wisconsin players had forfeited their amateur status. The Badgers were left with just two "big" games scheduled—a late October meeting with Minnesota and the Thanksgiving Day battle with Northwestern.

Meanwhile, in Madison, rumors continued to swirl that Maybury and Cochems had indeed profited from athletics. In July the university athletic council started to hear whispers that the two men had earned cash prizes at a track meet in the summer of 1895. The meet in question had taken place in the small Wisconsin town of Spring Green, not far from Madison.

In response the university dispatched three investigators, who spent several days in Spring Green deposing witnesses. They reached a disappointing and startling conclusion. "So far as they could see," university president Charles K. Adams admitted, "there was no reason to doubt that Maybury and Cochems had been present at the meet, had played for money, had received money, and had played under assumed names." As it turns out, the men had been fingered by fellow Wisconsin students, who said they had recognized Maybury and Cochems and actually spoken with them at the meet. Stagg had been right all along. Maybury and Cochems were ineligible.

Cochems, who was slated to be the football captain in the 1898 season, quickly admitted his culpability. He forfeited his position on the team and headed east to enroll in Harvard Law School. After some initial resistance, Maybury confessed as well. It was a confession that elicited some sympathy. The Wisconsin star said he had been left little choice, as he needed the money to help pay for his education. Unfounded rumors began to swirl that the university might rescind both men's undergraduate diplomas, which they had already earned. While Wisconsin took no such measures, its punishment of the players was swift, strong, and severe. Maybury and Cochems were banned from future competition, their records were vacated, and the university recommended that the faculty take whatever further disciplinary action it felt was appropriate against them.

In addition, Wisconsin issued a very public apology to all the schools that Maybury and Cochems had competed against during the past few seasons, assuring them that, had it been aware of the Spring Green meet, it would have declared the two men ineligible years before. "Painful as it is to relate these facts, I feel driven to the necessity of revealing them, since, by persistent misrepresentations, the university seems called upon for its defense. We cannot ignore the record without ignominy," Adams said. He added, "If I am to be convinced that intercollegiate athletics cannot be carried on without a sacrifice of absolute truth, honesty, and fair play, I shall be as earnestly in favor of their absolution as I have hitherto been in favor of their encouragement and support."

Having made its confession, Wisconsin next set about repairing its rift with Michigan, Illinois, and Chicago. The school crafted a letter to Harper and his university, asking Chicago to consider renewing athletic relations between the schools. Adams personally mailed the note from the post office in Madison and eagerly awaited a response.

Reaction in Chicago was mixed. On one hand, some believed that the Maroons ought to continue their boycott of Wisconsin, with the logic being that, were they simply to resume the series right away, the Madison school would not have suffered any material damage for its failure to manage the situation properly from the outset. Plus, Chicago didn't need Wisconsin. "We can get all the football we want," the *Chicago Tribune* said, paraphrasing the school's stance, "so why should we care what happens [with Wisconsin]?" Others felt it was best to just let bygones be bygones, contending that Wisconsin had done all it could do in the matter and had acted properly throughout given the information at its disposal. Either way, the *Tribune* reported that Wisconsin's declaration had "produced more of a sensation in local athletic circles than any occurrence in years."

Ultimately, those in favor of reconciliation prevailed. In a September 28 meeting at a Chicago hotel, the universities patched up their differences and joined together again as members of the Western Conference. Wisconsin and Chicago quickly scheduled a game for November 12. As part of the new conference agreement, the schools announced their belief that the rules governing amateurism were inadequate and proposed a committee to revisit the issue and come up with new solutions. Like many of the earnest and presumably well-intentioned declarations of the late 1890s, it sounded better in theory than it turned out to be in practice.

The dismissal of Maybury and Cochems had major on-the-field repercussions in Madison, as both men were expected to be among the stars of the Badgers' team. O'Dea was quickly elected the captain to replace Cochems, but that choice was far from a guarantee of success. O'Dea's skills, the *Milwaukee Sentinel* wrote, were beyond question. The Aussie, it noted, "has kicked his way into the hearts of . . . Wisconsin people who annually back the team with enthusiasm and ready cash." The issue, the paper contended, wasn't O'Dea's talent—it was his leadership skills, as he had "never been tested in an executive position."

Unfortunately, the team didn't have many other choices. Only three players from the previous season's squad would be returning to play for the Badgers. A run of bad luck cost the school several other key candidates, as a few players they had been counting on either failed to enroll or were talked out of playing by their parents. Expectations were low for the two-time defending Western Conference champions. "There is much discussion in university circles owing to a gloomy outlook for a creditable football team," the *Chicago Tribune* reported.

As the first big game against Minnesota approached, the situation reached the point of near-crisis, focusing more on the quantity of the "football material" than the quality. The Badgers simply needed more players. For a variety of reasons, eight men had quit the team during the early portions of the season. "There are men, leaders in athletics of this institution," the *Daily Cardinal* reported, "who advocate the cancelling of all games and the disbanding of the team." While the eligibility issues and defections were obviously part of the explanation, there was still much debate on campus over how exactly the Badgers had gotten themselves into this predicament.

"If this dearth of football material is due to an overconfidence acquired from two years of unbroken success it is high time this delusion was destroyed. Unbiased football critics pronounce our chances of winning from Chicago to be dubious in the extreme," the *Cardinal* asserted. "If you have ever played football, if you think you can play football, if you are strong enough to play, it is your duty to report to Coach King.... WE MUST HAVE MORE CANDIDATES OUT FOR PRACTICE."

O'Dea reinforced that notion, telling the paper, "What we want is more candidates out on the field, and when they come out to stay out; not come out for one night, then quit." It was precisely those quitters that King targeted when he said, "The varsity squad can use all the new men who will come out, but it needs most of all the return of those men who have been out at various times and who know the formations and signals."

It was a terrible time for a team to lose its star, but that's precisely what happened next to the Badgers. O'Dea cracked his ribs in practice, and the team announced that he would not be able to play against Minnesota. While Wisconsin's most familiar face was sidelined, some newer ones helped ensure that the game would actually be played. Thirty-two students came out for practice on Thursday night, a dramatic increase over the numbers from earlier in the week. Several of the newest players filled key roles in the Badgers' easy 29–0 win, a margin that, truthfully, was far more reflective of Minnesota's weakness than Wisconsin's strength. Still, the crisis had been averted. "That was a truly critical period in the history of football at Wisconsin," the *Cardinal* observed the following week, "but the method of arousing that lethargy proved most effectual." Now, the team could focus on its biggest match of the year—the showdown with Chicago, which loomed just two weeks away.

As that game drew nearer, it became clear that the antipathy that had surfaced between the two schools during the past summer still remained. It manifested itself in a borderline-comical sequence of protests and counterprotests regarding eligibility, which filled the pages of the Chicago and Wisconsin papers in the days leading up to the game.

Wisconsin questioned the eligibility of Chicago's Joseph Ewing. "It appears that Ewing played baseball in Farmer City, Ill. During one summer, and for two games he received a small sum for his expenses," the *Chicago Times-Herald* alleged, before clarifying the almost preposterous timeline. "This was about eight years ago, while he was in grammar school."

As that case played out, others surfaced. Wisconsin inquired about the amateur standing of Chicago's Orville Burnett, though the school did not file an official protest. Chicago countered by questioning the status of Wisconsin's Harvey Holmes. The *Times-Herald* reported that Minnesota's coach, Jack Minds, had evidence that Holmes had wrestled professionally, but he and King had made a side deal before the Minnesota–Wisconsin game. King agreed to keep Holmes out of the game if Minds kept the information to himself.

Wisconsin's team manager, John Fisher, was moved to comment on the affair, and told the *Times-Herald* that Holmes had already revealed the details to Wisconsin's athletic board: "The public was given to understand," said Fisher, "that the bouts were for a purse of $200, with a side bet of $300, but Holmes claims that the advertised purse was a 'fake' for the purpose of drawing spectators." Or maybe Fisher didn't say that at all. The next day, the same paper ran another story directly contradicting that tale. "Manager Fisher of the Wisconsin football team flatly denies that he ever had an interview while in Chicago in which he is said to have stated that Holmes had wrestled with professionals."

Meanwhile, the Chicago athletic board heard three cases regarding the allegations against Ewing, Burnett, and the school's captain, Walter Kennedy. Another case, that of Walter Cavanagh, was set to be heard later in the week. Chicago was also said to be standing by Clarence Rogers, whom Wisconsin contended had run out of eligibility after playing for Beloit.

In hindsight, the details of who was being accused, what they were being accused of, and whether or not the accusations were accurate aren't that important. It was all difficult to get to the bottom of in 1898, let alone more than a hundred years later. What the back-and-forth finger-pointing frenzy does show is the inadequacy of the procedures that were in place to enforce the eligibility rules. It is also further evidence of the underlying hostility between the schools, a rivalry that continued to call their future as athletic opponents into question. And while they may have been hiding behind accusations of professionalism, it's fairly clear that neither program was truly "pure," which leads one to conclude that the dispute was really about something else. And that something else, of course, was money.

"Some of the influential members of the Midway institution have made the assertion that Wisconsin and Chicago would not meet in any dual contests for the next ten years," the *Times-Herald* wrote just days before the Wisconsin–Chicago game. "Stagg seems to hold the whip hand," it continued. "Future contests are more to the advantage of the Badgers than to Chicago. The Badgers need the money more than do the Maroons, but the more radical students at the University of Chicago are bound to have revenge for what they call indiscriminate protests and slurs on practically every member of the Maroon team."

In the end the protests turned out to be a massive waste of everyone's time. Only one player, Chicago halfback Gordon Clarke, was kept out of the game. He actually quit the Maroon team in the days leading up to the showdown after admitting to having coached at Tarkio University in Missouri for pay several years before. Though such an arrangement had not been illegal under the amateurism rules in place when Clarke took the money, those guidelines had been changed to ban anyone who had ever been compensated for coaching. Learning he was being investigated by Wisconsin, Clarke went to Stagg, revealed his story, and withdrew from the team.

The rhetoric continued to escalate as game day drew nearer. While Chicago's anger revolved around the protests, Wisconsin's target was Stagg. The Chicago coach was still reviled in Madison for his comportment after the game the year before, when he had been less than gracious in defeat. The *Cardinal* published a song written by a law student that took numerous potshots at Stagg. It described the Wisconsin team marching into Chicago, and continued:

> And each one would pick out a man
> No matter what his name,
> For they all knew Stagg was a sham
> And his men were just the same.

> They carried him off the field on a slat
> When the slaughter had all been done.
> He stood on a barrel and said, "for a' that"
> Again the poorer team won.

The *Milwaukee Sentinel* took a more intellectual approach, though the message was similar. "How can a university faculty which would not tolerate Maybury and Cochems expose its amateurs to association with

Prof. Stagg? He is a professional athlete who does more professing than the majority of that class," it contended. "He bluffs like a prize fighter in the presence of defeat and hangs up cash offers for an extra game on occasion which would tempt world's champions in any line." The *Sentinel* concluded by asking a question about college coaches that has been repeated in various forms ever since, "Do the college faculties expect the eager and ambitious students to be more pure and high-minded than their instructors?"

The presumption of dishonesty extended to game preparations. Two days before the showdown, reporters arrived at Chicago's practice to find the field empty. Concerned that Wisconsin might be spying on the Maroons, Stagg had herded the team off on buses to practice in a secret location.

His paranoia was not unfounded. Weeks later, before their showdown with Michigan, the Maroons' practice was disrupted when the team noticed that a pile of hay alongside the field appeared to be moving. As the players ran toward the mysterious heap, a man in an overcoat and cap emerged and tried to run away. The players caught him and demanded an explanation, but the interloper wasn't talking. "I'll wager it's a spy," Walter Cavanagh exclaimed. "The players wanted to use him for a football, but Stagg objected," the *Chicago Chronicle* reported of the incident, "and the man was ejected forcibly from the grounds and then chased several blocks, when he boarded a street car and disappeared."

Lost in all the Chicago–Wisconsin suspicion and bickering was the fact that many were expecting an outstanding game. "It will be Herschberger against O'Dea. There will be twenty other men in the center, but they will be mere satellites," the *Times-Herald* proclaimed on game day. "The game should furnish the greatest kicking duel in the history of American football. Never before have two such giants of the pigskin met on the gridiron."

But the weather did not cooperate. Chicago was pummeled by heavy rains throughout the week leading up to the game. One local paper described Marshall Field as a "swamp" and "a mud hole," noting that

Chicago's team had been forced to spend some of its practice time inside the gymnasium due to field conditions.

Stagg did all he could to try to get the grass ready for the game. "His first device was to pour oil over the worst spots and set fire to it," the *Chicago Chronicle* reported. "The scheme did not work to perfection and the coach ordered the mud removed and sand drawn. This morning the field will be gone over with a steam roller." Unfortunately, all of that work only exacerbated the problems. In a last-ditch effort to make the field playable, Chicago spread pine shavings the morning of the game and simply hoped for the best.

The showdown did not go well for O'Dea and company. In front of a crowd of 9,000, including several thousand Wisconsin supporters, the significantly larger Maroons pulled out a 6–0 win, ending their two-game losing streak against the Badgers. Chicago scored in the first ten minutes of the game and held on from there in a contest that, by all accounts, was free of much in the way of interesting play.

The great kicking game that many had so eagerly anticipated never materialized due to the brutal field conditions. "Pat O'Dea was there, but his leg was crooked. Herschberger was there, but his leg had a slant," the *Times-Herald* reported the next day. "A pair of heroic limbs had gone wrong."

Stagg's behavior was clear evidence of just how much the game meant to him. "The coach stooped along the side lines all through the game, scarcely noticing anyone beside him, while at the most inopportune moments . . . he would jump to his feet, pull off his cap, and yell like a maniac as he saw his men accomplishing some little trick of play which he had taught them," the *Daily Inter Ocean* reported.

The Badgers accepted the painful defeat with dignity. "We were clearly outclassed," King said afterward. O'Dea agreed. "Chicago deserves the victory for it was earned by straight, hard football," he said, though he did mention the mud pile that was Marshall Field, saying, "I could do almost nothing on the ground in the condition it was in. The shavings seemed to clog my cleats, making a slip more certain than if no attempt had been made to make the field passably good." The national press took notice of the Badgers' sportsmanship, with Caspar Whitney noting in *Harper's* that "she took defeat far more handsomely than Chicago did in the previous year." Still, the underlying bitterness was a huge part of the story. "It was asserted on almost every hand," the *Times-Herald* reported, "that the two universities will be strangers to each other in athletics for the future."

Back on campus, the loss served only to further the O'Dea legend. He was repeatedly praised for his composure, particularly given that he was goaded by the Maroons throughout the game, with a Chicago player, Theron Mortimer, eventually getting ejected after he intentionally kicked O'Dea.

In class on Monday, O'Dea received a bouquet of roses from Dean Bryant of the law faculty. In the note, addressing the "champion football kicker of the world," Bryant wrote: "I honor the man who can take defeat like a man. I am proud of an athlete who comes out in true sportsmanlike manner and admits frankly that his opponent defeated him because of his superior ability under the existing conditions." Bryant concluded that, despite all the adulation, O'Dea "has not allowed his head to be turned by self-consciousness, begotten of praise."

If anything, the defeat seemed to galvanize the Badgers, who got right back on the practice field to prepare for their Thanksgiving Day showdown with Northwestern. The 47–0 rout, highlighted by O'Dea's record-setting "champagne kick," helped vault the Aussie from a regional to a national celebrity. "It was the most notable drop-kick goal of this season," Caspar Whitney marveled in *Harper's Weekly*, "and one of the most remarkable performances of its kind in football annals."

There was some debate over the actual length of the kick. Most reports settled on 60 yards, but there were a few contemporaneous accounts that claimed it was a bit farther, with Whitney, for instance, writing that O'Dea had "sixty-two yards to cover." Wisconsin's record book lists the kick at 62 yards, still the longest field goal in the school's history. There was certainly no debate over the significance of the achievement, though.

The *Times-Herald*'s assessment was typical, saying that O'Dea "by that single act has immortalized himself in the annals of football."

The Northwestern game was the last of the year for the Badgers, who finished with a mark of 9–1, though seven of the wins came against minor opponents. O'Dea truthfully hadn't had a great season. He was injured for one of the Badgers' three biggest games and played poorly in a second. But the remarkable kick against Northwestern seemed to overshadow much of that reality. The capper came when the Aussie was named to Walter Camp's All-American second team. It was a monumental achievement. The All-American team had been selected by Whitney starting in 1889 before Camp later joined him. None of the nearly two hundred spots on the first or second teams had been occupied by non-Easterners until O'Dea and a few others broke through in that 1898 season. "There is not yet equality," Whitney wrote in *Harper's* upon revealing the team, "it would be unreasonable to expect it—but the West is no longer the unthinking pupil of the East."

The establishment's interest in Western football as a whole and O'Dea in particular had been piqued. They'd get a chance to satisfy their curiosity in person in 1899.

CHAPTER FOURTEEN

EAST VS. WEST

THE BLEARY-EYED WISCONSIN FOOTBALL PLAYERS STUMBLED SLOWLY through the predawn blackness on their way to the Madison train station. It was approaching 5:00 a.m. on Monday, October 16, 1899. A forty-hour train trip awaited them. Later that week they would play the most anticipated game in school history—a chance for the Badgers to show the world that Western football had finally caught up to the Eastern game. As they arrived at the depot, the Wisconsin players were stunned by what they saw. Even at this early hour, a crowd of several hundred supporters had gathered to see them off. If they hadn't figured it out already, the Badgers now fully grasped the enormity of what lay before them. They were on their way to Connecticut to battle powerful Yale.

While there had been an actual championship on the line when they played for the Western title in previous years, the game against the Elis was about much more. It was a referendum on Western football as a whole and, to a certain extent, a referendum on Pat O'Dea's skills—a chance for the Eastern media to judge whether or not he had truly been worthy of his All-American selection at the end of the previous season. Put simply, the teams and players in the West were considered inferior to those of the traditional powers—and not just athletically. When Michigan played Harvard in 1895, the *Boston Herald* described the men from Ann Arbor as "crude blacksmiths, miners and backwoodsmen."

In an article he penned for *Outing* magazine previewing the 1899 season, Walter Camp discussed the perceived chasm in the game between the East and West. "Football has now reached a point in this country where there are certain classes," Camp wrote, "and those classes are becoming more and more well-defined, and for a team to get from one class into another is almost like changing caste in India."

The top class, Camp wrote, was made up of four schools—Yale, Harvard, Princeton, and Penn. Just beneath them were a couple of other Eastern schools—Cornell and West Point. And after that was a hodgepodge of colleges—Brown, Wesleyan, Carlisle, and others. Michigan, Chicago, and Wisconsin, Camp contended, "form a class by themselves and they are going to have an opportunity of bettering that class in certain of their contests this year," with Michigan and Chicago each scheduled to face Penn, and the Badgers taking on Yale.

The Maroons had earned the West some respect the previous season, traveling from Chicago to Philadelphia and giving the Quakers a good game—leading at the half before falling 23–11. Still, playing a team competitively and actually beating them were two very different things, and Camp contended that "there are few football enthusiasts on the Eastern seaboard who have given any consideration to this rivalry that is springing up or regard these matches with the Middle West teams as anything more than practice," though he seemed to be coming to the realization that this was a dangerous attitude to take. "Sooner or later," Camp concluded, "some of these teams will overcome a crack Eastern team. The interesting question is, 'How soon?'"

The hope in Madison was that the Badgers would be the team to pull off that monumental win. It was "an epochal occasion for those of us who were youngsters out in the Middle West at that time," *New York Times* sportswriter William Richardson remembered many years later. A local internal revenue collector named J. G. Monahan wasn't above resorting to superstition to help the Badgers, presenting the team "with 21 rabbits feet, all shot in dark of the moon in a graveyard" to protect them against bad luck.

Given the remarkable early morning crowd, the Badgers felt it simply wouldn't be right to board the train without addressing their fans, so Coach King got up and delivered a few impromptu thoughts. He was followed by O'Dea, who declared, "We are off to do our best. If the spirit of this crowd stays with the team, we shall surely come back winners." The throng erupted in cheers. Moments later, with a traveling party of twenty-four players and six coaches on board, the train pulled out of the station and headed east. Their arrival was eagerly anticipated in Connecticut, thanks to the presence of the Kangaroo Kicker. The *New Haven Evening Leader* said of O'Dea, "The interest which his advent in the East has aroused is as great or greater than the excitement which has been caused by the anticipation of the game itself."

O'Dea's star had risen exponentially since his remarkable kick against Northwestern the year before. He had become a full-fledged celebrity. On campus he got the royal treatment. While his teammates walked to practice, a particularly wealthy classmate sent his family's phaeton, a kind of sporty carriage, to transport Pat to the team's daily workout.

O'Dea had his fair share of female admirers as well. After big games his mailbox was jammed with letters from flirtatious women. The Aussie did all he could to impress them. In the 1890s in Madison, nothing got a young coed's attention more than renting a private carriage for a trip around the small city, and O'Dea quickly developed a reputation as "one of the greatest hirers of carriages the town ever knew." Seemingly every day, he would telephone the local stables and, playing up his irresistible Australian accent, loudly demand, "This is *Pot* O'Dea. Send up a carriage right away!" One friendship even made it into the gossip pages, as it linked perhaps the two best-known Australians in the United States, O'Dea and Dame Nellie Melba.

In the late 1890s, there were few women in the entire world as famous as Melba. She was born Helen "Nellie" Porter Mitchell just outside of Melbourne in 1861, eleven years before O'Dea, and she had left for Europe in the 1880s, determined to find success as a soprano. She assumed the stage name Nellie Melba, as a tribute to her hometown of Melbourne.

For the next five decades, she dazzled audiences worldwide, thanks to what was, according to the *New York Times,* "one of the loveliest voices that ever issued from a human throat . . . simply delicious in its fullness, richness and purity." She sang for the tsar of Russia, the king of Sweden, the emperor of Austria, the kaiser of Germany, and the queen of England. She had a highly publicized and scrutinized affair with the duke of Orleans, a well-known claimant to the French throne. She even had foods named after her—peach melba and melba toast. And as a result of her Australian connection with Pat O'Dea, Melba had a close friendship with the Kangaroo Kicker.

The press followed their interactions closely. In February 1899, the *New York World* noted that two famous Australians had been "chumming together" in Chicago. "They are Melba and Pat O'Dea, the famous football player. O'Dea and Melba, who was then Nellie Mitchell, knew each other in Melbourne," the paper explained.

Weeks later the *St. Paul Globe* wrote an expansive piece on their friendship under the headline MELBA AND PAT O'DEA—HOW THE GREAT WISCONSIN FOOTBALLIST WITHSTOOD THE PRIMA DONNA'S APPEAL. It documented how Melba had "failed signally in an earnest plea, calculated to rob American football of one of its particular stars." The great singer, the paper reported, "sought by every means to secure his promise that he would never again risk his life and limb in what she called 'this brutal football game you are playing here in America.'" O'Dea, readers were told, "stood firm" against Melba's rantings over "the heinous conduct of which she had heard in frightened letters from Melbourne, where O'Dea was almost daily reported as carried from the field as good as dead." The Aussies argued for two days, the *Globe* claimed, but Melba couldn't get O'Dea to cave. He would play again in the fall of 1899.

The Badgers had prepared for their October 21 matchup against Yale with three other games—topping Lake Forest, Beloit, and Northwestern by a combined total of 119–0. As always, O'Dea grabbed the headlines. Against Beloit, he ran 100 yards for a touchdown. In the win over the Methodists, as Northwestern was known at the time, O'Dea showed off one of the skills he had been honing all summer, his ability to spin and curve his punts. The *Chicago Tribune* spoke glowingly of the performance. "Once when Wisconsin punted the ball out from its twenty-five yard line," the *Tribune* reported, "Captain O'Dea tried his new twister, which goes high and then comes down almost in direct perpendicular. It was a puzzler for the Methodists and the Badgers got it on a fumble."

Though the 38–0 winning margin was impressive, the consensus afterward was that the Badgers were not, with the *Tribune* pointing out that the final score was "made only by the wonderful punting of Captain O'Dea." Northwestern had moved the ball effectively throughout the first half before seeing a number of drives fizzle out due to blocked kicks, and observers were harsh in their criticism of Wisconsin's defense. The *Chicago Times-Herald* said the Badgers "fell down sadly at times on defense," while the *Tribune* termed the Badgers' tackling "a disappointment," adding that "the Northwestern players all unite in saying unless it is greatly improved in the next week Yale will push the Badgers all over the field."

It is certainly possible that the looming Yale game may have impacted Wisconsin's effort. Northwestern simply wasn't a very good team—they would lose to Chicago 76–0 later in the season. It was clear within the first ten minutes of the game that Northwestern was outclassed, and perhaps the Badgers simply let up, knowing that they were going to get a win and that the more important contest was still a week away.

Fantastic kicking aside, that mentality was apparently reflected in O'Dea's play, with the *Times-Herald* saying he "did not play hard and appeared to be saving himself." The *Sentinel* elaborated on that opinion. "O'Dea saved himself in every possible way, neither hitting the line hard nor attempting to make open runs in the field," the paper told its readers, adding, "This was owing to his fear of being disabled before the Yale game . . . [as] an injury at this late day would be disastrous."

King said afterward that his team showed "every fault known," and O'Dea, to a great extent, agreed, saying, "The play in the first half was very poor and continued so in part of the second." He did conclude on an optimistic note, though, commenting, "Toward the end we had the first team work of this year and with two or three more practices we will be in much better condition to meet Yale."

Despite the criticism of their most recent performance, spirits were high as the Badgers rolled toward Connecticut. The team passed its time singing college songs and belting out the Wisconsin varsity yell. In an effort to stay loose, they also got off the train whenever the opportunity arose and took a few minutes to run around. They arrived in Hartford just before midnight the following day. The plan was to practice in Connecticut's capital city for three days before heading down to New Haven on Saturday morning.

After spending a rainy Wednesday morning touring Hartford, the Badgers headed to the practice field at Trinity College that afternoon. Due presumably to the Hartford school's rivalry with Yale, the Badgers were well received, with some Trinity students even going so far as to toss a couple of their New Haven counterparts off the field in an effort to prevent them from spying on Wisconsin. The efforts were only moderately successful. The spies climbed a tree outside the practice field and watched the proceedings through binoculars.

From that vantage point, the Yale men saw a group that the *Chicago Tribune* described as "an unusually fast, snappy team." The paper raved in particular about O'Dea, whose "kicking was a revelation to the onlookers." Coach King was less impressed, telling the *Tribune* that the men had not done well, as they were still feeling the aftereffects of the long journey. In addition, he was concerned about injuries. Center Nathan Comstock hurt his wrist in the workout, hampering his ability to snap the ball.

Still, reports of Wisconsin's strength were trickling down to New Haven, and Yale captain Malcolm McBride sprang into action, "scouring the country to find coaches to assist the team in its emergency." In addition to Camp, eight others were cited as being among those who helped the Elis through their practices during the course of the week. After overseeing Yale's Thursday practice, Camp was asked what he thought of the matchup. He "modestly declined even to hazard a guess." The *Daily Cardinal* concluded, "That Yale fears defeat there cannot be a shadow of a doubt." The *Chicago Chronicle* agreed. It reported that Camp's team was particularly focused on blocking kicks, an attempt to neutralize what obviously was perceived as Wisconsin's greatest strength.

Meanwhile, back in Madison, interest was at an all-time high. Arrangements had been made to chart the game in two different locations—the Library Hall and the local opera house. The band was slated to perform at the former building, while, thanks to continuous reports from Western Union, those on hand would be able to follow the game on a huge piece of canvas, which would be on display at the front of the room.

The technology at the opera house, though, promised to be even more exciting, as for the first time in the West, fans would have an opportunity to watch a football game on "Arthur Irwin's Patent Veriscope Board." Irwin was a former professional baseball player, who, at the time, was serving as the manager of the Washington Senators, and while he was best known as the man who had helped popularize the fielder's glove, he didn't confine his ingenuity to baseball. Irwin's board was a giant mockup of a football field, with a ball suspended from a cord and propelled by pulleys. Beneath that was a scoreboard that displayed all the information needed to follow the game. A local newspaper editor was hired to announce the play-by-play as it came in. King himself sang the praises of the device, calling it "a great 'Educator' of football." The promoters of the event had sold thirteen hundred seats in advance.

The Badgers got a special pep talk after supper on Thursday courtesy of King and a couple of former players. "They were told that every time the Yale yell was given they had only to brace themselves and know that although their own rooters were not present they were back in Wisconsin yelling hard for the Cardinal; and that in fact the entire West would be waiting anxiously but with confidence the result of the game," the *Daily Cardinal* reported. After a light practice Friday focusing on signals and the kicking game, the Badgers boarded a train on Saturday to head to New Haven.

Unfortunately, the train ride was not without incident. O'Dea jammed his hand in a car door, breaking his finger, though Wisconsin didn't announce that he was injured until after the game. O'Dea joined a list of wounded players for the Badgers that included Comstock and the quarterback, George Wilmarth. The injury Comstock suffered in Wednesday's practice turned out to be a fractured wrist, which was now encased in a plaster cast. Wilmarth, meanwhile, had dislocated his shoulder in practice and was wearing a leather harness that hampered his movements.

The banged-up Badgers arrived at the train station in New Haven just before 1:30, greeted at the depot by a crowd of rooters. Music, cheering, and confidence filled the air.

"I've got fifty here to put up on O'Dea's men," a Badger supporter yelled, trying to be heard above the din.

"What are you betting on? Even money on victory?" a young Yale student replied incredulously.

"Of course I'm betting on victory. Nothing less," the Wisconsin fan shouted, unsure whether to up the ante or go after the young man, whose lack of respect for the Westerners was evident in his manner.

It briefly looked as if a fight might break out, but the man's friends calmed him down "and assured him that it was Yale over-confidence and nothing else that led the callow youth to disparage Wisconsin."

The Badgers and their supporters made their way to the field, past stately houses adorned with Yale flags and banners. It was a gorgeous day for football, and the scene in New Haven was a festive one. A crowd of Yale students estimated at 2,500 marched to the stadium. They were celebrating not just the game but also the end of a huge week on campus that had included the inauguration of a new university president, Arthur Hadley. They had pulled out all the stops, with no fewer than four bands leading the procession.

The Badgers' fans were fronted, more modestly, by a single group of musicians. The band had not been easy to come by, as Yale supporters had hired most of the musical groups in town. All that was left was an Italian ensemble that, according to the *Daily Cardinal*, "furnished no end of amusement," particularly its bass drummer, which the paper, without compunction, described as "a fat little dago."

Pageantry and cultural insensitivity aside, the real story was, of course, the game. As the band blared martial music and well-coordinated cheers echoed throughout the stands, the Elis took the field. Though this was a very good Yale team—one that included three of the season's eleven first-team All-Americans—it was nowhere near the level of those the university had fielded earlier in the decade. Still, they made for an impressive sight as they trotted out, due, more than anything, to their sheer numbers. Yale had fully sixty men suited up for the game—nearly three times as many as the Badgers brought.

Ten minutes later Wisconsin's team made its entrance, and Eastern football fans got a glimpse of the player they had heard so much about. "'O'Dea, O'Dea!' everywhere was heard. 'Which is he? That tall, lank, youngish looking chap!' was the sum of the babel of talk," though O'Dea "seemed unconscious of the interest he aroused," the *Daily Cardinal* reported. His every movement was followed by a massive cadre of reporters, including the top writers from papers throughout the country. "Indeed," the *New Haven Register* observed, "it is not possible to remember when a Harvard or Princeton game here has called together such prominent newspaper men."

Yale won the toss, electing to take the ball and to play with what was described as a "stiff wind" at its back for the first half. The Elis didn't have the ball for long—fumbling the opening kick at their own 35-yard line. O'Dea tried for a dropkick goal from the field on Wisconsin's first play from scrimmage. But the kick was blocked, a theme that ran throughout the day, as, depending on which newspaper account you believe, O'Dea had anywhere from one to three of his boots knocked down. The Badger star recalled many years later that Comstock's injury had played a major role in his dropkicking struggles, as it "prevented him passing the ball back the usual distance, consequently drawing me closer to the line and thereby making the blocking of drop kicks an easy matter."

Yale's issue was holding onto the football. While the Elis moved it far more effectively than the Badgers did in the first half, three different drives were snuffed out inside the Wisconsin 25-yard line due to fumbles by Yale halfback George Chadwick. Whenever the Elis coughed it up, Wisconsin was quick to kick it back to them—the goal being to get out of the first half without giving up any points and then to score in the second half, when they would have the wind in their favor. The first part of that mission was accomplished. The game went to halftime scoreless, a partial result that was seen as a triumph for the Badgers. As the team trotted off the field, Hereward Peele threw his nose guard into the air and exclaimed, "Now we've got 'em beaten boys. They couldn't score with the wind to help them. We've got the wind and the game."

The halftime tie certainly raised some eyebrows. In Chicago a Yale alum, eager to learn of the progress of the game, made his way to the *Times-Herald* building, where updates of the battle in New Haven were being posted in the window. "The first half is a surprise—a big surprise to me," he said. "Wisconsin is holding our boys down in the hardest portion of the struggle. The Badgers are showing unexpected mettle and speed." In Madison this news was greeted with enthusiasm. Sitting in his box at the opera house, from which he enjoyed a wonderful view of the Veriscope Board, President Adams dispatched a halftime telegram to O'Dea. "P. O'Dea:" it read—"Every one glories in your success in the first half. With the wind we hope you will score."

The Badgers tried to do just that at the outset of the second half. Yale sent the kickoff to Wisconsin's 20-yard line and O'Dea weaved 35 yards on the return before being brought down around midfield. The Badgers were able to move the ball a bit before O'Dea tried a dropkick from 45 yards. It was blocked.

Yale lined up on offense for the first time in the half with one notable change—the fumbling Chadwick was out of the game, replaced by Howard Richards. Although Chadwick had obviously not played well, it was still a curious move. Richards had spent the previous two seasons as a substitute tackle. Just a week before, he had been playing with the third string. On the Thursday before the game, he was tried at halfback for the first time and impressed the coaches with his "terrific plunges into the scrub line." Now, he was in with the game hanging in the balance.

Richards and his teammates had some moderate success running the ball in the second half but found themselves unable to capitalize on their numerous opportunities. Fumbles continued to be an issue, but the Elis also had several drives simply stall out or end on failed kick attempts. Wisconsin, meanwhile, had no luck at all offensively, unable to gain a single first down on its attempts to send the ball through the line. It all set the stage for O'Dea, who "displayed a kicking prowess which has never been equaled on the Yale field."

The first truly amazing kick came after Yale's Malcolm McBride punted to the Wisconsin 25-yard line. O'Dea returned a kick of his own on Wisconsin's first play from scrimmage, and the ball "looked as though it intended taking an aerial journey, but finally descended on Yale's ten yard line," eventually coming to rest on the five—a boot of 80 yards on the 110-yard field. When the remarkable distance of the kick was announced back at the opera house in Madison, "the house fairly went crazy." But O'Dea wasn't done. Later in the half, the Elis saw yet another drive stall out in Wisconsin territory and punted the ball to the Wisconsin 18-yard line. O'Dea kicked it right back to the Yale 15-yard line—a drive of 77 yards.

As the half went on, it seemed that the combination of O'Dea's leg and the Badgers' "bend but don't break" defense would be enough to keep Yale out of scoring position and earn Wisconsin a tie. But in the final five minutes, disaster struck.

With the ball at its own 45-yard line, Yale handed off to Richards, the halftime substitute at halfback. Thanks to some "splendid interferences," or blocking, he made his way around the right end. Yale had its fair share of eight- to ten-yard runs in the game, and it seemed this would be another one, but Richards wasn't done. He broke into the open field "with four Wisconsin backs after him. The first man he dodged, a second he eluded with a clever foot movement, the third he proceeded to bowl over with his free arm." That left only O'Dea between Richards and the goal line. "Here, the inexplicable happened. Pat, the surest of tacklers, handicapped by a broken finger, for the first time in his football career at

Wisconsin, failed to bring down his man." Richards took it all the way to the goal line, planting the ball right between the posts. The 65-yard run and the goal after touchdown gave Yale a 6–0 lead that it would not relinquish. Yale had won the game "that in many respects was the best ever witnessed on the Yale gridiron."

Richards, the unlikely hero, was carried off the field on the shoulders of his fellow students, though many who witnessed the contest were reticent to give him too much credit. It "will not go down in football history as one of the few truly great runs," the *Boston Globe* asserted. "This is due to the fact that Richards could have never covered this distance . . . had the Badgers known enough to 'tackle low.'"

O'Dea shared that opinion. "I am willing to take the blame," he told the *New York Sun* afterward. "I should have got Richards as he came down the field, and it is the first time that I have missed a man under similar circumstances." Coach Phil King, though, quickly leaped to his star's defense. "To show the pluck of Wisconsin's captain," he said of O'Dea, "I should like it known that he played through the entire game with a broken finger and played the game of his life notwithstanding."

The Eastern scribes seemed to agree with King, lavishing praise on the Wisconsin star. The *Sun* called him "the prince of all kickers," while the *Boston Eagle* described him as a "marvelous man." The *New York Press* confirmed, "Capt. O'Dea proved himself to be the great punter he was reported to be." The *Boston Globe* proclaimed "in punting . . . O'Dea is a wonder." And the *Philadelphia Inquirer* stated "O'Dea's punting for Wisconsin was marvelous."

The problem, according to the Easterners, was that O'Dea was essentially all Wisconsin had. "O'Dea . . . was the whole Badger team," the *Globe* stated. The *New York Times* criticized the Badgers for "their sole dependence . . . upon Capt. O'Dea's kicking ability," complaining that they only tried to rush the ball about a dozen times in the entire game. "Wisconsin was made up principally of O'Dea," the *New York Journal* observed. "O'Dea's kicks gained the only ground she made, and O'Dea's kicks took her out of whatever danger she was in." The *Sun* contended, "if O'Dea were replaced by an ordinary kicker [Wisconsin] would fall an easy prey to at least two of the smaller New England colleges."

O'Dea saw it differently. "We should have won without a doubt," the Wisconsin star said. "We traveled 1,200 miles and got out of condition . . . let the Yale team come to Madison and the result will be reversed."

All the journalists seemed to agree that the strategy of having O'Dea punt at every opportunity, while keeping the Badgers in the game, ultimately led to their downfall. "Something more than kicking prowess is needed to vanquish a team like Yale," the *New York Press* observed, "and the Badgers found it out today."

Of course, Wisconsin's strategy involved more than O'Dea's punting—it also included his phenomenal drop-kicking. But, on this day, that part of his game was anything but phenomenal. Whether the issue was Comstock's wrist, O'Dea's finger, Yale's focus during practice on blocking kicks, the wind, or a combination of all of the factors, the record-setting Aussie simply couldn't get it going. The *Philadelphia Inquirer* called that part of his game "a disappointment." The *New York Journal* said that, if O'Dea is a great drop-kicker, "he certainly did not show it in to-day's game," and the same *Boston Globe* writer who described him as "a wonder" in punting referred to him as "fatally slow" and "terribly overrated" as a drop-kicker. The *Globe* described one of O'Dea's dropkicks as "a failure," another as "worse than a failure," and it dropped in a highly technical term when it offered that he had made a "poo fizzle" of a third.

Despite the unsuccessful drop-kicking in New Haven, the Yale game actually helped cement O'Dea's status as a superstar. Along with the Northwestern contest of the year before, which saw him execute his record-setting dropkick, it was one of the two defining moments of his career. And though that career was certainly significant at the time, it took on further significance in the years to come. While O'Dea is a forgotten figure in the twenty-first century, he was a legend in the first half of the 1900s—a larger-than-life hero whose exploits helped put an entire region on the athletic map. The 1898 Northwestern game and the 1899 Yale game combined to create that legend. Those two contests are connected by an obvious thread—the difficulty of separating myth from reality.

What is fascinating about the games is how sharply memories of them years later diverged from the contemporaneous accounts. In 1917 the *Atlanta Journal Constitution*'s Malcolm McLean wrote an item on O'Dea in his column. "Isn't it strange," McLean began, "how the thrills in sporting events are remembered with vividness for such a long period?" The columnist said he recalled the Wisconsin–Yale battle "as it had happened only yesterday."

Early in the game, McLean remembered, Wisconsin had the ball in a position that was "something like sixty or sixty-five yards to Yale's goal— maybe it was closer to seventy." O'Dea dropped back for what the crowd assumed would be a punt. Instead, though, in his "peculiar fashion" the "tall giant" attempted a dropkick. "As the ball soared straight as a die for the goal every heart quickened. To begin with, the distance attempted was something unheard of in the east. Yet there the ball went—on and on. It swerved a trifle and missed going between the posts by a yard, perhaps. The carry was sufficient, but Pat had missed by a hair's breadth. Even yet we can hear the muffled roar as all exhaled their breath. This may sound like an overdrawn statement, but it was actually a roar. And every man and woman—all had arisen—sank back breathless. That thrill exceeded anything we can remember at a ballgame." It's a great story—other than the fact that there is not a single contemporaneous account that even comes close to supporting it. Still, it was picked up in a syndicated column, running verbatim a dozen years later in newspapers across the country.

Grantland Rice, considered by many to be the greatest sportswriter of all time, told a similar story in 1944, as he pondered the question, "who is the greatest all-around kicker football has produced so far?" Of O'Dea, Rice wrote, "As I recall the fog-hidden details, O'Dea hit the crossbar against Yale from 64 yards." That's a long way from a "poo fizzle."

While that "near miss" obviously doesn't show up in the record books, Wisconsin does list a 100-yard punt by O'Dea from the Yale game—20 yards longer than what was described in the game reports. And if you go by what was in the papers years after the fact, it seems O'Dea's alma mater might be shortchanging him. In 1934 famed *New York Times* writer Allison Danzig wrote, "against Yale in 1899, when the field measured 110 yards in length, O'Dea got off a punt that measured 117 yards, with the aid of the wind, and he was credited with another kick of 110 yards."

Just seven years after the game, in 1906, O'Dea's former teammate Edward Cochems recounted for the *Fort Worth Star Telegram* that Pat "booted the ball from behind the goal line to Yale's 5 yard line." In 1934 the Associated Press spoke of a punt "in the Yale game at New Haven in 1899 that went 117 yards."

Another 1934 account details a 110-yard punt in New Haven, though it claimed that it came in warm-ups. "Pat, at a run, dropped the ball and booted it just as he passed under the goal posts. It zoomed high into the autumn air, plunked to the earth on the 10 yard line at the other end of the field, and rolled over the goal line . . . [while] the Yale stands groaned a unanimous groan and sat down!"

The record "champagne" boot against Northwestern took on a life of its own as well. Right after it happened, the press raved about the kick, calling it "a performance never equaled on any gridiron in the world." O'Dea downplayed his remarkable achievement, saying he would try a dropkick from anywhere within 70 yards "on decent ground."

The mention of "decent ground" is critical, as it got less and less "decent" as the years went on. A fable of sorts grew up around the weather. Though it was quite cold, newspapers of the day noted that "a more perfect day could not have been chosen for a football game" and that the gridiron was in "fine condition." The weather report for the Chicago area shows a grand total of one one-hundredth of an inch of precipitation in the three days before the contest. The setting, however, deteriorated significantly upon retelling.

A feature in Wisconsin's homecoming game program in 1934 mentioned that the Northwestern kick had come "on a muddy field with a heavy ball," and the *Montana Standard* of the same year reported that the kick "was made from the sidelines with a slippery ball." O'Dea's National Football Foundation Hall of Fame write-up reports that the boot was converted "in a driving blizzard," and his UPI obituary took it one step further, not only mentioning the blizzard but also reporting that the Aussie was "on the run from scrimmage" when he kicked it.

Legendary sportswriter John Lardner wrote a *New York Times* column in 1955 debunking some of the great myths in sports. He included stories such as Abner Doubleday's "invention" of baseball and Babe Ruth's famous called shot against the Cubs' Charlie Root in the 1932 World Series. Of O'Dea's kick against Northwestern, Lardner wrote: "The day that Pat O'Dea of the University of Wisconsin kicked the most celebrated of his long field goals lives in a curious way in the minds of old-time football fans: the snow gets deeper with every year. With one conservative faction it became stabilized . . . at six inches." Unlike Doubleday and Ruth, O'Dea was still around at the time and, upon questioning, told Lardner that the kick "was made from relatively bare ground."

Though the length of the kick wasn't subject to quite the same embellishment as the weather reports, there were also some differing opinions on that front. Cochems, who was the younger brother of Henry Cochems, one of the two Wisconsin players ruled ineligible before the 1898 season, always insisted that the kick against Northwestern came from 65 yards, rather than the 60 yards that most of the papers reported or the 62 yards that Wisconsin credited him with in its record books. And while the general consensus at the time was that the ball traveled 70 yards in the air, Cochems insisted that it was "easily an 80 yard drop."

What to make of the disparities in the accounts of the Northwestern and Yale performances? One thing to keep in mind when it comes to the Yale game is that virtually none of the newspaper stories of the day gave any length approximations at all for any of the O'Dea punts. In fact, of the myriad of newspaper accounts cited here, only two discussed actual distances. The *Daily Cardinal* had a play-by-play account of the game where, under the heading O'DEA'S GREAT PUNT, it described "a kick of 80 yards." Later in the same paragraph, it reported, "McBride punts to the 18 yard line and O'Dea punts back to Yale's 15 yard line," which is the 77-yard boot described earlier. Embedded in its game story, the *Boston Globe* wrote, "once he punted from his 25-yard line over the heads of Yale's backs to Yale's 8 yard line." Though the writer didn't feel it was worthwhile to do the math, that too would have been a 77-yard punt.

Equally telling is the lack of a consensus in the reporting of Richards's game-winning run. While the distance of the dash was reported in every game story, and the general conclusion was that it covered 65 yards, there were certainly some dissenting opinions. The *Philadelphia Inquirer*'s headline spoke of RICHARDS' 70 YARD RUN, while the *Daily Cardinal*—the only paper to specifically mention the punt distance—wrote of the game-winning play, "Richards grabs the ball and runs around the end 95 yds for a touchdown." Obviously, a significant variation from what others had reported.

There are all kinds of possible explanations for the discrepancies. Though there were yard markers on the sidelines, the numbers weren't painted onto the field like they are today, so it was easy to lose track of the spot where a play originated. The typed play-by-play accounts that today are part of the postgame box scores didn't exist. With the limits in technology and the many steps it took to get a game story from a stadium into a newspaper, simple issues like typos can't be ruled out.

There may be something else at work, too. The lack of video evidence put a tremendous amount of power in the hands of newspaper writers. It was a time when myth could quickly become reality. We all know what the greatest athletes and sports moments of the last half-century looked like because we can watch them whenever we want. We don't need a reporter to describe "The Miracle on Ice," Michael Jordan's flu-ridden NBA Finals performance against the Jazz, or even Bill Mazeroski's 1960 World Series–winning home run. That wasn't the case in 1899, or many years later when writers discussed the events of that bygone era.

As has certainly become obvious by now, O'Dea was truly great. There are too many independent accounts stating so to believe otherwise. Yet, it's also obvious that, like any athlete, there were some days when he was

better than others. But people want to talk about having witnessed phenomenal athletes at their greatest moments. So, if twenty or even forty
years after the fact, a writer decides to reflect on the time he saw a superstar in action, why not stretch the truth a little? Why not pretend that the
kick that happened in warm-ups actually occurred in the game? After all,
it makes for a better story. It adds to the legend. And it was the legend,
both on the field and off, that defined O'Dea.

It would be disingenuous to suggest that these inconsistencies aren't
relevant. After all, there is a massive difference between an 80-yard punt
and a 117-yard one, just as a kick in a driving blizzard is more impressive than one made in placid conditions. But given the unanimous praise
heaped upon his punting by the reporters who covered the Yale game, it
does seem fair to conclude that, however far his kicks traveled, O'Dea's
punting that day was truly remarkable. In summarizing the Elis' performance, the *Philadelphia Inquirer* wrote of O'Dea's "immense superiority"
over his Yale counterpart McBride, who would be named a first-team
All-American at the end of the season. "It must be borne in mind, however," the paper pointed out, "that O'Dea is an exceptional punter and
when compared with any other standard ... McBride ... [is] considerably
above average." The *New York Herald* reached a more sweeping conclusion, saying simply, "The game conclusively proved that, in 'Pat' O'Dea,
Wisconsin has the greatest kicker who ever played football."

O'Dea aside, conclusions regarding what the Badgers' performance
meant for Western football as a whole were less uniform. As we've seen,
there were some who dismissed them as a one-man team. The general consensus, however, was that Wisconsin had helped earn its region a measure
of respect. "The West is working hard to take the football supremacy away
from this part of the country, where it has remained ever since the first
pigskin was kicked by an intercollegiate toe," the *New York Sun* concluded.

As would be expected, the strongest opinions came from the West.
Wisconsin manager Fisher said that, in playing Yale so close, Wisconsin has "clearly shown there is practically no difference between the east
and the west." The *Chicago Times-Herald* saw it as a milestone game.

"A tottering tradition has been completely overthrown," the paper proclaimed. After all, it reasoned, in previous years, Harvard, Yale, and Princeton had beaten one another more soundly than the Elis beat Wisconsin. Therefore, there was no more difference between Yale and Wisconsin than there might have been in a given year between any of the Eastern powers. "Admit that Yale has the better team, and the proof of the collapse of the tradition is still convincing."

In a conclusion that would certainly resonate with today's college football fans, the *Times-Herald* stated that the only way to really resolve the debate was with a playoff of sorts. "The final game of the year," the paper predicted, "will be fought out between the strongest team of the West and the strongest team of the East."

CHAPTER FIFTEEN

A PREMATURE END

Upon returning home from New Haven, Pat O'Dea dropped a bombshell. This would be his last year playing for the Badgers. Though, under the rules of the time, he was still eligible to participate in intercollegiate athletics for another season, he had decided to call it a career.

Today's sportswriters would call it a "quality of life" decision. "Every year I have worked hard in the interests of Wisconsin, keeping in training steadfastly," O'Dea told the *Milwaukee Sentinel*. "Now I am tired of it and desire to enjoy my last year in the university prior to graduating instead of working hard to condition myself for athletic contests."

O'Dea outlined the many sacrifices he had made to participate in football—everything from eschewing pastries and sweets to missing out on the social aspects of college life. A *Milwaukee Journal* reporter, oblivious to O'Dea's reputation as a ladies man, noted sympathetically that the football star "had no time to call on girls." The story of the impending retirement of "the greatest punter and drop-kicker college athletics has ever known" made national news, appearing in newspapers as far-flung as Dallas, New Orleans, and Boston.

Though the *Sentinel* reported that O'Dea planned to practice law in either Milwaukee or Madison after graduation, speculation began that he would succeed King, who, several papers reported, might step down from his position as Wisconsin's coach. "In all these years," the *Minneapolis*

Journal said of O'Dea, "he has not drawn any pecuniary benefit from his labors in helping to bring Wisconsin into the foreground of western football history, and now there is an opportunity to, in a measure, recognize his services in giving him a remunerative position it seems that that should be done, if he desires it." O'Dea shrugged off talk of succeeding his coach, saying respectfully, "all I know now I have learned from Phil King." He did note, however, that he would like to help the team in some capacity, perhaps as a kicking coach.

There was still the matter of finishing his final season, though. It was a season that seemed unlikely to include a showdown with archrival Chicago. Tired of Stagg's heavy-handedness on financial issues, Wisconsin, Michigan, and Illinois announced a joint boycott of the Maroons in March of 1899. The three state universities said they would not resume relations with Chicago unless the school agreed to an even split of gate receipts and gave its opponents the right to choose the location for half of their matches with the Maroons. In other words, the schools demanded financial equality with Chicago. "We decline to compete with universities of our own rank which are unwilling to admit the principle that intercollegiate contests are established primarily for the sake of sport and not for financial gain," Wisconsin manager John Fisher said.

O'Dea articulated a similar position. "I should like to play Chicago before my football career is ended," he said, "but a game cannot be arranged unless Stagg accedes to the conditions comprised in Manager Fisher's statement." But the concept of sharing equally was one that Stagg had long scoffed at as "socialistic philanthropy." In a letter to University of Chicago president William Rainey Harper, frustrated Wisconsin president Charles Adams complained that negotiations with Stagg were marked by an "assumption of superiority" on the part of the Chicago coach.

Reluctant to give up the lucrative Chicago market, Wisconsin and Michigan scheduled a Windy City game for Thanksgiving Day. It was to be played at West Side Park, then home of the Chicago Orphans, the city's National League baseball team, which, within a few years, would come to be known as the Cubs. The contest would be the first meeting between the two schools since 1893. As former Badgers star "Ikey" Karel noted, like Wisconsin, Michigan had "had enough of Stagg and Staggism." In response to the boycott, Stagg turned eastward, lining up games against three solid opponents—Cornell, Pennsylvania, and Brown, the latter of which would visit Chicago on Thanksgiving afternoon. Stagg believed that a battle between his eminently popular local team and an Eastern opponent, even a second-tier one, would prove to be a bigger draw than a game between two out-of-town teams. That hubris, as it turned out, would cost him dearly.

Wisconsin had two more games scheduled against conference foes before the big showdown with Michigan, and those two games provided two of the most memorable moments of O'Dea's career.

The first came in the Badgers' matchup with Illinois on a windy November day in Milwaukee. Early in the game, after O'Dea had punted deep into Illinois territory, the Illini quickly kicked back to the Badgers. While the ball was in the air, O'Dea yelled to his teammate William Juneau, "fair catch, Bill, fair catch!" Juneau did as he was told, raising his hand and, in accordance with the rules of the day, digging in his heel to mark the spot of the catch. He grabbed the ball near the sideline at Wisconsin's 53-yard line, meaning he was at a sharp angle 57 yards away from the goalposts. The rules at the time in college football, as they still do in the National Football League to this day, allowed a team making a fair catch to immediately attempt a field goal from the spot of the catch—an uncontested kick that the defense cannot rush. Given the circumstances, no one expected O'Dea to invoke the rule. The game referee reportedly turned to the Aussie and quipped, "I think you're crazy if you're trying to score in this wind."

And, yet, that's exactly what O'Dea was trying to do. Juneau assumed the position for holding a placekick attempt. He lay down on his stomach and extended his right arm, placing a fingertip on top of the ball. Taking the wind into account, O'Dea lined up for the attempt. "I aimed the ball for a spot between the goal posts and the sideline to allow for the drift," he later recounted. A twenty-year-old named Robert Zuppke, later a Hall of Fame football coach at Illinois, had paid the princely sum of a nickel to watch the game from a nearby rooftop. "It was a mighty boot," Zuppke recalled. "The ball soared far above the goal posts, almost squarely between them, and sailed on above the crowd in the stands and landed outside the park."

It was the longest successful placekick in college football at the time, officially credited at 57 yards, though, thanks to the angle and the fact that the ball flew well beyond the posts, it was estimated to have traveled roughly 75 yards. Reaction to the kick was overwhelming. One Illinois assistant coach called it "the prettiest piece of football I have ever seen," while another said simply, "O'Dea's kick was wonderful."

And unlike many of O'Dea's hyperbole-aided efforts, the contemporaneous accounts tell the same story that was relayed many years later. For instance, an article in an Ann Arbor newspaper described the kick this way. "O'Dea established a new world's record by a goal kick which was little short of marvelous. Juneau made a fair catch on Wisconsin's 53 yard line near the edge of the gridiron. From this point O'Dea made a place-kick scoring a clean goal at a distance of 57 yards, and that too, from near the edge of the field."

The Badgers won the game 23–0, holding the Illini to just one first down in the process, prompting the *Chicago Tribune* to remark that "Illinois' offense was about as helpless an article as ever happened on a football field." It was a group, the paper remarked, that at times was "seized with intense stupidity" and at others seemed "to have not the slightest idea what to do." The Badgers, on the other hand, were clicking, taking a 6–1 mark into their game at Minnesota.

That contest was only marginally closer, and once again, O'Dea was the story. Early in the second half, the Badgers' captain fielded a Minnesota punt on Wisconsin's side of midfield. He then executed a move that another future Hall of Fame coach, Gil Dobie, who was playing for the Gophers that day, always maintained was "the greatest individual play he ever saw." Dobie saw some good plays, by the way. He later coached sixty-one games at the University of Washington and didn't lose a single one of them.

As O'Dea caught the ball, Dobie was bearing down on him, in perfect position to make the tackle. He dove at O'Dea, who sidestepped him beautifully. "After eluding me," Dobie remembered, "O'Dea ran toward the sideline. He did not kick until several Minnesota players were almost upon him. The boot was therefore at a difficult angle, made harder by the fact that O'Dea, a right-footed kicker, was running to his left." Oscar Erickson, a Badger freshman athlete at the time, remembered the kick similarly, recalling, "It is safe to say the ball covered all of 70 yards. I have had my share of athletics as player, coach and spectator, but that play as a spectacle will always stay with me."

And much like the kick against Illinois from the week before, the accounts of the time jibe nicely with the legend. The *Minneapolis Journal*'s description of the play in its game story read, "The ball flew straight to O'Dea 10 yards beyond center and with Gil Dobie right under it. Great was the surprise of the Minnesota men to see O'Dea dodge an attack from Dobie and then deliberately kick a drop from the center of the field. A nicer kick could not have been made and Wisconsin had a score, 5–0." The kick is officially listed as a 60-yarder, the second longest of O'Dea's career. The Badgers won 19–0. They were still unbeaten against Western foes heading into their Thanksgiving Day showdown with Michigan in Chicago.

As the appointed 11:00 hour for kickoff of that game came and went, Stagg fidgeted uncomfortably in the stands. He had decided to drop by the West Side grounds to work off some of his nervous energy as he awaited the mid-afternoon kickoff between his Maroons and Brown, but if anything, the scene was making him more agitated.

Stagg had come early, in part, to exchange what were almost certainly strained greetings with the management of the Michigan and Wisconsin teams. Though both schools were still boycotting Chicago, he harbored hopes of talking the winner into playing a championship game the following weekend. None of the three teams had lost to a Western squad all season, and the fan bases were unhappy that, due to the boycott, they would not get a clear-cut champion.

As upsetting as that prospect was to Stagg, it was the size of the crowd that really disturbed him. The wooden bleachers were absolutely packed with Wisconsin and Michigan supporters, who had poured in by the trainload and taken over the Windy City. Stagg had hoped that the Wisconsin–Michigan game would prove less attractive than a game between the Wolverines and his Maroons, who had played the last six Thanksgiving Days in Chicago. As was clear from the throng in the stadium and the many thousands who snaked through the streets and vacant lots outside trying to get in, he had miscalculated.

The final attendance that day was estimated (not all that precisely) at between 13,000 and 22,000. Whatever the number, it was the largest crowd ever to see a football game in the West, and Stagg knew it would dwarf the attendance at Marshall Field that afternoon, which ended up numbering less than 8,000. He had hoped that fans would be able to attend both games, but as the minutes ticked away, it became more and more apparent that wouldn't be possible. Though management attributed the delay to the throngs who were backed up at the ticket windows, there was a small part of Stagg that wondered whether it was aimed at him—an attempt to further diminish his turnstile count.

Brass bands from the two schools filled the void, marching around the field to entertain the fans, who responded with tin horns and even an occasional cowbell. When the two teams finally emerged at 11:30, the wooden stands shook with the sounds of music and cheering, as fans waved banners and streamers decorated in school colors. The field ran sideways across the baseball lot, with one goalpost placed right around the spot where first base would be and the other in left center field.

The fans had all paid handsomely for the right to be in the ballpark, with ticket prices ranging between $1.00 for general admission and $10.00 for the boxes, which were arranged under a covered grandstand behind the home plate area. Each school ended up netting $6,000—making it the most lucrative gate ever for a football game in Chicago. It was a number that showed just how far the sport had come in the Midwest during the 1890s. When the two schools had last met, six years earlier in Ann Arbor, the attendance totaled 360. After Wisconsin's team had returned to Madison back then, it was forced to ask the student body to chip in cash to pay off the debt from the journey.

As always, the pregame hype and attention had centered on Wisconsin's star kicker. The Wolverines' strategy, the *Milwaukee Journal* reported on the morning of the game, "will be to keep Pat O'Dea so far away from their goal that he will be unable to use his famous kicking leg to advantage in scoring." The Badgers, the paper said, "will play a defensive game, making its effort to keep Michigan away from the danger line and trusting to Pat O'Dea for the rest." The *Chicago Tribune* asserted that the Badgers might be overly reliant on their great kicker, noting that Wisconsin "depends so much on O'Dea that the offensive work has suffered." Michigan captain Allen Steckle concurred, saying simply, "O'Dea is our greatest fear."

The Wolverines had a plan for O'Dea, and the Badgers' star was well aware of it. "The Michigan men had threatened, through letters sent to our people, to disable me, to get me out of the game," he said afterward. That the threats were more than just idle chatter became evident just minutes into the game. O'Dea called for a fair catch on a Michigan punt, but the Wolverines' David Gill ignored his hand signal "and tackled the Australian foully." The ensuing 10-yard penalty gave the Badgers the ball at Michigan's 35-yard line. "With the wind blowing rather stiffly at his back and the center of the goal posts directly before him O'Dea's task seemed a foregone conclusion," the *Chicago Chronicle* reported. "The ball rose straight as a shot from the Australian's cleated toe and sailed between the uprights with an aim and directness that seemed almost stereotyped." The Badgers had an early 5–0 lead.

Michigan was undeterred by the penalty against Gill and continued its rough play on O'Dea. "Every time that O'Dea punted opposing men would break through and rush upon him needlessly," the *Chronicle* observed. "Efforts to block a kick are most praiseworthy, but there is no excuse for the rough work of the Michigan men," the *Tribune* admonished. "It was dirty football, as dirty as ever was seen without actual slugging." O'Dea said afterward that he could overhear the Michigan players urging one another to "cripple me if possible so I would have to retire," but each time he complained to the game officials, his pleas were ignored.

Finally, he could take it no more. Late in the first half, O'Dea boomed a punt from midfield. It slipped through the arms of Michigan's John McClean and rolled over the goal line, where Wisconsin's Frank Hyman recovered it for a touchdown. Back behind the line of scrimmage, O'Dea "was attacked by Snow, Gill, France and Richardson," who, according to the *Milwaukee Sentinel*, "dug their elbows into his ribs with terrific force." O'Dea swung his arms in an effort to fight off his assailants and, depending on what account you believe, either accidentally or purposefully nailed France in the face. At that moment the umpire, Laurie Bliss, whose job it was to maintain order, "whirled about on his heel and ordered O'Dea out of the game."

The ejection was roundly criticized. The *Sentinel* condemned the decision as "autocratic and unjust." The *Tribune* agreed, saying, "No man ever had more provocation or was more justified in hitting back than was O'Dea at this time." The *Chronicle* shared that stance. "Ordinarily slugging is reprehensible," the paper opined, before adding that "in this case O'Dea was not disgraced in the eyes of his admirers."

His absence, as it turned out, made little difference. The Badgers rolled to a 17–5 win. Afterward, they celebrated at the bar of the team hotel. Coach Phil King was hoisted onto a chair and paraded around the room before being placed triumphantly upon a table. As the crowd called for order, King rose to his feet, the small man now towering over the happy celebrants.

"Quiet! Quiet!" the men shouted, removing their hats in a show of mock solemnity.

King paused dramatically, waiting for the room to silence.

"It goes without saying that I am immensely pleased with the work of the team to-day, and the last half showed that we could beat them without Pat," he said, before glancing fondly at his star player.

"What would we have done with O'Dea?" a member of the crowd shouted, eliciting cheers and laughter.

King continued, "[T]he captain was, I am absolutely certain, ruled off unjustly."

O'Dea gave his side of the story. "Michigan was sending five and six men against me repeatedly with the evident purpose of putting me out of the game," he said. "I simply put out my hands to ward them off and the officials thought I was slugging when I was not."

Even Charles Kendall Adams, the president of the university, weighed in on the O'Dea ejection. "We who know Patrick know that he didn't do anything that either he or we should be ashamed of," he said, placing his arm on his star's shoulder. "Patrick, I'm proud of you; we're all proud of you," he added, as the room again erupted in cheers.

Adams's business in Chicago wasn't done. He and the rest of the conference's presidents brokered a peace agreement at a city hotel the next day. It included renewed relations between Chicago and Wisconsin, Michigan, and Illinois. Humbled by the financial losses his obstinacy had caused, Stagg essentially agreed to the terms he had long opposed. His school would host Thanksgiving games every year, alternating between Wisconsin and Michigan as its opponents. On years they weren't playing in Chicago, the Badgers and Wolverines would have the right to choose the locale for their game with the Maroons. Most important, the universities would split their gate receipts equally, though, in an effort to placate Stagg and help him save some face, the other three schools agreed that the visitor would always be guaranteed at least $1,000.

Given the kind of money they were all pulling in, that portion of the agreement seemed almost pointless, and yet it rankled the devoted amateur Caspar Whitney. "This is really such an absurd and puerile sub-contract as to be amusing," he wrote. "Fancy mature men, and supposedly sportsmen at that, embarking on such boyish bickering! The pot-hunting spirit larks in this agreement." Still, there was no doubt that, at least for the time being, Stagg had been put in his place. "The failure of games with Eastern teams to interest the public so much as those between Western elevens is not only complimentary to the growth of a real football spirit in Chicago, but also a straw to show Professor Stagg which way the wind is blowing," Whitney observed.

As part of the agreement, Chicago and Wisconsin agreed to play a Western championship game the following Saturday in Madison. It was a mob scene. The small city was overwhelmed, with visitors forced to sleep on cots in the lobbies of the jammed hotels and restaurant space proving virtually impossible to come by. Still, it was a festive atmosphere. "The shops that face on Capitol square were ablaze with cardinal," the *Daily Inter Ocean* reported. "Every window was decorated with color dear to Wisconsin men." A reported $20,000 changed hands in wagering.

Those who bet on the Maroons took home the cash. With 10,000 fans jammed into Camp Randall, and many thousand more watching from the surrounding hillsides, Chicago dominated the game from start to finish. The Badgers came out flat and simply never recovered. The Maroons, on the other hand, played like they had a score to settle. "Every man took a hand in the game, and the runner, after being tackled, was always dragged and pushed along for a yard or more. The fierce aggressiveness of the Chicago players bewildered their opponents."

The Maroons' strategy was a simple one. They repeatedly pounded the ball at Wisconsin's young tackles, Arthur Curtis and Edwin Blair. "Blair was found to offer the line of least resistance," the *Tribune* reported, "so against him the attack of Chicago . . . was directed." Wisconsin, noted all year for its defense, was powerless to stop the Maroons' attack. "Our mass plays worked smoothly," Stagg observed afterward.

Wisconsin, as always, relied on O'Dea, but perhaps impacted by the drizzly, dreary conditions, the Australian, making his final appearance in a Wisconsin uniform, was largely ineffective. "O'Dea certainly was not in form," the *Inter Ocean* observed, "and many of his punts fell woefully short." Beloit College coach John Hollister, who had come to Madison to watch the game, concurred, observing, "O'Dea's kicking was poor." The playing career of one of the game's biggest stars ended with an uncharacteristic whimper, though it was not the last that college football fans would hear from Pat O'Dea.

As time expired, the thousand or so Chicago students who had made the journey northward rushed the field and hoisted the Maroons on their shoulders, carrying them a full mile to the team hotel, where they celebrated long into the night. Joyous Chicago president William Rainey Harper was hauled away in a similar fashion, though not everyone saw it as a triumph worth celebrating. "It is a fact that in the last two years Chicago has had more athletes of questionable eligibility . . . than all the leading Middle-Western universities put together," Whitney wrote later that month in *Harper's Weekly*. "Surely not an enviable record for a university which started with such promise and protested such righteousness."

Whitney wasn't the only one who objected to the direction that football was taking. The voices that joined him became more widespread and powerful. They would soon threaten the game's very survival.

CHAPTER SIXTEEN

"THE MOST DISGRACEFUL SCANDAL EVER KNOWN"

Wisconsin wasn't the only notable school to see its 1899 season end in disappointment. The Yale team that had beaten the Badgers in October ended up dropping two games that year, tying for the most in the history of the program, which had begun in 1872.

One of the losses came in Yale's annual showdown with Princeton. There was no great shame in that defeat. It was the Elis' fourth setback in their last seven meetings with the Tigers, dating from the huge upset on Thanksgiving Day in 1893. The other defeat was a shocker, as it came against a school Yale had beaten by a combined 155–0 the last two times they had met—a school that hadn't even had a football team for most of the prior decade.

Columbia had been a part of the early evolution of the game, playing its first intercollegiate match in 1870, just one year after the historic meeting between Princeton and Rutgers. The New York school participated in some of the early rules meetings and fielded a team for much of the 1870s and 1880s. It was a perennial doormat. The 1891 team lost its last five games by a combined total of 220–0. Not surprisingly, there was no 1892 team. The school dropped the game, choosing to focus its athletic efforts on the crew team.

By the late 1890s, though, it became evident that eliminating football might not have been the wisest move. Columbia looked at the crowds, revenue, and publicity that Yale, Princeton, and Harvard were generating and decided to give the game another shot. "Columbia saw greater advertising possibilities in football—successful football of course," Henry Beach Needham observed in *McClure's Magazine* in 1905. "Played in New York, the games would attract large crowds, and sufficient revenue would result to support athletics in general." The school hired former Yale star George Foster Sanford as head coach and organized a team for the 1899 season. In the words of the *New York Times,* Sanford's team was "an experimental one, formed to see if Columbia might not develop an athletic record such as is an honor to other universities."

On October 28, just one week after the Elis beat Wisconsin, they journeyed to Manhattan to battle Sanford's team. The result sent shock waves through the Eastern football establishment. Midway through the second half in a scoreless game, Harold Weekes, a talented freshman from Long Island, ran 50 yards straight through the Yale defense for what would prove to be the only score of the game. The 5–0 Columbia win was no fluke. "They outplayed, both offensively and defensively, the arrogant sons of Eli," the *Times* reported. It was the first time since the advent of the scrimmage that any school other than Harvard or Princeton had beaten Yale.

The resulting celebration showed the impact that a successful football team could have on a university. On the sidelines, one Columbia grad hugged another while exclaiming, "It's the first time that Columbia has scored against Yale since 1873, and I played in that game." He was off by two years, but who was going to correct him at a moment like this?

"What is Yale anyway?" another grad yelled. He quickly answered his own question. "One of those minor colleges located somewhere down in Connecticut!"

"The victory means everything to the local university," the *New York Sun* asserted. "It will serve to boom Columbia as a football college in the estimation of thousands of young players who are in the various preparatory schools throughout the United States." It also helped the school's immediate bottom line, as the team's manager, William Mitchell, reported box office revenues of $12,000.

But the result did not meet with universal acclaim. "I am unable to endorse it as a *bona fide* university team in the ethical sense understood and accepted at all colleges where the wholesomeness of the college sport is considered," Whitney wrote in *Harper's Weekly*. He contended that several of Columbia's players were not genuine students. The men, he said, were enrolled in the School of Political Science, "where there is no daily roll-call or entrance examinations," and were there solely due to their football ability.

The Faculty Committee on Athletics demanded an investigation. The results were disturbing. Upon questioning by university officials, Mitchell admitted that he had paid the tuition, board, and lodgings of five men on the football team, a move that, in the days before athletic scholarships, was a blatant violation of the amateur code. The tuition payments were made from the football budget and were hidden with false bookkeeping. For instance, after the two schools met in Manhattan in October, Columbia claimed to have paid $226 more to Princeton in gate receipts than it actually had. That amount was then funneled to the school as tuition payments for the men in question.

Not that it was tuition the men were particularly interested in having paid for them. Two of the players, R. E. Larendon and G. H. Miller, wrote a signed letter to the *New York Tribune* in March of 1900 countering the notion that they had benefitted in any way from Columbia's chicanery. "We wish to emphatically deny the current rumors that we received any pecuniary or educational benefit from playing football with Columbia last season," they wrote. "It is a well-known fact that we did not attend lectures and never had any intention of so doing. We played as a favor to Columbia."

It was an incident that one university grad, in a letter to a member of the Athletic Committee, referred to as "the most disgraceful scandal ever known in College Athletics." He added that he and other alums "were subjected to the deepest mortification and humiliation." In response, Columbia fired the team manager, William Mitchell, and kicked him out of school. As for Coach Sanford? He got a raise. After all, he had defeated Yale.

— ⁓

Football's physical danger escalated along with its corruption. In 1900 Sanford and Weekes devised a play they termed the high hurdle. They unveiled it in the team's second impressive upset in as many seasons, a 6–5 home victory over Princeton. Weekes, lined up five yards behind the line, took the handoff and, pushed forward by four of his teammates and using his center's back as a springboard, "leaped feet foremost into space." In his 1955 book *The Saga of American Football*, Alexander Weyand recalled that "Weekes was frequently catapulted over the heads of the linemen, sometimes rising to a height of five and a half feet off the ground." Two years later, Princeton attempted to stop the play by launching a player of its own at Weekes, causing a midair collision. Not surprisingly, both players left the game with injuries.

Though Columbia's return to the sport ultimately proved to be brief, it perfectly encapsulated both the positive and negative aspects of intercollegiate football that had developed during the prior decade. It showed the vast power of the game and its ability to generate publicity and revenue for a university while providing excitement for the students and alums. It also showed the game's sordid side—the emphasis on winning at all costs, the neglect of academic integrity, the taint of professionalism, and the growing violence inherent in the sport. It was far from an isolated example. Between 1900 and 1905, football was under almost constant attack, as years of troubles escalated to the point of crisis—a crisis that nearly led to the abolition of the sport.

As was often the case in the early years of the game, Yale was at the forefront. In 1901 the school enrolled a 26-year-old freshman named James J. Hogan. As his age would indicate, Hogan had taken an indirect path to New Haven. A native of County Tipperary in Ireland, Hogan had come to the United States with his family at age five. They settled in Torrington, Connecticut, where his father found work as a stonemason.

The 5'10" 210-pound fireplug graduated from high school and then went to work in the hardware business before a friend, noting his size and athleticism, suggested that he might have potential as a football player. Though well into his twenties at the time, Hogan enrolled at Phillips Exeter Academy, where he received a full scholarship. To his credit, he worked hard to master his studies, which did not come easily. He was "always on the edge of his seat fighting for every bit of information that he could get," one instructor recalled, adding, "It was interesting and almost amusing at times to watch him."

Though Hogan wasn't a natural in the classroom, he certainly was on the gridiron—literally and figuratively a man among boys. Sleeves rolled up to display his muscular forearms, his massive chest and neck muscles bulging with exertion, Hogan was the driving force behind a Yale team that went 32–2–1 in his last three years in New Haven. An "almost irresistible" ball carrier, Hogan coupled his skill with remarkable intensity, often screaming "from sheer Celtic emotion" when the moment got particularly tense.

The Irishman was named a first-team All-American in each of his final three seasons in New Haven, though his rewards went far beyond simple mention in a magazine. Hogan lived a life of luxury at Yale. He had his own suite at Vanderbilt Hall, the most upscale student dormitory, got his meals free at the ordinarily pricey University Club, and received free tuition and spending money. By today's standards, such treatment might not seem so egregious, but it flew in the face of the principles of the time, arrived at during an 1898 conference at Brown University, which stated: "The practice of assisting young men through college in order that they may strengthen the athletic teams is degrading to amateur sport."

Hogan's deal was about more than just tuition, room, and board, though. He also worked out a side agreement with the American Tobacco Company that gave him a cut of all of its cigarettes that were sold in New Haven. Hogan was an effective salesman. He managed to persuade Mory's, a local grille room frequented by Yale men, to sell the company's smokes. "But his efforts did not end there," J. T. Wilcox, the American Tobacco Company's assistant secretary noted. "He talks cigarettes to his friends. They appreciate and like him; they realize he is a poor fellow, working his way through college, and they want to help him. So they buy our cigarettes, knowing that Hogan gets a commission on every box sold in New Haven. We are satisfied with our arrangement, and I am sure that Hogan is." As a token of thanks at the end of his career, the university's boosters sent him on an all-expenses-paid Cuban vacation.

In fairness, Hogan and Yale weren't the only ones bending the rules in the early years of the twentieth century. But their transgressions might have never come to light were it not for another development in journalism—the rise of the muckrakers. "Muckraker" was a name applied to a group of magazine writers in the first decade of the 1900s and popularized in a 1906 speech by President Theodore Roosevelt. Though he commended the work of journalists in search of the truth, Roosevelt initially meant for the description to have a negative connotation, indicative of those who raked "the filth of the floor." The movement was, in some ways, an offshoot of yellow journalism, as it looked to stir up emotion in its readers. There was one significant difference, though. Whereas the "yellows" were simply in competition for circulation, with no regard for whether their articles contained much in the way of truth, the muckrakers were crusaders, looking to expose society's wrongs.

McClure's Magazine published the first significant muckraking articles in late 1902. Among them was a nineteen-part series on the Standard Oil Company written by a woman named Ida Tarbell. Tarbell grew up in the oil-producing region of western Pennsylvania. Her father, Frank, had, for a time, been a successful oilman, but his business suffered a major blow in the 1870s. John D. Rockefeller, president of the Standard Oil Company and later the benefactor of the University of Chicago, reached a secret deal with a number of railroads. In the scheme, the railroads jacked up their shipping rates but agreed to pay rebates to Rockefeller, meaning he spent significantly less to transport his oil than other companies. As one would expect, the collusion had a disastrous effect on the smaller refiners, including Frank Tarbell, who patiently explained the reasons behind the family's reversal of fortune to his young daughter. "Out of the alarm and bitterness and confusion, I gathered from my father's talk a conviction to which I still hold that what had been undertaken was wrong," Tarbell wrote many years later in her autobiography.

She ended up being uniquely positioned to do something about it. Tarbell was a trailblazer. In 1880, a time when very few women continued their education past high school, Tarbell graduated from Allegheny College, not far from her western Pennsylvania home. She eventually became a writer, ultimately hired by *McClure's* in 1894. She wrote a number of serialized life histories for the magazine, including a glowing profile on Abraham Lincoln that helped establish her as one of the nation's foremost biographers. The magazine's founder, Samuel McClure, then assigned her to write a piece on Standard Oil.

Though Tarbell's life experience would suggest otherwise, the goal at the outset, it seems, was not to expose maleficence in the company, but to use Standard Oil "as an example of the achievements of business in production and efficient distribution." That's certainly what the company believed. Tarbell received tremendous help from Standard Oil, which opened its records to her. After five years of investigation and writing, she produced a series that blew the lid off the company's operation. "The articles," James Wood wrote in his 1956 book *Magazines in the United States,* "showed that Standard Oil was magnificently organized, that it functioned superbly, but that the methods by which the corporation had been built included bribery, fraud, violence, the corruption of public officials and railroads, and the wrecking of competitors by fair means and foul."

Tarbell's series started a tidal wave. The muckrakers and the magazines that employed them "wrested from the daily newspapers the influencing of public opinion by the direct discussion of public affairs," Wood wrote. As a result, "All the important general weeklies and monthlies began to give more coverage and more thorough discussion to public matters and thus to exert a greater influence on the minds of their readers." College football was one of their targets.

McClure's struck the first blow. Starting in June 1905, the magazine published a lengthy two-part indictment of the sport authored by Henry Beach Needham. The first portion of Needham's series, entitled "The

College Athlete: How Commercialism Is Making Him a Professional," was particularly damning. Though there had been some reporting done in 1899 and 1900 on the Columbia scandal, Needham went into greater depth. He described the role of the fired manager, Mitchell, labeling him as a "scapegoat," quoting an anonymous Columbia professor who said, "the manager and captain are clay in the hands of the potter—and the coach is the potter." In other words, he refused to buy the explanation that Coach Sanford had played no role in the recruitment of nonstudents to Columbia's team. George Kirchwey, the dean of the Columbia Law School and the chair of the Athletic Committee, agreed that the issues were deeper than simply a rogue manager and a few hired-gun players. In a 1902 letter to Columbia president Nicholas Murray Butler, he wrote, "I believe the whole present system to rest on a false basis and its evils to be incurable."

Needham and *McClure's* also exposed Hogan's story at Yale, including details of the athlete's deal with the American Tobacco Company. As it turns out, the arrangement wasn't unique. At Princeton, for instance, the athletic association gave certain athletes the privilege of selling advertisements in the scorecards that were sold at baseball games. They were allowed to keep the profits as well as the revenue from the sale of the cards themselves. "When the association gives away this privilege," Needham wrote, "it puts its hand in its pocket and *pays the athletes.*"

As Needham revealed, though, the inducements for athletes began well before they arrived on campus. He spoke of a new "class of students tainted with commercialism." These young men, Needham wrote, "are resolved that their athletic ability shall put them through college, and they propose to go to the institution offering the best 'opportunities'—a gentle word, elastic and covering many sins."

Included among the sinners was Penn, historically a school not quite as obsessed with athletic success as some of its counterparts. As the school newspaper wrote in 1899, "every student must learn that Pennsylvania goes into sport for sport's sake—that sport is primary, winning secondary." It sounded nice, but Needham reported it was an attitude that had been changing. An anonymous Penn alum said of his alma mater, "we had to do as the other colleges were doing. It is all summed up in these words: Couldn't stand losing."

As an example, Needham gave the story of a Penn football player named Edward Greene, who returned to his alma mater of Exeter in 1904 to pursue some promising young prospects, including an underclassman named Edward Hart, whom he brought back to Philadelphia for what amounted to a recruiting trip. "They certainly gave us a slick time," Hart recalled afterward. "Why our dinner cost nine dollars! They must have spent $200 setting us up. I tell you they are good fellows at Penn. It ain't just the students either. The city folks take an interest in the boys. One man offered Greene his room and board, and he bought him a sixty-dollar overcoat." Enticing as it all seemed to Hart, it wasn't enough. The future College Football Hall of Famer eventually went to Princeton.

Though Needham's exposé focused on the East, the Midwest didn't escape the scrutiny of the muckrakers. In the fall of 1905, *Collier's* magazine published a four-part series entitled "Buying Football Victories," which centered on the schools of the Western Conference. The articles, written by a recent Wisconsin grad named Edward S. Jordan, went into great detail, though they were essentially summarized in the statement of University of Illinois coach George Huff, who asserted that "victory in the West today depended upon the ability of the colleges to sustain men by devious means."

Not surprisingly, Chicago was at the center of the report. "Western educators who have helplessly watched this campaign," Jordan wrote, "place the University of Chicago first among the violators of the trust which rests upon all universities for the conservation of academic ideals." Jordan described a fund of $80,000 that the university held in a trust to aid "needy students." He reported that the fund was being used to pay tuition for athletes, with no actual demonstration of neediness. The money, Jordan said, was being given out "for athletic qualifications alone." Theoretically, the recipients were supposed to do university service in exchange for the grants, but the reality was altogether different. "In some instances no work is required of athletes," Jordan wrote.

The plan was being executed at the highest reaches of the school, as the dean of the Senior College reported that he had "arranged the student service scholarships for Stagg's men, according to [President] Harper's instructions." Before the beginning of the 1904 school year, Stagg wrote to Harper, "Provision should be made so that eighteen new students can work out their tuition free. This is very important." In a return letter, Harper responded, "We will of course do what is necessary to be done." And it seems Harper was true to his word. One player reportedly told a Northwestern recruiter during the courting process, "You fellows can't get me at Northwestern, and they can't get me at Wisconsin. You haven't got the money." The player, Walter Steffen, went to Chicago, where he became an All-American. Like Princeton's Hart, he's enshrined in the College Football Hall of Fame.

No single player exemplified Chicago's strategy quite like Walter Eckersall. Eckersall was a gifted athlete at Hyde Park High School, which sat in the shadow of the university's campus. In addition to quarterbacking the football team, he also set the state record in the 100-yard dash at ten seconds flat, a mark that stood for twenty-five years. In his final season, Hyde Park played what was billed as a high school national championship game against Brooklyn Poly Tech at Chicago's Marshall Field. With Eckersall leading the way before leaving late in the game with a broken collarbone, the Chicago team won rather convincingly. The final score was 105–0.

The subject of an intense recruiting battle between Michigan and Chicago, Eckersall ultimately decided to enroll at his hometown school, though, it seems, he had some help in making the decision. Stagg later admitted to grabbing the star player off a Chicago train platform as he prepared to leave for a campus visit to Ann Arbor.

Eckersall was a student at Chicago in name only. To begin with, he was grossly unqualified academically. He was initially categorized as a "sub-freshman," as he had yet to complete his college prep work, having entered school "short three of the minimum number of credits for the admission of the most poorly prepared freshman." He compounded that lack of preparation with an acute lack of interest in academic pursuits. According to Robin Lester's book *Stagg's University,* in his first quarter at Chicago, Eckersall had the worst grades and most classroom absences of any player on the football team. And it's not like the rest of the group was full of academic overachievers. Only three of the team's twenty-three members took a full load of courses that quarter. Undaunted, Eckersall registered for classes with the same professors the next quarter, "but his political science instructor, Charles Merriam, reported that 'he never appeared in class.'"

Eckersall was a disaster in other areas of life as well, gaining a reputation on campus as a carouser and a con artist. But the Chicago native lived up to his promise on the field, as perhaps the greatest player Stagg ever coached. A three-time All-American, he at times seemed like a one-man team, as evidenced by a Wisconsin newspaper headline after a particularly dominating performance during his freshman year that read, ECKERSALL, 15; WISCONSIN, 6.

When Eckersall finally used up his eligibility in the fall of 1906, he was nowhere near graduation, having earned just fourteen course credits of the thirty-six needed for a diploma. Eckersall's last game came against Nebraska in late November 1906. At halftime the faculty presented him with a gold watch in appreciation for his "service in the University." Less than two months later, the school put a notation on Eckersall's transcript reading, "Mr. Eckersall is not permitted to register in the Univ. again— for cause." President William Rainey Harper died during Eckersall's time at Chicago, so the order was signed by Acting President Henry Pratt Judson.

The nature of that "cause" was, and still is, unclear. An older alum of the university, George Buckley, wrote an angry note to Judson in March 1907. While he acknowledged the "many deplorable and unfortunate actions of Mr. Eckersall," he also took the school to task. Chicago had been derelict in its duties, he wrote. "Derelict in so far as their having knowledge of his loose morals, and yet willing to use him for advertising purposes until he had completed his college career."

That issue was at the crux of Edward Jordan's *Collier's* series. Eckersall, he said of the man who was still playing for the school when the piece was published, "is simply an 'athletic ward' of the University of Chicago. . . . Eckersall entered Chicago, and received free tuition during his entire course, with no return except in kicking and tackling ability. He has demanded nothing. Chicago has provided for his retention and that is enough."

Jordan did not limit his attacks to Chicago, though, next turning his attention to Michigan. In 1901 the Ann Arbor school had hired Fielding Yost, who had gained a reputation as a "tramp athlete" in college after his well-publicized midseason switch between West Virginia and Lafayette. Upon his graduation, Yost quickly found success as a coach, producing outstanding teams in one-year stints at Ohio Wesleyan, Nebraska, Kansas, and Stanford. His methods, Jordan reported, were a bit suspect. "Four men on his Wesleyan team were reputed to receive pay. Two players who appeared and disappeared within a few days are said to have saved his reputation at Nebraska in the great annual game with Kansas." As for his year at Stanford, the article quoted university president David Starr Jordan as saying of his then-former coach, "All of us who have had Yost or any Yost-like man are not to be counted as sinless." Yost, of course, went on to become one of the most accomplished coaches in college football history. His first Michigan team outscored its eleven foes by a combined total of 555–0.

But it wasn't the game-day results that *Collier's* writer Edward Jordan questioned; it was the methods. Jordan told the story of Yost's first great star, Willie Heston, who, like Hogan at Yale, got a portion of local tobacco sales through a product branded as "Willie Heston's cigars." The star halfback, Jordan reported, had a succession of easy jobs as well, and "in all positions Heston was well paid." Jordan quoted a former state senator named James Murfin, later a university regent, who admitted he "took care of Heston while in college." Murfin said of the law student, "I don't suppose he knows much about law, but you ought to see that boy hit the line."

By the end of the *Collier's* series, Jordan had essentially taken all of the Western Conference schools to task, pointing out transgressions at Illinois, Northwestern, Wisconsin, and Minnesota as well as Chicago and Michigan. "These fellows are so crazy to win that they forget what colleges are established for," said former Yale star Pudge Heffelfinger, then working as an assistant coach at Minnesota.

While not the focus of the pieces, the violence that had stolen the headlines during Heffelfinger's time at Yale more than a decade earlier had a place in the muckrakers' stories as well. Needham, for instance, described an incident from the Dartmouth–Princeton game of 1903. Dartmouth's star player was an end named Matthew Bullock, the son of two former slaves. An African American was a rare sight on college campuses of the era, let alone on the playing field. Though it is typically impossible to discuss the history of sport in America without touching on race, the sad truth is that African Americans were so excluded from elite institutions in the late nineteenth and early twentieth centuries that there is precious little to say about their role in the early years of the college game. With only a very few rare exceptions, they simply weren't a part of it.

The inclusion of Bullock on the roster caused a travel hardship for the New Hampshire team. The group was forced to take the train to Princeton from New York City on the day of the game, as the Princeton Inn refused to provide rooming for African Americans. When Bullock and his teammates arrived for the contest, Needham recalled, they received a rude greeting. On the first play of the game, a number of Princeton men piled on Bullock, breaking his collarbone. An angry friend of Bullock's accused a Princeton player of being a part of a racist attack. "You put him out because he is a black man," he said of Bullock. In a response that foretold incidents like the New Orleans Saints' bounty scandal a century later, the Princeton man replied, "We didn't put him out because he is a black man. We're coached to pick out the most dangerous man on the opposing team and put him out in the first five minutes of play."

Indeed, efforts to combat against the ongoing violence in the sport continued during the critical years between 1900 and 1905. In an effort to promote open play and reduce the number of injuries sustained in mass plays, the rules committee made an unusual adjustment in 1903, creating separate rules depending on where the ball was on the field. Between the 25-yard lines, the new rule stated that at least seven players on the offensive team had to be on the line of scrimmage. In addition, the player receiving the snap, who, in the past, had been prohibited from running with the ball, now could carry it, providing he crossed the line at least five yards to the left or right of the spot at which the ball had been snapped. In order to help the officials in enforcing the new regulation, the field was marked with vertical lines in addition to the horizontal yard lines, giving it a checkerboard effect. Inside the 25-yard lines, the old rules applied, meaning teams needed only five players on the line and could continue with mass plays.

Opinion was divided as to whether the new rules would help curb the violence. At least one well-known former football star said they would not. "The new rules do not improve the game. Instead of lessening the danger, they increase it," Pat O'Dea told the *Dallas Morning News* at the outset of the 1903 season, voicing the opinion that open-field running was actually more dangerous than mass plays.

O'Dea was about to begin his first season as the head coach at the American School of Osteopathy in Kirksville, Missouri. It was hardly the position he had imagined for himself when he left Wisconsin three years before.

Though O'Dea, finished as a college football player, had said he would stay in Madison to continue his studies for another year, he actually graduated with a law degree in the spring of 1900. He then announced his intention to head back to Australia, while rumors circulated that the motivation for his return was "to get his share of a great fortune to which he was one of the heirs."

Though he refused to comment on that speculation, O'Dea did mention that, after sorting out some affairs in his native country, he hoped to journey to Africa to fight the Boers, a group of Dutch descendants who had formed their own independent colonies in the British-held southern portion of that continent.

Instead, O'Dea headed for a significantly less-distant destination—South Bend, Indiana. He accepted a position as the football coach at Notre Dame. While today that is considered one of the elite jobs in college football, at the time Notre Dame was barely a factor in the sport, enjoying limited success in its battles with high schools and other colleges.

In his two years in South Bend, O'Dea elevated the program, largely due to the exploits of Louis "Red" Salmon.

Legend has it that, while walking around campus one day with one of the Notre Dame priests, O'Dea discovered Salmon kicking in a field and was impressed with his form. He asked the father why Salmon wasn't out for football and was told, "He isn't a student. He's a waiter."

"I don't care what he is," O'Dea responded. "I want him."

Sure enough, Salmon showed up for football practice the next day and embarked on a career that would end with his selection as Notre Dame's first-ever All-American. As O'Dea remembered many years later, "He learned to kick so well that later, in a Purdue game, the Purdue boys half scalped him trying to pull his hair off. They thought I was out there kicking disguised by a red wig."

Led by O'Dea and Salmon, the 1901 team won the "Indiana championship" for the first time, defeating the other two major football-playing institutions in the state, Indiana and Purdue. Notre Dame's *Scholastic* magazine raved about the success of that team, proclaiming, "all hail to them (and) to Coach O'Dea."

But O'Dea's tenure ended badly in South Bend. Notre Dame concluded the 1901 season with a game against the South Bend Studebakers, a professional team that O'Dea had been playing for on the side. Coached by Salmon, the Notre Dame team defeated the Studebakers 22–6. "The surprised and humiliated Studebakers blamed O'Dea for not knowing what to expect from his own team," Notre Dame historian Herb Juliano wrote. "O'Dea blamed his Studebaker cohorts and a brawl ensued with some serious punches thrown." Embarrassed by the unfavorable light cast upon the Golden Dome, university president Father Andrew Morrissey fired O'Dea.

But losing his job turned out to be the least of O'Dea's issues. Just weeks later, playing for the Studebakers in a game against the Rensselear Athletic Club, O'Dea injured his shoulder early in the second half. He played the rest of the game, but it was determined afterward that the shoulder was broken and would need to be in a sling for six weeks. A few weeks later, O'Dea was mugged while walking in downtown Chicago—knocked unconscious by two men who proceeded to rob him.

Just days after the assault, right after New Year's, O'Dea was severely burned after stepping into a bathtub of scalding water. O'Dea had been staying at a Chicago hotel and had ordered a bath to be drawn. "When he came to take his plunge he neglected to notice that the boy had turned on only the hot faucet. To make matters worse, his foot slipped as he sprang out of the tub and he fell partly into the water, severely burning his back as well as one of his legs."

For a while it appeared O'Dea might not survive. Reporters showed up outside his hospital room hoping to get word from the doctors regarding his condition. Upon learning of their presence, O'Dea scowled, "Go out there and make them a bet that they're wasting their time." Which, apparently, they were.

In March 1902, the University of Missouri announced the hiring of O'Dea as its coach, and the immediate reaction in Columbia was a positive one. "O'Dea has a fine reputation both as a coach and a player," the *Omaha World Herald* reported, "and great things are predicted of the Tigers next season." The team did improve under O'Dea's tutelage, winning five games, as compared to just one the year before. Still, O'Dea did not return to Missouri for a second campaign. While there were newspaper accounts indicating that the school unsuccessfully tried to sign him to a new two-year contract, family lore presents a differing picture, with accusations that O'Dea had "sold" the season-ending game against Kansas and, in fact, needed to carry a pistol in town for his safety. Either way,

O'Dea left Columbia and took a new coaching job about 90 miles to the north in Kirksville.

He arrived with a new bride by his side, having married the former Agnes McConnell on Valentine's Day of 1903. The wedding was a small affair held at Agnes's uncle's house in St. Louis. The bride, it was reported, was in poor health and was "just able to sit up during the hurried ceremony."

The inauspicious beginning was a portent of things to come. The marriage quickly disintegrated. In personal letters with her aunt, Agnes expressed her unhappiness, reporting that Pat was often away for many days at a time without informing her about where he was going or when he might return. Agnes also believed Pat to be involved with another woman in Columbia, and after giving her new husband an ultimatum, the now-pregnant Agnes left Kirksville and moved to a relative's home in upstate New York, where she gave birth to a daughter, Teresa, in November. Pat did not travel to the baptism, though his brother Andy did, beginning a long and close relationship with the baby and her mother. Appalled by Pat's behavior, Andy apparently never spoke with his brother again.

Pat coached the Osteopaths for just one year, a season that saw them play impressively in defeat against both Wisconsin and Notre Dame. The school's catalog listed him as the Director of Athletics, erroneously crediting him with having received a bachelor's degree from Melbourne University in 1893, the same year that school had actually rejected him on three separate occasions. He departed Kirksville soon after graduation in the spring of 1903. His life, like that of the sport that had made him famous, was reaching the point of crisis.

⌐•⌐

None of the changes that O'Dea had criticized in the *Dallas Morning News* in 1903 had a significant impact on the game. Football violence continued to escalate, and the game's detractors continued to voice their disgust. "Disabling opponents by kneeing and kicking, and by heavy blows on the head and particularly about the eyes, nose, and jaw, are unquestionably profitable toward victory; and no means have been found of preventing these violations of rules," Harvard president Charles Eliot complained in his annual report on the 1903–04 school year.

Though Eliot disapproved of the violence, his real issue was the lack of morals that pervaded the game. It was not a new position for Eliot. Thirty years before, he had threatened to shut down the Harvard baseball program for its "deceptive" practices. "I heard that this year we won the championship because we have a pitcher who has a fine curve ball," he said. "I am further instructed that the purpose of the curve ball is to deliberately deceive the batter. Harvard is not in the business of teaching deception."

Despite Eliot's strong objections, the school *was* in the business of teaching football. Frustrated by his team's struggles against Yale, whom Harvard had failed to score upon in three straight meetings, the school's football captain asked the athletic committee to hire alum Bill Reid to coach the team in 1905. Reid was a Harvard hero, the team's fullback as a student between 1898 and 1900. Upon graduation, he became the coach, leading the 1901 team to a perfect 12–0 mark, including a 22–0 win over Yale. That margin of defeat was, at the time, the largest ever experienced by the New Haven school.

Motivated by grumbling from frustrated grads, and hopeful that Reid could repeat his past success, the committee acquiesced. Reid was offered $3,500 to come from his home in California to coach the team, a salary that would likely have made him the second-highest-paid coach in the country, behind only Columbia's Sanford. Reid turned them down. Undeterred, a group of alums raised another $3,500, meaning Reid would earn $7,000, which, as historian Ronald Smith observes, was "nearly double the salary of the average professor at Harvard, 30 percent more than the highest paid professor and nearly as much as Charles Eliot, Harvard's president since 1869."

Reid arrived in Boston in March of 1905 and immediately set about the task of trying to assemble a team. Though Harvard had always professed to operate differently than archrival Yale, a few excerpts from

Reid's diary show quite clearly that he was not dealing with the cream of the academic crop. "Unless one keeps everlastingly after them," Reid said of his potential team members, "there is very little possibility of having them pass through their examinations. I have had to do more police duty this spring than anyone would have considered possible."

Among those troubling Reid was 225-pound tackle Preston Upham, who had already been expelled from Harvard due to behavioral issues and then readmitted. Upham's conduct was deplorable. "He cut, went in town continually, and stayed in for three or four nights at a time," Reid wrote. "[He] got into street rows, into automobile scrapes, and bad repute in money matters, into gambling, and other forms of trouble. . . . The fellow seemed to lack all idea of responsibility or sense of decency, and all interest in things except loud women." Yet Reid continued to make efforts to get Upham eligible for the team. Even after a street fight in which Upham knocked out three policemen, the school attempted to work with him. But to no avail. Upham left Harvard and went to Kansas City to work installing telegraph lines.

Though his behavior was extreme, Upham's scholastic indifference seemed to be the rule rather than the exception. Another potential star, Walter Harrison, "has impressed me as being very lazy in nature, and is lacking in ambition in many ways," Reid wrote. "However, as the last year's full back leaves this year, and we shall need a good man, I made up my mind to try to get him eligible." Reid worked tirelessly with Harrison, ultimately getting him to the point where he needed only to pass a summer-school geometry class to become eligible. Instead of taking the class, Harrison left Cambridge, opting to spend the summer at the seashore in Maine, leaving an exasperated Reid to observe, "The utter helplessness of these big fellows is disgustingly ludicrous."

And then there was the odd case of Harry LeMoyne. LeMoyne was one of the greatest schoolboy athletes of his time, having set numerous American records as a short-distance swimmer while simultaneously holding the national mark in the 16-pound shot put. He was a star guard and kicker on the Harvard football team as a freshman in 1903 before academic struggles led him to leave the school. He eventually made his way to tiny Hagerman, Idaho, where he went to work on a sheep ranch. Reid tried everything to get him back, lining up tutors, jobs, and a train ticket and, after repeatedly getting no response from his would-be star, arranging for a Hagerman storekeeper to deliver his appeals on horse-back. LeMoyne stayed in Idaho.

As a result, Harvard didn't have the team its coach had hoped for as the 1905 season dawned. But eligibility issues turned out to be the least of the concerns facing Reid and the rest of those who ran the game. 1905 would prove to be the most trying season in the history of the sport.

CHAPTER SEVENTEEN

"THE SILENT PROTEST OF THE NINETEEN GRAVES"

HARVARD COACH WILLIAM REID'S TRAIN ROLLED INTO WASHINGTON, DC, just after 9:00 a.m. on October 9, 1905, a full four and a half hours before he was due to join other football power brokers in a summit with President Theodore Roosevelt. The invitations had come just a week earlier and were somewhat cryptic in nature. "I want to talk over certain football matters with you," the president had written, "and I very earnestly hope that you will be able to come." Reid's primary concern, as it had been from the moment he took the Harvard job the previous spring, was preparing for the year-end showdown with Yale. But when the president beckons, you figure out a way to make some time. So Reid and Dr. Edward Nichols, the team physician and assistant coach, had boarded the Federal Express train out of Boston's Back Bay Station on the evening of October 8 and headed toward the nation's capital

They spent their spare time on the journey going over Yale's defense, poring through their notes in hopes of finding some sort of weakness in their archrival. But once they arrived in Washington, they allowed themselves a little bit of time for sightseeing. They stopped briefly at The Cosmos Club, an elite social club that still exists to this day. After freshening up there, they took in some of the sights, including a visit to the top of the Washington Monument. From there it was a short walk over to the White House for their lunch with the president.

The visitors were greeted at the entrance by an usher, who took them into the main reception hall, an imposing room featuring the seal of the President of the United States embedded in the floor and immense portraits of Roosevelt and his predecessor, the late William McKinley. They were then led to the main corridor, past more presidential portraits, to the site of their meeting, the State Dining Room.

It was an impressive place, having just been expanded and refurbished three years earlier. The enormous room measured 2,400 square feet, with a 21-foot ceiling that made it seem even larger. The decor was vintage Roosevelt. The first thing that caught the visitor's eye was an immense moose head mounted high above the lightly colored stone mantel. Flanking it on either side were matching ram trophies, both set into the natural oak paneling. Seventeenth-century Flemish tapestries depicting outdoor scenes adorned the walls. They blended nicely with the color scheme—green carpeting and oak chairs with green velvet cushions and backs.

Despite the massive space, it was an intimate gathering, with just eight places set at the table. The president and his secretary of state, Elihu Root, occupied the middle spots on the long sides of the table. They were surrounded by six football men, two from each of the "Big Three" powers of Harvard, Yale, and Princeton. Walter Camp and John Owsley, who was Yale's coach that year, represented the New Haven school. Coach Arthur Hillenbrand and athletic committee head John Fine had made the journey from New Jersey.

The meeting was partly a reaction to Henry Beech Needham's muckraking series in *McClure's*. The articles were an embarrassment to the game—so much so that Yale had unsuccessfully appealed to the magazine not to publish them. While Roosevelt didn't hold the entire class of new crusading journalists in particularly lofty regard, he did think highly of Needham. In fact, the writer had joined him at the president's retreat in Oyster Bay, Long Island, just a month or so after the exposé was published. After reading the articles himself, Endicott Peabody, Roosevelt's son Kermit's headmaster at the elite Groton School, suggested a meeting of the "Big Three." The president immediately sprang into action.

Roosevelt felt strongly that football did more good than harm, particularly when it came to developing physical and mental toughness. He feared that the trend away from more labor-intensive occupations was creating an effete national population, and he believed football could help counteract that trend. "We were tending steadily in America to produce in our leisure and sedentary classes a type of man not much above the Bengalee baboo," he had told Camp ten years earlier, "and from this the athletic spirit has saved us." He had no issues with the sport's inherent danger. "No fellow is worth his salt if he minds an occasional bruise or cut," he wrote. In Roosevelt's mind, football helped create the kind of men America needed—tough men of character. As he told Camp, "The rough play, if confined within manly and honorable limits, is an advantage."

But Needham had described a game that was distinctly dishonorable, on and off the field, and dishonor bothered Roosevelt a great deal. The president wanted his guests to repair the sport's disrepute. He cited a number of examples—everything from violence on the line, which was easy to hide due to the closely packed nature of the scrimmage—to attempts to deceive and injure the opposition. After sending the group out to the porch while he tended to some other business, Roosevelt rejoined them and made a request. "Will each of you," he asked, "give your word to me, as President of the United States, that you will obey the rules of the season, both in letter and spirit?" The men said they would and pledged to draw up an agreement to that effect on the train.

Camp forwarded the resulting one-sentence note to Roosevelt for his approval later that day. It read: "At a meeting with the President of the United States it was agreed that we consider an honorable obligation exists to carry out in letter and in spirit the rules of the game of foot ball relating to roughness, holding, and foul play, and the active coaches of our Universities being present with us pledge themselves to so regard it, and to do their utmost to carry out these obligations." Roosevelt wired back that he approved of the memo and thanked the men for their service.

Word of the White House summit was met with approbation. The *New York Times* was particularly complimentary of Roosevelt's initiative, praising his "superabundant vitality" and calling the move "the most important step yet" in eliminating the game's brutality. But not everyone was convinced that the president had entrusted the job to the right group of men. While complimenting Roosevelt's vigor, Harvard president Charles Eliot told the *Times*, "It is hard to bring about a reform through the very men who have long known about the existing evils, and have been largely responsible for their continuance." Indeed, after Reid sent a note to Yale's Owsley several days later looking to elucidate what exactly constituted holding and rough play, the Elis' coach showed little interest in furthering the discussion, responding, "these matters will have to be left to the officials of the game, as they are all dealt with in the rules."

Therein lay the fundamental conflict. The very men charged with overseeing the game were those who were being enriched by it. Out of pure self-interest, they were reticent to make any significant changes. As the *Princeton Alumni Weekly* wrote, "It has been plain for some time that, unless football is radically reformed, this great American college sport is doomed." It was a fact, the magazine commented, that was apparent "to most every one but a few of those entangled in the dominant theory and practice of the game itself."

As the secretary of the rules committee, Camp was the ringleader of the old guard. For years the committee had operated under the premise that any changes needed to be unanimous. The net result, as Reid complained to Eliot in the fall of 1905, was that the committee was "merely a tool of Camp's." It was an opinion shared by the chairman of Columbia's Committee on Athletics, Francis Bangs, who, in a fall letter to university president Nicholas Murray Butler, referred to Camp's committee as "self-perpetuating, non-representative, pig-headed, oblivious to public opinion and obstinate in refusing to modify the rules of play as demanded by public sentiment."

Less than a week later, Butler replied to Bangs in a note of his own, quoting a letter he had received from Harvard president Charles Eliot. Of the possibility of reforming the rules, Eliot wrote that Camp "has the matter completely in his own hands. He has always controlled the existing irresponsible committee on rules." As a result, Eliot felt that meaningful change was impossible. "The trouble with him," Eliot had written of Camp, is "that he is deficient in moral sensibility—a trouble not likely to be cured at his age." As it turned out, though, circumstances were about to force Camp's hand.

In late September 1905, William Beebe, a member of the Yale faculty, sent a letter to university president Arthur Hadley alleging financial abuses in the school's athletics operation. While still technically run by the students, athletics at Yale were overseen by the alumni, a group headed by Camp. He had accepted the position of treasurer of the Yale Financial Union in 1892, a role that gave him control of the school's athletic finances. So, any questioning of the operation of Yale's athletics was a de facto questioning of Camp himself.

Within a month, the allegations hit the newspapers, with word that Hadley had formed a committee to investigate the charges. "The whole matter of what is termed athletic abuses will be gone over," the *New York Times* reported, "including the matter of the predominating influence of the undergraduate's life at Yale . . . the relations of athletics to scholarship, and the charge of financial extravagance in connection with athletics." Camp's impeccable public reputation had taken a hit.

Football was coming under fire in Cambridge as well. In early November Reid received an urgent late-evening phone call from Herbert White, a former graduate manager of the Harvard football team, who said that he needed to speak with the Harvard coach immediately. Not comfortable sharing his news over the phone, White drove to Reid's house. Once there he told Reid that he had received word "from an authoritative source that the Harvard Corporation had voted to abolish football." The source had told White that the group had not yet decided when it would publicize the results of the vote.

Reid, White, and a couple of other football men decided to make a preemptive strike. They prepared a letter, signed by Reid, which was released to the Boston papers. In an effort to appease the sport's opponents within the university, it used language borrowed from Eliot's criticisms of football. "I have become convinced that the game as it is played today has fundamental faults which cannot be removed by any mere technical revision of the rules," the Harvard coach wrote. "Although I am willing to admit that the necessary roughness of the game may be objectionable to some people, that appears to me to be much less serious than the fact that there is a distinct advantage to be gained by brutality and evasion of the rules, because they are committed when the player and the ball also are hidden from the eyes of the umpire. For these reasons, I have come to believe that the game ought to be radically changed." Reid appealed to the Harvard Corporation to form a committee to help reform, rather than abolish, the sport.

Just days later Reid found himself at the center of an on-the-field controversy. After repeatedly complaining to the referee that he was being struck by an opponent "in an illegal and extremely painful manner" during a game against Penn, Harvard's center, Bartol Parker, fought back. In full view of the official, he slugged the offending Quaker player in the face and was summarily kicked out of the game.

News of the incident quickly reached the White House, and Reid was again summoned to Washington, sharing an informal dinner with a group that included the Roosevelt family, a number of US military officers, and the German ambassador. Reid remembered later that the president had been in fine humor, at one point looking to his end of the table and quipping, "You getting enough to eat down there, Reid? My wife doesn't know what these football appetites are like, you know."

Roosevelt's mood turned serious after the meal, though, as he ushered the coach into the library. "Now, Reid," he said, "what's this I see in the papers about a Harvard man slugging? You and I are both Harvard men, and it puts me in a very awkward position—after our agreement—to have a Harvard man the first one to violate the agreement. What happened anyway?"

"Mr. President," Reid responded. "I will tell you exactly what happened without mincing words." He did exactly that, emphasizing that Parker had been provoked. "What would you have done, Mr. President," Reid asked, "if you had been placed in a similar position?"

"He paused a moment," Reid recalled many years later, "and then, turning to me, said through his teeth, as was his custom, 'It wouldn't be policy for me to state.'" Reid made a third and final visit to the White House again at the end of the season to discuss an incident that occurred in Harvard's loss to Yale. The Crimson's Francis Burr suffered a broken nose after Yale's Jim Quill ignored a fair-catch signal and struck the Harvard guard in the face.

Much has been made of the president's role in the crisis, with some going so far as to suggest that Roosevelt "saved" the game of football. Though Roosevelt did continue to exert his influence in writing, particularly when it came to the composition of the rules committee, the Reid meetings appear to have been his final face-to-face discussions with any of the game's power brokers.

He certainly had an abiding interest in football's future, and he kept in touch with the principals. For instance, as the the sport's leaders continued to look for solutions to their difficulties, the president forwarded several suggestions for modifying the game to Camp, including one from the head of an Australian Rules Football league recommending that the United States adopt that country's game.

But Roosevelt left the ultimate decision making to the football men. "Now that the matter is in your hands," he wrote to Camp after the initial White House meeting, "I am more than content to abide by whatever you do." A later correspondence concluded, "I am sure you are doing everything that can be done, and I won't venture to make a suggestion." Historian Guy M. Lewis put it aptly when he called Roosevelt's role "a significant, but not a crucial one." As the president watched anxiously from the sidelines, public perception of the game went from bad to worse.

In the first half of a November 25 game between New York University and Union College, Union's William Moore suffered what proved to be a fatal injury. Moore was tackled hard and buried under a horde of men. When the group was finally separated, the nineteen-year-old Moore remained motionless, facedown on the turf. He was rushed to Fordham

Hospital, where he died later that evening. An autopsy showed he had suffered a cerebral hemorrhage.

Moore's death was cited in reports of the day as the nineteenth on football fields across all levels of competition in the fall of 1905, though later articles put the toll at eighteen. It was one of three fatalities on the college gridiron. Due to the fact that it had occurred in the nation's largest media center and involved two well-known universities, though, Moore's death caused more outrage than the rest of the year's fatalities combined.

Under the headline THE HOMICIDAL PASTIME, the *New York Times* published a strongly worded editorial against the game just days after Moore's death. "In theory boys play football for their health," the paper asserted. "The breaking of a youngster's leg, the twisting of his spine, and the fracturing of his skull are of doubtful advantage to his health. To kill him is indeed a very bad thing for his health." Citing "the silent protest of the nineteen graves," the paper contended that the game had to be reformed "by attacking the evils which afflict it in their source. The source of them is the insane rivalry that has grown up among the colleges and universities, the ferocious pursuit of the honor and distinction of supremacy." The *Times* concluded, "Football has degenerated into a savage, brutal, bloody fight between men animated with the passions of pugilists, seeking to win, not by demonstrations of skill and strength, but by the blackguardly expedient of physically disabling as many of their adversaries as possible. Kick the ball or kick a head—it is all in the game."

It was an attitude that was shared by many educators. In a widely repeated quotation, University of Chicago professor Shailer Matthews said of the game, "Football to-day is a social obsession—a boy-killing, man-mutilating, education-prostituting, gladiatorial sport. It teaches virility and courage," he added, "but so does war." The forces that had criticized football for years coalesced after Moore's death, further escalating the game's ongoing crisis. It was, historian John Watterson has observed, "a crisis of public confidence fanned by newspaper headlines and exploited by groups that disliked the existing gridiron system."

Columbia University, which had resumed playing the sport just six years earlier, struck the first blow. On November 28, just days after Moore's death, the school announced that it was abolishing the game. In explaining the action, Professor H. G. Lord, chairman of the Committee on Student Organizations, said it had been an easy decision, as the sport had "proved itself harmful to academic standing and dangerous to human life." The student newspaper, the *Columbia Spectator*, responded with disappointment. "The solution to the football problem lies in constructive not in destructive action," the paper editorialized.

NYU chancellor Henry MacCracken shared that opinion. Horrified that his school had been involved in the game that had caused Moore's death and convinced that action had to be taken, he called for an early December conference in New York to discuss the football question. Interestingly, Harvard's Eliot declined the invitation, saying he didn't feel the university presidents had it in their power to abolish the game. He also thought the timing was bad. "There should be an interval for cooling down," he wrote to MacCracken. "Deaths and injuries are not the strongest argument against football. That cheating and brutality are profitable is the main evil."

MacCracken carried on without him. His December 8 meeting was made up only of schools that NYU had played in the past. That group of thirteen voted to reform rather than abolish the game. Sensing they needed a broader mandate, though, they adjourned, calling for a national meeting in late December.

In an address delivered at the school's alumni dinner just days before that next scheduled meeting, MacCracken made it clear what his tack would be. He placed the blame for the game's struggles squarely on the shoulders of Camp's rules committee, a group he likened to Russian grand dukes. "[They] call themselves a committee on rules. They are really a committee of misrule. They have reigned for years by virtue of their descent from a defunct ancestor," he said of the group, adding, "I forgive the grand dukes, every one. They think and act according to their points of view and antecedents. But I do not forgive the universities which deliver themselves over to this narrow committee."

The second New York meeting, held on December 28, was strong in numbers but weak in stature. It was composed of roughly sixty universities, but none of the traditional powers. It was almost exclusively an Eastern gathering, though Minnesota, Texas, Colorado College, and South Dakota also sent representatives. The schools formed a new organization, called the Intercollegiate Athletic Association, or ICAA. It would be renamed the National Collegiate Athletic Association, or NCAA, five years later. Significant as that move proved to be in the long term, it was the decision to form a second football rules committee that stole the headlines. The action, a clear shot at Camp and his old guard, was an attempt to give more schools a voice in the game's future. The new committee proposed a merger. The members of the old committee said they wanted to meet with their group before agreeing to combine forces.

Believing that it could only truly revamp the sport by combining the two groups, Harvard forced the issue. On January 8, 1906, the school proposed a list of changes aimed at radically overhauling football. The recommendations were focused on spreading the players out on the field, which, it was believed, would cut down on the injuries caused by mass plays. Among other things, they advised extending the yardage needed for a first down from five to ten yards, allowing the forward pass, adding a neutral zone between the offensive and defensive lines, adding an extra official to root out brutality, and strengthening the penalties against players found guilty of foul play. The message was clear: Were the changes not made, Harvard would abolish football. The Cambridge school was setting up for a showdown with Camp, who favored just one rule change—the ten-yard rule.

It was a showdown the *New York Times* believed Harvard could not win. "Camp is determined not to abandon the one-man veto rule, which in operation in the past meant one-man domination with Walter Camp in the position of dictator," the paper wrote just days before the two rules committees were scheduled to meet separately in New York. "It is a well-known fact that football men at Yale, in spite of Camp's professions to the contrary, do not want to see any changes in the rules that will alter the present style of the game."

But Harvard had a trick up its sleeve. The two committees were scheduled to meet simultaneously at neighboring Manhattan hotels on January 12, 1906. Just prior to that meeting, Reid called some members of the old committee together. It was a gathering that did not include Walter Camp. He told that group of Harvard's proposed changes and then issued what amounted to a threat. "Either the rules go through," he told them, "or there will be no football at Harvard; and if Harvard throws out the game, many other colleges will follow Harvard's lead, and an important blow will be dealt to the game." While Yale had the superior football team, Harvard was still the most prestigious university in the nation, and the school believed that prestige was enough to force its agenda through.

As the two committees met, Reid, a member of the old established committee, showed up outside the room where the new committee was assembled and asked to join their group. The extraordinary request was granted. Contact was then made with the old committee, which agreed to gather with the reformers.

When the groups got together, Reid pulled an end around. A member of the new group was elected secretary of the combined organization, the role long held by Walter Camp. It was seen as a compromise. But the new secretary, Haverford's James Babbitt, immediately resigned his newly elected post and named Reid as his replacement. Harvard's man now held the most powerful position in the newly formed joint committee. If football were to continue, it would be on Harvard's terms.

Camp's position was further weakened just days later by a startling revelation. On January 18, 1906, the *New York Evening Post* published the details of the athletic abuses at Yale, which had been hinted at in the papers the previous fall. Muckraking journalist Clarence Deming disclosed that Camp had what amounted to a slush fund. He had been collecting the money, which was made up of the accumulated yearly athletic surpluses, ever since the formation of the Yale Financial Union in 1892. The fund now totaled nearly $100,000.

The paper also uncovered deceptive accounting processes within the fund. The expenses for star player James Hogan's trip to Cuba, for instance, were filed under the catch-all category "miscellaneous." Along the same lines, Camp's salary was included under "maintenance of the field." Furthermore, Camp was using money from the cache to finance private tutoring for players. These expenses were buried under the heading of "maintenance."

More newspapers quickly jumped on the story. DEMING AFTER WALTER CAMP, the *New Haven Evening Register* screamed on page one the next day. Referring to the "scandalous concealment of its administration," the *New York Press* saw the enormous fund as a sign of "the frantic commercialism which has brutalized" football. The *New York Times* reported that Yale's faculty was sharply divided on the game's future at the school. The paper spoke with professors who exposed a culture of graft within the football program, revealing "that the coaches have received free trips to New York for mere pleasure jaunts during the season; that they have had carriages for the least excuse; [and] that they have, with the teams, attended theatres at the expense of the associations." Much of the fund, the *Times* revealed, came directly out of students' pockets, as the undergraduates were forced "on pain of ostracism in some cases" to pay $8 each to support athletics.

The revelation led to a series of athletic meetings in New Haven. Speaking before a gathering of alums in New York just two days after the slush-fund story broke, President Hadley promised that a group was looking into ways of "cutting off unnecessary expense," though he seemed shockingly oblivious to some of the broader issues the sport was facing. "Football has, among all major sports, the double advantage of being the most democratic and the least dangerous," Hadley told the group, less than two months after the end of a season that had seen nearly twenty men killed on the gridiron. He continued, "At Yale we have had no deaths from football, and, to my knowledge, no grave permanent injuries. This shows that hard football is not necessarily attended with overwhelming physical danger."

Hadley was clearly on Camp's side, joining with his coach in resisting massive alterations of the playing rules. In a February letter to Camp, he advised his athletic advisor to cooperate with the new committee on some of its broader reforms. "We should take a position about eligibility which the public will approve," Hadley wrote. "Then we can deal with the matter of rules as we please." Evidently, Hadley, like Camp, was most concerned with continuing Yale's winning ways.

And while it seems fair to commend Harvard's reform-minded stance, there were certainly those who believed they too were operating out of self-interest. Penn's athletic trainer, Michael Murphy, a friend of Camp, wrote that "Harvard would not play any more football under Camp's Rules, they are sick of being licked and want a change of any kind." He concluded that the Cambridge school was "playing the baby as usual and ought to be spanked this time."

Whatever its motivation, Harvard helped push through a sweeping set of reforms. The newly combined rules committee met six times between early January and mid-April of 1906. They emerged with a new rule book that promised to dramatically change the nature of the game. The yardage needed for a first down was increased from five to ten yards. Runners were now considered down when any part of their body other than their hand or their foot hit the ground. A neutral zone, which neither team could cross before the snap of the ball, was established between the linemen. Stricter definitions were adopted regarding personal fouls, unnecessary roughness, and unsportsmanlike conduct. And, finally, the forward pass was now permitted, though with severe limitations: It had to be made at least five yards to the side of the center, passes could not cross the goal line, and an incomplete pass resulted in a turnover.

Harvard, Yale, and Princeton also worked out a new series of eligibility rules. "The main purpose of these rules," the *Harvard Graduates' Magazine* wrote in June 1906, "is to limit participation in intercollegiate sports to undergraduates in regular academic standing and to shut out the men who come to college solely to engage in athletics." The new rules barred graduate students and freshmen from participating in intercollegiate sports, thus limiting eligibility to three years total. The changes were deemed satisfactory by Harvard. The university's Board of Overseers voted in early May to allow football to continue at the school.

The schools of the Western Conference went through a concurrent crisis. In early January the Wisconsin faculty elected outspoken football critic Frederick Jackson Turner to represent their group at a meeting of Midwestern schools to be held in Chicago. The faculty asked Turner to propose a two-year suspension of intercollegiate games, "to the end that rational, moral, and normal relations between athletics and intellectual activities may develop in each institution." They had a good spokesman in Turner, who in early January told a group of alums that football had "become a business, carried on far too often by professionals supported by levies on the public, bringing in vast gate receipts, demoralizing student ethics, and confusing the ideals of sport, manliness, and decency."

Though Turner's suggestion of a two-year ban on the game failed to gather support, the schools did push through a series of reforms that fundamentally changed the nature of the competition in the Midwest. In January they adopted a new eligibility code that became the basis for the later agreement between Harvard, Yale, and Princeton. They also limited the number of intercollegiate games to five per season, banned preseason practice, capped the cost of student and faculty tickets at fifty cents, and mandated that the season must end before Thanksgiving. In addition, non-faculty members were prohibited from coaching their teams, though those already under contract, including Michigan's Yost, were grandfathered in.

Though massive in scope, the reforms were not enough for Northwestern, which suspended the sport in March. The fear in Madison was that Wisconsin might do the same, and the school's students reacted with violence. On the evening of March 27, 1906, a group of protestors, armed with rifles and revolvers, marched through town shouting "death to the faculty!" When they arrived at Turner's home, the noted historian walked out onto his porch, where he was greeted with hisses.

"When can we have football?" a student yelled.

"When you can have a clean game," Turner replied. "It's been so rotten for the last ten years that it is impossible to purge it." Before the night was over, the angry mob burned effigies of Turner and two other Wisconsin professors. After a protracted series of meetings, Turner eventually helped broker a compromise to keep the sport. The agreement came at a price, though. The biggest matches—battles with Chicago, Minnesota, and Michigan—were all canceled.

The attempts to overhaul the game got mixed reviews. The *Yale Daily News,* for instance, lampooned the changes. In the new sport, it said, the ground should be as soft as possible and covered by a red carpet, tickets should cost whatever spectators want to pay, fans should stay quiet in the stands, and "the time between halves should be devoted to tests in high class literature." In this new farcical football world, players would need at least an 85 percent classroom average to be eligible, and, if they were carrying more than two dollars, they would be disqualified as professionals. All tackles, the article concluded, would be preceded by the waving of a flag and the statement, "Tweedledum, tweedledee, I now tackle thee."

But most people recognized the changes for what they were—an honest effort to save a troubled sport. "We have endeavored to reform the game in earnest and adopt measures which will prevent the continuance of the old grinding game," Reid said as the 1906 season loomed. "If the game does not stand the test it will be rooted out completely at Harvard and elsewhere."

That test proved to be a lengthy and difficult one.

CHAPTER EIGHTEEN

FOOTBALL'S NEW RULES

THREE HUNDRED CADETS STOOD IN SILENCE, THEIR GRAY ARMY UNIFORMS mirroring the mood in the late morning of November 2, 1909. More than a thousand more men, women, and children congregated with them. They couldn't hear the service going on inside the tiny Catholic chapel on the gorgeous grounds of the United States Military Academy in West Point, New York, so they simply stood and waited. An empty artillery caisson drawn by seven horses waited nearby. The West Point band, instruments in hand, lingered alongside.

For nearly an hour, they waited. Then, just before noon, the church door opened. A single cadet emerged carrying a shield-shaped arrangement of red, white, and blue flowers. He placed it gently on the wagon. That was the cue for the band, which began playing the somber hymn "Nearer My God to Thee."

Moments later, seven cadets emerged through the doorway, eyes red with tears, together bearing a coffin as some in the gathering quietly sang the poignant words.

> Though like the wanderer, the sun gone down,
> Darkness be over me, my rest a stone;
> Yet in my dreams I'd be nearer, my God, to Thee

They lifted the casket onto the caisson and carefully strapped it down. The horses were urged slowly forward, and the wagon rolled down the steep hill toward the academy's famed cemetery, carrying 21-year-old Cadet Eugene Alexis Byrne to his final resting place.

Just four days earlier, Byrne had been playing left tackle for Army in a game against Harvard in front of 10,000 fans, the largest crowd ever to witness a game at West Point. The Crimson pounded the ball straight at him throughout the game, building a 9–0 lead, and the merciless smashes began to take their toll in the final ten minutes of play. Byrne was briefly shaken up after making a tackle on a short gain by Harvard, but he stayed in the action. On the next play, Crimson fullback Wayland Minot took a handoff and followed the blocks of tackle Hamilton Fish and guard Robert Fisher, who crushed Byrne between them. The players all ended up in a pile just beyond the line of scrimmage.

As the men untangled, Minot and Byrne remained down. Trainers from both sides rushed onto the field. Minot eventually sat up, invigorated by a dousing of water on his face. Byrne didn't move. He was rolled off the field on a cot and died fourteen hours later. Posthumous X-rays revealed two crushed vertebrae.

Byrne's death came just two weeks after a similar tragedy had befallen rival Navy. Midshipman Earl Wilson injured his spine in a loss to Villanova. He fought valiantly for six months before passing away in April. Two weeks after Byrne's injury, Virginia fullback Archer Christian was killed in a game against Georgetown. In all, twenty-six players died from football-related injuries in 1909, ten of them college players. The death total was double the number that had perished just a year earlier.

The new rules of 1906 had led to a temporary decrease in casualties and a brief sense that football had emerged from its crisis. Caspar Whitney called the 1906 season "the most satisfactory year I have known in football," while Walter Camp basked in "the reinstatement of Foot Ball in popular favor." Even one of the game's harshest critics, Harvard president Charles Eliot, begrudgingly admitted, "the game of football was somewhat improved by the new rules."

But in truth, the game hadn't changed very dramatically. The forward pass proved unpopular as an offensive strategy, due in large part to the fact that an incompletion resulted in a turnover. A few scattered coaches embraced the new tactics. St. Louis University's Edward Cochems, a former teammate of Pat O'Dea at Wisconsin, was particularly innovative, designing plays he termed the "Parabola Pass" and the catchy "Overhead Projectile Spiral Pass." When Iowa beat Illinois 25–12 in November of 1907, the *Chicago Tribune* attributed the win to "a remarkable development of the forward pass." The Illini showed mastery of the new approach the next season, as quarterback "Pom" Sinnock completed fourteen of seventeen passes in a 64–8 drubbing of Northwestern's newly reinstated team.

But most of the Eastern powers continued to play the game much like they had before, pushing and pulling runners through the line, a strategy that remained legal and, particularly against lighter and less talented opponents, largely effective. As evidenced by the 1909 fatalities, it was also quite dangerous.

As it had when the crisis began in 1905, the press attacked the game vigorously. "After three such accidents to experienced and skillful players in the 'leading teams' the public has the right to demand that football be abolished or completely reformed forthwith," the *New York Times* proclaimed in an editorial, published just days after Christian's fatal injury. The paper noted that presidents of the affected universities were quick to cancel the season after one of their players perished, but that the leaders of the other schools were blind "to the greater propriety of canceling all games before the next boy is killed."

Two Harvard athletic coaches expressed their dismay at the ongoing carnage. "I believe that the new rules did little or nothing toward making the game clean," crew coach James Wray told the *Times*. "I think that Byrne's death and Wilson's fatal injury will prove the undoing of the game unless further modified." Track coach W. E. Quinn echoed that sentiment, saying in the days after Byrne's death, "The accident is the last straw. Football, to my mind, is henceforth a doomed sport."

Even amid the latest crisis, there was resistance among the old guard. Walter Camp's Yale team was coming off a 10–0 season, which had seen the Elis outscore their opponents 209–0. As proposals to further reform the game circulated in the off-season, Princeton's athletic advisor, Bill Roper, complained to university (and future US) president Woodrow Wilson that Camp was, once again, far more concerned with his own self-interest than that of the sport as a whole. "Mr. Camp is violently opposed to the new rules," Roper wrote, "because Yale's style of play is practically destroyed, there being no further pushing and pulling of the runner." It got to the point, though, where there was little Camp could do to block further reform. "We have certainly got to do something, Walter," his old friend and longtime ally Amos Alonzo Stagg wrote, "for the season has been a mighty bad one for a number of individuals as well as for the game."

Over the subsequent four months, the rules committee met repeatedly with a goal of again overhauling football. The results of those meetings ushered the game into the modern era. The new rules essentially outlawed mass plays, requiring seven offensive players to be positioned on the line of scrimmage and prohibiting the pushing and pulling of ball carriers. The quarterback was now allowed to carry the ball across the line of scrimmage at any point.

But the most significant alterations surrounded the forward pass. Balls could now be thrown over the line of scrimmage at any point, rather than the previously mandated five yards to the left or right of the snapper. In addition, the rules eliminated the penal aspects of the incomplete forward pass, which had initially resulted in a turnover and had subsequently been changed to a 15-yard penalty. An incomplete pass now simply counted as a down. The new rules promised to open up the game dramatically. Not everyone was pleased with these developments. Though he was a member of the committee that had drawn them up, Walter Camp refused to sign the new rules.

The committee made more tweaks over the next few years. The dimensions of the field were changed to their modern configuration with the addition of 10-yard-deep end zones and the reduction of the distance between the goal lines from 110 to 100 yards. Passes over the goal line, which were previously prohibited, were legalized. The size of the ball was reduced as well, as a means of further facilitating the passing game. While the sport would obviously undergo many changes over the next hundred years, the football played in 1913 would be instantly recognizable to today's fans.

The possibilities of the new rules were on full display on November 1, 1913. That afternoon's matchup at West Point between Notre Dame and Army didn't figure to be a revolutionary one. Notre Dame was in its first season under new coach Jesse Harper, who had played for Stagg at Chicago, serving as the backup to quarterback Walter Eckersall. Though his new school hadn't lost a game since 1910, its schedule hardly inspired fear—looking largely similar to the one it had played at the turn of the century, when Pat O'Dea had coached in South Bend. Notre Dame's opponents in 1912 had included mostly tiny regional colleges: Adrian, Morris Harvey, St. Viator, and a Wabash College team coached by Harper.

Those foes generated little excitement on campus, and as a result, Notre Dame's attendance and cash flow were underwhelming. Harper immediately set out to upgrade the schedule, sending notes to a number of higher profile schools hoping to secure a game.

Somewhat surprisingly, he got a positive response from Army. The Cadets continued to occupy a spot in the second tier of the Eastern football hierarchy. They were certainly not a powerhouse. The week before Notre Dame showed up, they had managed only a safety in a narrow shutout win over Tufts. They had dropped three games the year before, including a shocking 27–6 defeat against Carlisle, a game in which the Indians' remarkable Jim Thorpe, in the words of the *New York Times,* "simply ran wild." But Army would be a clear step up in competition for the small Catholic school from northern Indiana. The academy's student manager, Dan Sultan, who scheduled the game, recalled afterward that he had agreed to the contest because he felt the Cadets "needed a breather" before their game against Navy. They promised Notre Dame $1,000 for its troubles.

It was hardly an impressive group that rolled into West Point. Due to the severely limited storage space on the train, many of the men wore their uniforms under their coats. Each player was forced to carry his own equipment. They dined on sandwiches packed by the nuns in the university cafeteria. Future Irish coaching legend Knute Rockne, a player on the 1913 team, recalled: "Our only extra equipment was a roll of tape, a jug of liniment and a bottle of iodine."

What the Notre Dame team lacked in style, it more than made up for in substance. Rockne, a talented end, and quarterback Gus Dorais had worked that summer at Cedar Point, a resort town in Ohio. They spent their spare time at the beach trying to perfect the passing game. "I'd run along the beach," Rockne remembered, and "Dorais would throw from all angles. People who didn't know we were two college seniors making painstaking preparations for our final season probably thought we were crazy."

Those skills they honed over the summer were perfected in Harper's practices. "The pass plays were rehearsed for weeks by the entire squad," Harper recalled. Careful observers knew this was a better Notre Dame team than they were getting credit for. "There are many who believe the South Bend aggregation will walk off the field a winner," the *Chicago Tribune* reported. "The Westerners are expected to flash an open field attack," the *New York Times* wrote, "and the Cadets are wondering what it consists of."

They found out soon enough. Late in the first quarter, in a scoreless game, Dorais faded back to pass and hit Rockne in stride at the Army two-yard line. He waltzed into the end zone for the first touchdown of the game, a play variously reported at between 25 and 40 yards. "Everyone seemed astonished," Rockne recalled. "There had been no hurdling, no tackling, no plunging, no crushing of fiber and sinew. Just a long-distance touchdown by rapid transit."

By the time the game was over, Dorais had completed a remarkable thirteen of seventeen passes for 243 yards. Notre Dame won 35–13, with the forward pass playing a role in all five touchdowns. "The Army players were hopelessly confused and chagrined before Notre Dame's great playing," the *New York Times* reported, "and their style of old-fashioned close line-smashing play was no match for the spectacular and highly perfected attack of the Indiana collegians." Eastern observers were flabbergasted. Former Princeton head coach Bill Roper, who served as one of the game officials, said afterward he "had always believed that such playing was possible under the new rules, but that he had never seen the forward pass developed to such a state of perfection."

The new game wasn't just aesthetically pleasing; it was also demonstrably safer. After peaking at ten in 1909, the number of deaths in college football declined to just one by 1912. Fatalities at all levels of the sport dropped from twenty-six to eleven in the same three-year span. By 1915 the threat of death on the college gridiron had been minimized to the point where the NCAA decided to abolish its committee on casualties. The sport had successfully navigated a massive crisis.

Which isn't to say the game didn't still have problems. The concerns in 1905, remember, had been about much more than injuries. Understandably, the reforms of 1910 to 1912 focused on player safety. It was an issue that, had it not been satisfactorily solved, might very well have killed the sport. The new rules didn't just help football escape that fate, though. They birthed a game that would grow virtually unencumbered for the next century, despite the fact that many of its other warts remained. The road had been paved for college football to become an American institution.

Over a span of twenty-five years, the sport had evolved in ways its early advocates could have never imagined. It grew from a sparsely attended, mostly regional game into a spectacle that filled stadiums from coast to coast. It unified student bodies. It alienated some academicians. It left some universities questioning their academic mission and led others to ignore theirs in pursuit of gate receipts and glory. It captivated some influential members of the media. It appalled others. In 1890 college football was a curiosity. By 1915 it was an institution. But as the ensuing century has taught us, institutions are not beyond reproach. College football survived the problems that dominated its early existence, but it didn't solve them. Sadly, it still hasn't.

Epilogue

The bespectacled man stared out at the adoring throng—5,000 fans braving the chilly Midwestern November night—all there to see him. An enormous bonfire raged in front of him, its flames leaping four stories into the air. All around him, people craned their necks just to catch a glimpse of his crease-lined face, of his graying hair, of his fedora hat. He was, after all, a legend. For decades young boys growing up in Wisconsin had known his name before they knew the president's. Yet, they had never expected to get this chance—the chance to lay eyes on the greatest hero their state had ever known. There was a simple reason for that. They had thought he was dead.

But Pat O'Dea was very much alive. He was sixty-two years old, carrying the same 170 pounds on his 6' 1½" frame that he had thirty-five years earlier, when crowds like this one had last cheered him—a football player described as "the closest thing to a Paul Bunyan that the game has produced."

That had all been so long ago, though, before he'd made a mess of his life. Before the disintegrated marriage. Before his failure first as a coach and then as a businessman. Before the indictment. Before he ran away from it all, changing his name and slinking off in shame. Somewhere he had a daughter that he had never met. Did she know of his fame? Perhaps she was out there now, among the adoring masses.

The last time O'Dea had set foot in this town, in his beloved Madison, he had taken the cheers for granted—seen them as a birthright. But it had been ages since he'd been in the spotlight. And now, the player who Walter Camp, the father of the modern game, once said, "put the foot in football as no man ever has or as no man probably ever will again" was back in front of the reverent masses.

O'Dea's eyes began to moisten as the memories flooded back to him.

And then he spoke. His words were not profound. He had told himself he wouldn't reveal much. The fans knew his legend. But they did not know his secrets. Besides, when it came to Pat O'Dea's life, it was hard to separate the myth from the reality. His silence on the most important matters simply added more mystique to an already fantastic story.

"They told me the Wisconsin spirit had changed," he said into the microphone from his perch on the balcony outside the old library building. "But I want to tell you that you have the same Wisconsin spirit we knew and loved years ago."

And then, as he had so many times before, Pat O'Dea heard the cheers.

———

After leaving his job as the head coach of the American School of Osteopathy in 1905, Pat O'Dea faded from public view. In fact, in December of 1905, a *Kansas City Star* reporter naming O'Dea "the greatest long distance goal kicker ever seen in football" inquired with his now-estranged brother Andy about his whereabouts and got this sarcastic response: "He is in the employ of the Japanese government and assigned to Honolulu, where he is giving the emperor of the island kingdom the benefit of the years of study at Madison." The former Wisconsin crew coach added that his brother "expects to remain in the Japanese government service as a commercial expert—he will try to make long goals from the mercantile field for the Japanese."

Pat had indeed headed west, though not quite that far. He had landed in the San Francisco area, where he survived the 1906 earthquake and occasionally surfaced on the periphery of the athletic scene. He umpired some high school football matches, got involved with a local rugby team, and even took a job coaching Lowell High School, where, upon announcing his hiring, the local paper was quick to point out that heretofore he had been "a failure as a coach." O'Dea was mugged again in November of 1908 (as he had been seven years before) and showed up to court drunk.

By 1913 he had turned things around sufficiently to be formally admitted to practice law in California. That same year he was named the crew coach at Stanford, a position he held for one season. He also helped coach a young society girl named Celia Zwillinger, who shattered the national walking record for a woman. Cheered on by crowds lining the roads along the way, she hiked the 66 miles between the Northern California towns of Burlingame and Gilroy in a little less than eighteen hours. O'Dea said afterward that, in all his athletic experience, he had "never encountered a more gritty athlete than Miss Zwillinger."

Not much more was heard of O'Dea in the next few years. He worked in the fruit business—employed in the San Jose office of the California Prune and Apricot growers, the antecedent to Sunsweet. Then in 1919 he was charged with embezzlement by a Sonoma County woman named Elsie Waters, the daughter of a prominent area family. Waters claimed she had given O'Dea some money to invest and some stock to hold, and when she asked for it back, the former football star fled to Seattle.

A San Francisco grand jury brought charges against him. The case was heard in May 1919. Among the witnesses was J. F. Brennan, a friend of O'Dea, who testified that the former football star had originally told him he planned on returning the money. Later, though, Brennan received a letter from O'Dea "in which he said he would make no further explanation and that 'by the time you receive this I will have passed into the great beyond where I will find rest.'" O'Dea was indicted. Not that it mattered. With his life now in a shambles, Pat O'Dea had disappeared. His second wife, Emma, filed for divorce on the grounds of desertion. The divorce was granted, but it turned out she knew where her husband was all along.

Around the same time, the town of Westwood, California, gained two new residents—a husband and his wife. Their names were Charles and Emma Mitchell. Or, at least, that was what they claimed. Not that anyone was particularly inclined to press them on the issue. As a fellow Westwood resident named Dick Pershing recalled in a letter many years later, "At that time (before Social Security) people used any name they chose—and nobody asked any questions. I'd guess 10% of the people in Westwood travelled under another name than their own." The town's residents were all there for one reason: The Red River Lumber Company.

The company had been founded in Minnesota in the 1870s by Thomas Barlow Walker. By the 1890s it expanded its operations to the West, where the supply of timber was seemingly unlimited. Red River went on a buying spree and eventually owned more timberlands than any other private concern in Northern California—more than 900,000 acres. With the 1916 publication of its pamphlet, "Introducing Mr. Paul Bunyan of Westwood, California," the company launched a modern legend, creating an advertising campaign around the long-circulated tale of a lumber-camp folk hero.

Bunyan's "home" hadn't even existed a handful of years earlier. But after negotiating an agreement for the Southern Pacific Railroad to construct a rail line into the area in exchange for exclusive shipping rights, Walker built a company town in Westwood, adjacent to what would become one of the most active sawmills in the nation. Westwood was Red River and vice versa. Everyone who lived there worked for the company, which provided housing, health care, and all the other necessities, including a massive company store. It was a highly restrictive operation that sought to control every aspect of its employees' lives. For instance, if a Red River worker made purchases via mail order or in the closest town, located about 20 miles away, they were immediately fired.

T. B. Walker's son Willis was in charge of the Westwood operation. He had played football for Minnesota in the 1890s, which presumably was when he first met O'Dea. Walker moved west in 1915, originally working out of San Francisco, where he again could have come in contact with his former football foe.

As O'Dea's life began to deteriorate, culminating in his impending indictment, Walker made him an offer: He could disappear to Westwood. Red River needed some help. As one would expect in an environment as confining as the one the Walker family had established, maintaining control of the workers was paramount. The threat of union organization, in particular, was a constant concern. Walker apparently intended to use his old acquaintance as an informant.

Many years later, O'Dea described his mission to Milt Bruhn, Wisconsin's football coach for a portion of the 1950s and 1960s. "He said his boss, an industrialist, needed someone to do an undercover job at his lumber mill," Bruhn recalled. "The company was having lots of trouble and it was necessary that Pat's identity not be known or he couldn't have gotten the information needed." It was not an assignment for the faint of heart. "I could have been done away with if certain people knew who I was and what I was doing," O'Dea told Bruhn.

With the offer of the covert assignment, Patrick J. O'Dea became Charles J. Mitchell. Though the "Charles" could have been a tribute to any number of friends from O'Dea's past, the origins of "Mitchell" are far easier to discern. Though it was not his mother's maiden name, as O'Dea would claim many years later, it was, in fact, the birth surname of his good friend Dame Nellie Melba.

Mitchell held a variety of positions at Red River during the next fifteen years. Dressed in his signature cap and leather puttees and with his distinctive accent, he was a well-liked member of the community. He had a number of different titles in the Westwood Auto Club, the town's version of a chamber of commerce, whose primary goal was to bring improved roads to their little pocket of the world. Mitchell also wrote feature and sports stories for the *Sugar Pine,* the local newspaper, and served as a special correspondent for several other publications.

While his identity remained a secret within Westwood, there were a select few from his former life who knew of his whereabouts. Among them was famed Wisconsin senator Robert La Follette Sr., who, according to an article in the *Wisconsin News,* "several times during O'Dea's voluntary masquerade saw and talked to O'Dea in California." In fact, O'Dea later revealed that he spent a great deal of time with La Follette during his failed presidential campaign in 1924.

While in Westwood, Mitchell passed his time listening to operas on his phonograph and reading the half-dozen newspapers to which he subscribed. In his reading, he would have almost certainly come across any number of the many tributes to his talents that appeared in print throughout his exile. Perhaps he would have seen the 1924 *Boston Globe* article that mentioned those "who would give O'Dea the palm for all time" as the greatest kicker in football history. Maybe he stumbled across the *Atlanta Constitution* in 1925, when it cited him as "perhaps the greatest kicker of all time," marveling at "how he could boot the ball, shooting goals from all angles." And perhaps he bristled when, in the same article, the author derided him for his fragility, claiming that "his teammates had to treat him like an egg in an egg and spoon race."

But what might have pained him most was his occasional inclusion in articles about the fleeting nature of fame, like one written by former major league pitcher Al Demaree in the *Washington Post* in 1925 under the headline HERO ONE DAY—BUM THE NEXT—ISN'T LIFE TOUGH? The same paper mentioned him again in a similar vein the next year, including him among a group of athletes who "just flickered and died."

And while the reference to death in that article was purely metaphorical, the truth was that almost everyone believed Pat O'Dea was actually dead. On March 17, 1934, the day O'Dea would claim as his sixty-second birthday, *Literary Digest,* one of the most popular and widely read general-interest publications in the country, included a tribute to O'Dea, "the greatest American college kicker." The publication told the story that, at this point, had become accepted as the truth regarding his demise: "In 1917 when the Australian army passed through San Francisco, where he was practicing law, O'Dea joined . . . without informing even his brother, thus leaving the country as unostentatiously as he came. He has not been heard from since. Andy, who is now employed in a New York sporting goods firm, is certain he is an unknown soldier."

That *Literary Digest* story bothered O'Dea tremendously, so much so that he mentioned it upon his return. At around the same time, the former star learned that Wisconsin was debating erecting a plaque at Camp Randall Stadium and naming the field in his honor. The plaque would mention that he had died in the war. As Dick Pershing related in a letter, O'Dea "simply *couldn't* take that, he'd never been in the army!"

This man who had once known such fame, for whom the possibilities in life had seemed endless, now toiled in absolute anonymity, presumed dead. While fifteen years earlier, it had seemed to be his only option, it now felt confining—an unsatisfactory way to conclude what had once been a great story. So Pat O'Dea decided to change the ending.

The word went out, setting into motion the chain of events that brought Pat O'Dea back from the dead and sent Charles J. Mitchell to the grave in his place. Certainly, he knew it would be a big story, though he admitted later that he was "unprepared for the furor that did ensue."

On September 19, 1934, San Franciscans awoke to a headline that screamed: O'DEA, LOST GRID IMMORTAL, COMES TO LIFE. The *San Francisco Chronicle's* Bill Leiser had the scoop of his career.

"Out of the past he came smiling to sit across the dinner table last night. I could hardly believe it," Leiser wrote. "This man who crashed through with football records never surpassed or equaled in the whole gridiron history of America and then vanished as completely and mysteriously as Aladdin's Genie."

Despite his assertion that the "whole world remembers" Pat O'Dea's greatness, Leiser went on to regale his readers with the story of the football star's remarkable life. He spoke of O'Dea's arrival in America in 1896—just years after he was almost "cut to pieces by sharks" while saving a young girl from drowning in his native Australia—and of his incredible feats as a kicker at the University of Wisconsin at a time when the kicker could impact the game like no other player on the field.

He wrote of O'Dea's "world record" 63-yard dropkick field goal against Northwestern in 1898, a kick, Leiser reported, that flew 20 yards beyond the uprights. He told of a 55-yard placekick through a "twenty mile gale" against Illinois in 1899, a boot he dubbed "the most impossible kick in football history." He recounted a man who once rifled a 110-yard punt; a man who "could curve a football as a pitcher curves his throws"; a man who "displayed a ravishing, kicking, smothering type of football that

America never knew before and may never know again"; a man who, in short, was "the most spectacular and greatest athlete of his time." In fact, Lesier contended it wasn't just his own time that the Aussie dominated, asserting that "the names of Jim Thorpe and Red Grange, even, mean little alongside Wisconsin's Pat O'Dea."

But according to Leiser's account, the fame that came with these accomplishments became too much for O'Dea to bear. "I wanted to get away from what seemed to me to be all in the past," O'Dea told Leiser. "I seemed very much just an ex-Wisconsin football player."

And so he did get away; away to Westwood. He became Charles J. Mitchell. "Mitchell was my mother's name," O'Dea explained, "and Charley that of a cousin I like." And now, at the urging of his boss, who, readers were told, had just learned Mitchell's true identity, Pat O'Dea was back among the living.

The reaction to the news was fast and furious; the wire service version of the story ran on the front page of newspapers from coast to coast. As would be expected, O'Dea's resurrection got the most coverage in Wisconsin. The *Wisconsin State Journal* ran a picture of him on the front page of that afternoon's paper above a caption reading simply, "Found?" and talked of his punts, which the paper said "drew gasps from followers of opposing teams."

Not everyone was buying the story, though—most notably Pat's brother Andy, whose presence in Madison had prompted his brother to visit and eventually enroll at Wisconsin all those years earlier. "I don't believe it's Pat," he told the United Press, saying that men claiming to be his brother had surfaced many times since the grid star's disappearance in 1919. Andy, who was living in New York, added that he had no plans to try to verify the man's identity.

The *Chronicle* ran another piece the next day, this one penned by sports editor Harry Smith. In it Smith described the chaos that ensued in his paper's newsroom after the story broke—with phone calls, wires, and requests for information on the O'Dea scoop pouring in. To those who might doubt the validity of Leiser's piece, Smith spoke of the volumes of records, documents, and certificates that Mitchell had brought along to prove his identity.

All doubts were put to rest the next day by *Wisconsin State Journal* sports editor Henry McCormick, who, with the help of some of O'Dea's former friends and teammates, had compiled a list of questions to which "no imposter would know the answers." Not only did "Charley Mitchell" respond to them satisfactorily, he added details that led one friend to conclude, "I don't think there's any doubt of that being Pat O'Dea."

There didn't seem to be any doubt regarding the reasons for O'Dea's disappearance, either—at least none that made their way into the mainstream press. Two days after he revealed his true identity, the *New York Times* asserted that it "is easy to understand the feelings of Patrick O'Dea, the Wisconsin football hero of long ago." The *Times* recounted the words of Teddy Roosevelt, who once told the boys of the prestigious Groton School, "It is a mighty good thing to be a halfback on a varsity eleven, but it is a mighty poor thing when a man reaches 40 only to be able to say that he was once a halfback on a varsity eleven." The *Times* asserted that, if the story isn't true, "it ought to be."

Wisconsin's *La Crosse Tribune and Leader-Press* took a similar approach the next week, saying, "The Pat O'Dea case does emphasize the very great wrong which football can do to a young man. It hands him his life wrong-end to. The summit comes right at the beginning. Everything afterward must go downhill," adding, "The game that attaches itself to an All-American halfback is a load no youngster ought to be compelled to carry through life."

In Madison a movement quickly grew to bring O'Dea back for the Badgers' homecoming game against Illinois scheduled for mid-November. The former Wisconsin great immediately accepted the invitation.

In the weeks leading up to his return, O'Dea's story was told and retold throughout the country. The former footballer himself penned a newspaper article, where he said of his decision to disappear: "As Pat O'Dea I was a has-been. A football star at the University of Wisconsin once, with my name known everywhere—but now a has-been. It began to annoy me."

His explanation for his decision to disappear was universally accepted. There were a few quibbles with the details. The *Kilmore Advertiser* in his hometown in Australia mentioned that O'Dea's "statement about his mother's pre-marriage name is not correct," but it failed to make the connection to opera star Dame Nellie Melba and never suggested that O'Dea had any intent to deceive.

The United Press wrote a story that cast some doubt on Willis Walker's claims that he was unaware of his staff member's actual background: "Some say the Minnesota man knew O'Dea's true identity and others say he had no idea that his employee was his famous opponent." But no one mentioned O'Dea's indictment or his troubled past.

As for Andy O'Dea, he eventually admitted that his long-lost sibling had been found. Pat sent a letter to his brother in New York City, and Andy said he "recognized his writing instantly." Still, Andy said that he had no plans to reunite with Pat, who he hadn't seen in thirty-one years. Of the possibility of traveling to Madison for the big homecoming gala, Andy said simply, "That's his celebration, and I do not want to interfere."

And what a celebration Wisconsin was planning. Upon learning that O'Dea had accepted the invitation to return to campus, Athletic Director Walter Meanwell couldn't hide his excitement. "I think we should make this a great occasion," Meanwell said. "We want to do the thing up right."

The anticipation in Madison was palpable. In the week before O'Dea's arrival, the *Wisconsin State Journal* joked, "Pat O'Dea is sure selling them football tickets. The school should find Pat about every ten years. It sure brings them in the dough." By the day of O'Dea's scheduled arrival in town, the paper reported that "the Pat O'Dea hysteria which has been gathering momentum all these months is reaching a crescendo today." The *State Journal* spoke of boys walking to school while chanting, "Hey! Hey! Pat O'Dea!" It told of a woman who, when asked who the first white man to come to Wisconsin was, answered, with complete earnestness: "Pat O'Dea." And it spoke of a child who tried to soothe a screaming infant by saying, "Don't cry, baby, don't cry. Pat O'Dea is coming."

The story continued to generate national coverage, too, with the *New York Times* previewing Wisconsin's tribute to one of the "three greatest field goal kickers football has known" and the *Los Angeles Times* mentioning him alongside George Gipp and Red Grange "among the greatest middle western gridiron heroes of all time."

In fact, it was such a big story that the national press actually covered O'Dea en route. A quick stop-over in Omaha on his train journey warranted an AP story, with the reporter detailing that O'Dea "modestly recounted when he punted 110 yards against Yale," while also criticizing the concept of the huddle—"How can you call a play in a huddle and know it's the one?" The United Press reported that "crowds gathered at railroad stations to cheer him" along the way.

O'Dea finally arrived in Chicago on Thursday morning, November 15, stepping off the Overland Limited in the Northwestern train station at nine o'clock. He was immediately swarmed by newspaper photographers, who lined him up against a wall reserved for visiting dignitaries and snapped their all-important photos. O'Dea then chatted with reporters, all the while greeting friends and former teammates who had gathered to welcome him.

From there it was on to the sold-out Crystal Ball Room in Chicago, where a crowd of six hundred assembled to hear O'Dea speak—at a cost of $3.50 per person. The organizers were kicking themselves afterward for not charging more. They did manage to squeeze an extra $1,000 for the entertainment budget out of WGN Radio, which agreed to pay that amount in exchange for an exclusive interview with the famous Aussie. When O'Dea was finally introduced to speak at the banquet, "he received a thundering standing ovation" and spoke for about fifteen minutes—"a talk of quiet confidence, courage and modest pride in Wisconsin and her achievements." O'Dea made a great impression. *Wisconsin State Journal* writer Henry McCormick reported to readers back in Madison, "You're going to like Pat O'Dea, and you're going to be glad he's back when you see him."

O'Dea spoke at a similar function the next day in Milwaukee and then headed to Madison for several more receptions followed by the massive bonfire. There the crowd "uttered a frenzied cheer when he rose. The sky rocket of a thousand student voices echoed across the massed field and the band, too excited to bother about harmony, broke into a pealing serenade." They played a new song, written specially for the occasion, with a musical arrangement prepared by the local orchestra leader. Fans left the bonfire singing the chorus: "For Pat O'Dea has shown the way to glory and to victory." And the local papers reported with pride that in this, the first homecoming since the repeal of Prohibition, "only one person was arrested for drunkenness and he was not connected with the homecoming celebration."

Game day arrived. The threat of rain may have kept some fans away, but nearly 30,000 still piled into Camp Randall Stadium—considered a large turnout for a team that hadn't won a conference home game in nearly two years. O'Dea received "tumultuous applause" in the pregame, as the Wisconsin band marched in, its formation spelling out the words "Pat O'Dea." While facing the gridiron hero of yesteryear and his teammates, the musicians belted out renditions of "When Irish Eyes Are Smiling" and "Auld Lang Syne."

"For more than 20 minutes before the game he was photographed continuously, in virtually every imaginable pose," the *Wisconsin State Journal* reported. He spoke for the newsreel cameras, was driven around the field in an open car, and was awarded a cardinal blanket and a lifetime membership in the Wisconsin Athletic Association. Even opponent Illinois got into the act, as mascot Chief Illiniwek presented O'Dea with an Indian headdress at halftime and dubbed him "Chief Four Leaf Clover." The legendary star addressed the crowd at the half as well and was just as humble as he had been all weekend. "If it hadn't been for these other men on the team," O'Dea said, "I would have been no more than useless."

O'Dea and his teammates sat on a special bench at field level and watched the Badgers pull off a stunning upset, handing the sixth-ranked Illini what would be their only loss of the year—a 7–3 defeat. The return to Madison, O'Dea said, was "the finest thing ever to happen to me," adding, "When I was in school, I came to expect honors. This was unexpected." Afterward, he put off plans to return to California, instead choosing to stay in Madison for the season finale against Minnesota. Pat O'Dea was back in the public eye and loving every minute of it.

—◆—

The game O'Dea watched on that Saturday in 1934 was dramatically different from the one he had left behind. The forward pass had evolved considerably since its introduction in the early part of the century. Illinois's coach, Bob Zuppke, was particularly noted for his ingenious use of aerial strategies. The Illini featured a play known as the "Flying Trapeze," a series of handoffs, reverses, and laterals that culminated in a long pass to a streaking receiver. Wisconsin's win was attributed in part to its ability to slow down that play and others like it.

The rules weren't all that had changed. Everything surrounding the game was bigger and grander than in O'Dea's time. The battle with Illinois was played at the seventeen-year-old Camp Randall Stadium, which had replaced the wooden bleachers and grandstand of the 1890s. The current stadium had already been expanded three times since its original construction, and it now boasted a capacity of slightly more than 38,000. As massive as that would have seemed thirty years earlier, Camp Randall was fairly modest compared to the other concrete structures that sprung up across the country in the 1910s and 1920s. The Yale Bowl, built on land that Walter Camp bought out of his once-secret slush fund, boasted a capacity of 78,000. Ohio State drew 85,500 for star halfback Red Grange's final game in an Illinois uniform, a 14–9 Illini win in November of 1925. Immediately after the game, Grange, who had played in front of nearly three quarters of a million fans over the previous three seasons, announced his intention to forego the rest of his education and sign a professional contract.

Just five days later, Grange made his debut for the Chicago Bears. He did so in front of a crowd of 36,000 at Chicago's Wrigley Field, which, at the time, was the largest ever to see a professional football game. For years the pro game had been an afterthought, the province of small industrial towns throughout the Midwest. With Grange in the fold, though, the burgeoning National Football League threatened the monopoly enjoyed by the college game. On December 6, 1925, a crowd of 70,000 fans—including 100 reporters—crammed into New York's Polo Grounds to watch Grange and the Bears top the Giants 19–7. The star back, who just weeks before had been playing in college, pocketed $30,000 in gate receipts.

Grange was seen as the exception rather than the rule, and it was still tough to imagine the NFL ever eclipsing college football in popularity. College coaches, however, instantly recognized the challenge a successful pro game would provide. "I'd be glad to see Grange do anything except play professional football," Michigan coach Fielding Yost had said while the Illinois star was pondering his football future. The coaching fraternity was simply horrified at the prospect that their amateur sportsmen might make money off the game. The hypocrisy of that stance was readily apparent, as the coaches themselves were earning huge salaries from their involvement with the sport. Notre Dame's Knute Rockne, for instance, was offered $25,000 to coach Columbia in 1925, more than $330,000 in today's currency.

Some of the players were profiting off the game, as well, although far more modestly than their coaches. The system of covert payments, like the ones made to Yale's James Hogan around the turn of the century, became more widespread throughout the 1920s, a poorly kept secret that was revealed to the nation in October 1929. The Carnegie Foundation for the Advancement of Teaching, an organization endowed by steel magnate Andrew Carnegie, released a report entitled, rather innocuously, *Bulletin Number Twenty-Three*. Throughout the course of nearly four hundred pages, the report, which was the product of four years of investigations and interviews, exposed the sordid underbelly of college athletics. Its author, Howard Savage, alleged that 102 of the 130 schools that investigators visited illegally subsidized their athletes in some form. The subsidies varied from cash handouts to tuition waivers to jobs, both legitimate and bogus. It cited the involvement of the universities themselves, as well as booster clubs made up of alumni, many of which orchestrated underhanded recruiting efforts. The substance of the report was impressive. The timing of its release was not. The stock market crashed just days later, and the nation turned its attention from college football indiscretions to survival.

After a significant attendance dip due to the Depression, the game rebounded in the mid-1930s, around the time of O'Dea's return. The balance of power had shifted considerably in his absence. The first ever AP college football poll was released just two days before the Illinois–Wisconsin game that O'Dea witnessed in 1934. The Midwest, which had struggled for respect in O'Dea's time, was well-represented, boasting three of the top nine teams, including number one Minnesota. Perhaps most startling, though, was the rise of the South, a complete afterthought thirty-five years before. Alabama was ranked third, Rice was twelfth, Louisiana State thirteenth, and Southern Methodist fifteenth. Alabama and LSU were part of the newly formed Southeastern Conference, which, a year later, rocked the college football world with the announcement that it would begin offering athletic scholarships, directly undermining what was left of the amateur ideal.

Of the traditional "Big Three" of Harvard, Yale, and Princeton, only the Tigers were listed among the twenty-two ranked teams, checking in at number five. Those schools were still major players in the game, though. For instance, in 1936, Yale sold its radio rights for $20,000, the first such deal in the history of the sport, and one that foretold the impact that TV money would have on the sport in later years. Still, none of the "Big Three" ever won an AP National Championship.

But the decline of those schools paled in comparison to that of the University of Chicago. Amos Alonzo Stagg was forced into retirement in 1933. New president Robert Hutchins was far more interested in academics than athletics, overhauling the curriculum in a manner that made it virtually impossible to "hide" academically deficient student athletes. Though the team had a few successful years thanks to the remarkable exploits of Jay Berwanger, the first Heisman Trophy winner, its fortunes plummeted after his graduation in 1936.

In 1938 Hutchins penned a scathing indictment of the sport for the *Saturday Evening Post* entitled "Gate Receipts and Glory." College football's ills were well known, he wrote, as they had been for the last fifty years. So, he asked, why has no one done anything to cure them? In his mind, the explanation was simple: "[N]obody wants to give up the gate receipts." Nobody, that is, except Hutchins.

At the end of the next season, one that saw the Maroons fall 85–0 to Michigan and 61–0 to Ohio State, Chicago dropped football. Appalled by the world it had helped create, the school that had hired its football coach before opening its academic doors and had played its first game just days after holding its first class left major college football behind forever.

⌐⌐

While the game lost a former powerhouse in the 1930s, it regained long-lost superstar Pat O'Dea. After his reappearance in 1934, he became a regular fixture on the college football scene—always available to lend his thoughts to a newspaper writer in search of a quote. Though associated with Stanford on the West Coast as that school's former crew coach, O'Dea's primary loyalty fell to Wisconsin. He was heavily involved in the school's Alumni Association for the rest of his life.

In 1935 O'Dea's wife, Emma, began to develop health problems, and her doctor told her she should leave the altitude of Westwood. So, after sixteen years, O'Dea resigned his position with the Red River Lumber company and moved back to San Francisco, "the city I love second only to Madison." He was given a warm send-off in Westwood, where the locals held a banquet in his honor and presented him with gifts upon his departure.

Months later, with Wisconsin in search of a new football coach, O'Dea's name briefly surfaced, but nothing ever materialized. Instead, Wisconsin hired Harry Stuhldreher, one of Notre Dame's famed "Four Horsemen," a pick that O'Dea quickly endorsed. In a message to Wisconsin fans, O'Dea urged the faithful to stand "solidly behind Harry and his boys by letting them know we believe in them." O'Dea preached patience, a theme he emphasized again in 1940 when Stanford hired a new coach.

When Wisconsin went to Berkeley to take on the California Golden Bears in 1946, O'Dea was not only there, but spent the months leading up to the game handling ticket requests for local Badger alums. Jokingly mentioning that he still had his 1899 football uniform, O'Dea even offered his on-field services, saying, "just let 'em know that Pat O'Dea is standing by, awaiting orders." When the Badgers finally broke through and made their first-ever Rose Bowl appearance in the 1952 season, there was seemingly no Badger fan more excited than O'Dea, who told the United Press he'd be in the front row for the battle with USC. "I wouldn't miss that fun for anything," O'Dea said. When Stanford opened its season in Madison in 1959, the school flew the 87-year-old O'Dea out to Wisconsin with them, and the legendary star kept up a frenetic pace while at his alma mater. The Badgers made a return visit to the Rose Bowl that season, and "The Kangaroo Kicker" was once again in Pasadena for the game.

But O'Dea did far more than just attend games. In 1950 he was elected president of the Big Ten Club of San Francisco, and the next year he was the first inductee into the state of Wisconsin's Athletic Hall of Fame. He joined Bob Hope on his TV show as a celebrity guest when the famed comedian introduced his All-American team. He was a frequent presence at banquets, sharing the spotlight with the likes of Pop Warner and Wisconsin's old nemesis, Amos Alonzo Stagg—whom he hadn't seen since their memorable 1899 battle before the two were honored together at a gathering in 1957.

Whenever O'Dea's name was brought up in the press, a recounting of the legend inevitably followed. To one writer, he was "the patron saint of all kickers." Another called him "the most versatile kicker that the game of football has ever known." While still another saw him as the man who "not only did the impossible, but did it under the most trying of circumstances."

O'Dea held a variety of jobs after leaving Westwood, retiring in May of 1958 from his final position at Gerhardt's, a men's clothing store. His wife had passed away in 1956, and with some time now on his hands, O'Dea wrote to a friend in Madison telling him that he had begun work on his autobiography. Though some publishing companies reportedly expressed interest in telling O'Dea's story, it was never completed, and no traces of it have ever been located.

O'Dea's health began to decline in 1960. He was hit by a taxicab late that year. In a letter to Wisconsin football coach Milt Bruhn, the 88-year-old O'Dea reported that he was recovering well. Later in 1961, he traveled to Idaho to vacation with his daughter, Teresa, and her family—having finally established a relationship with the child he abandoned before her birth so many years before.

By early 1962, though, O'Dea was back in the hospital, diagnosed with cancer. In late March, just after his ninetieth birthday, while lying ill at the University of California Medical Center, the former superstar received a rather extraordinary message. No fewer than five nurses arrived at room 912 to deliver it. In their possession was a note from President John F. Kennedy. "As a fellow son of Erin and a longtime admirer of your fine sports record, I wanted to wish you a belated but a very sincere happy birthday," the president wrote. "I was sorry to hear of your illness and hope you will be on your feet again." O'Dea requested that the letter be saved—not for him, but "for the children." He was concerned, apparently, with more pressing matters, telling his son-in-law to "get the phone numbers of all the pretty girls" who might call to wish him well.

On April 3, 1962, Pat O'Dea's election to the College Football Hall of Fame was made public, though he had learned of the honor some time before, and friends said the news "brightened his final days." The day after his Hall of Fame election was officially announced, Pat O'Dea died at the age of ninety.

In the days after the star's death, Bruhn recalled trying to track down O'Dea a few years before on a visit to San Francisco. All of the letters that he got from his friend had the same return address, so the Wisconsin coach figured it would be an easy enough task. He went to the building indicated on the envelopes. When he arrived, he found an old, locked, abandoned warehouse. In an observation laced with understatement, Bruhn said of O'Dea, "he was hard to find." Hard to figure out, too.

Afterword

The date was January 4, 2006. The number two Texas Longhorns trailed number one USC 38–33 late in the fourth quarter of the ninety-second Rose Bowl Game, which was doubling as the Bowl Championship Series National Championship.

It was a dream matchup. The Trojans were riding a thirty-four-game winning streak, the longest in college football in more than three decades. Texas had won nineteen straight games. USC had been ranked number one in the AP Poll every week of the season. The Longhorns were second in every poll. USC boasted Heisman Trophy–winner Reggie Bush. Texas had Heisman runner-up Vince Young. Each team had a high-profile coach. USC was led by the dynamic Pete Carroll, who was in search of his third straight national title. Texas's Mack Brown was looking for his first championship—trying to shed the reputation of a fabulous recruiter who couldn't win the big one. The two teams' fan bases, among the most passionate in the country, were packed into the historic stadium, with the San Gabriel Mountains providing arguably the most beautiful backdrop in all of sports. Those who weren't fortunate enough to have a ticket were glued to their TV sets, helping make it the highest-rated BCS championship game in history.

As the pregame, halftime, and postgame host for ESPN Radio's national broadcast of the game, I was seated in the radio booth right at the 50-yard line. Moments earlier Young had scrambled 17 yards for a touchdown to pull Texas within five. Now, after USC had turned the ball over on downs near midfield, the brilliant Longhorns quarterback was trying to lead his team to the go-ahead touchdown.

After Young ran out of bounds on a beautifully improvised quarterback draw, the game's color commentator, Bob Davie, who was seated directly in front of me, turned around and handed me a scrap of paper. On it he had written three simple words: "best game ever." It was tough to debate that assertion. As an obsessive college football fan, I had spent weeks looking forward to this game, relishing the opportunity to be a part of a fabulous matchup. Bob's note only crystallized what I was thinking. This was sports at its best—a game those of us who were fortunate enough to attend will never forget. Moments later, on an all-or-nothing fourth and goal, Young, seeing his receivers covered, scrambled right and raced into the end zone. The Horns held on for the 41–38 win.

College football had done it again. It had captivated the nation, providing a thrilling, dramatic, and supremely satisfying spectacle. It had done so at one of the most majestic venues in all of sport. The battle in Pasadena was the most highly anticipated college football game in years, and it had lived up to the hype, perfectly exemplifying everything Americans had loved about the game for more than a century. But it was also a contest that highlighted many of the same ills that had challenged college football a hundred years earlier.

Taken as a group, neither team's players were overly successful in the classroom. USC's graduation rate for football at the end of the 2005–2006 season stood at 55 percent—certainly not appalling, but well below the mark for the student body as a whole. Quarterback Matt Leinart, the 2004 Heisman winner, had taken some flack a few months earlier after it was revealed that he was enrolled in just one class during the football season: ballroom dancing. Although, to his credit, it was the only class Leinart needed to get his degree. Texas, meanwhile, graduated just 40 percent of its football team.

Soon after the Rose Bowl game, allegations began to swirl that, while at USC, Bush had received illegal gifts from sports marketers, hoping to cash in on his impending professional fortune. The payments included the use of a Southern California home for his family. In 2010 USC was slapped with significant penalties by the NCAA for violations related to Bush's time on campus. Amid rumors that he was going to be stripped of the award, Bush voluntarily returned his Heisman Trophy. Carroll eventually fled Los Angeles for the NFL, just months before the NCAA slapped the program with wide-ranging sanctions.

Texas played in the BCS Championship Game again four years later before suffering several below-average seasons. The program remained as popular as ever, though. So popular, in fact, that in 2010 the university and ESPN agreed to a joint venture called the Longhorn Network, a 24-hour-a-day station devoted to Texas sports. The deal was worth $300 million to the school over twenty years, but the windfall came with plenty of controversy.

Texas's quest for more cash led to a further destabilization of the already fracturing college football landscape. Within months, incensed by the inequities in the conference revenue structure brought on by the Longhorns' new deal, Texas A&M announced it was leaving the Big 12 Conference, essentially ending its more than 100-year-old rivalry with the Longhorns. It was one in a series of realignment moves brought on by the chase for larger chunks of TV cash.

Tragedy visited the programs as well. In May of 2012, much-beloved former Trojan star Junior Seau, an All-American in his final season at USC and a twelve-time Pro Bowler, shot himself in the chest. Examinations of Seau's brain showed that he suffered from CTE, a degenerative brain disorder that can lead to memory loss, early onset dementia, and depression. While football has essentially eradicated deaths on the field, Seau's suicide shed light on the game's biggest injury crisis since 1909.

On its surface, the USC–Texas spectacle bore little resemblance to the Princeton–Yale Thanksgiving Day battle in 1893—a game of carriage rides, dropkicks, and chrysanthemum hairstyles. And yet, in many ways, very little had changed.

ACKNOWLEDGMENTS

I HAVE MIXED EMOTIONS AS I WRITE THIS. IT MEANS THE BOOK IS DONE. There have been many times over the last few years when I've wondered if I'd manage to get it to this point, so there's obviously a part of me that feels relieved. On the other hand, this has been an absolute labor of love. It is a topic that has proven unendingly fascinating for me. I'm sad to see it go.

Significance of the moment aside, one thing is clear: I could have never arrived here without the help of many people.

Thanks first to my colleagues at the Big Ten Network—particularly President Mark Silverman. From the moment I first mentioned this endeavor to him in 2010, he has been incredibly supportive—trusting me not to let it get in the way of my "real" job. Thanks too to Mark Hulsey, Quentin Carter, and Marc Carman, who never batted an eye when I told them what I was up to. I'm also thankful to Big Ten commissioner Jim Delany, who not only approved the project, but also proved to have great insight into the early history of college athletics. His perspective, as always, was invaluable.

I spent more time researching this book than I did writing it, and many people helped me along the way, though one did so unknowingly. Michael D. Shutko was a freelance photojournalist who stumbled upon the story of Pat O'Dea in the early 1980s and became determined to tell it. He worked on it on and off for 25 years before passing away unexpectedly in 2007. He did some fine work, particularly in the area of genealogy. His son Mike and daughter-in-law Shannon were kind enough to share his papers with me. Though he never got to present the story to a widespread audience, I am pleased to acknowledge his contributions to this work.

University of Wisconsin archivist David Null was extraordinarily helpful. David was the first to pull O'Dea's file for me back in 2010 and has aided me innumerable times since then. I appreciate his diligence. Northwestern University archivist Kevin Leonard has also been a huge help.

Others who assisted me in research included: Melba biographer Ann Blainey, O'Dea descendant Wendy Bolz, Phil King descendant Ken Luchs, Kent Stephens from the College Football Hall of Fame, Wendy Kramer of the San Francisco Public Library, Sue Braden of the Hedberg Public Library, Westwood authority Tim Purdy, Kilmore historian Grahame Thom, Frank Merriwell expert Ryan Anderson, Bill Bushong at the White House, Mark Rudner at the Big Ten, Jenni Wilson of Alexander Street Press, and Wisconsin football historian Dave Vitale.

I also employed three paid researchers, who were all fantastic: Stephen Morgan at Notre Dame, David Allen at Columbia, and Ally Brantley at Yale. Ally, in particular, did a fabulous job finding each and every note, telegram, and letter that I requested in the vast Walter Camp papers.

Several others provided guidance along the way. Eric Hagerman, Joseph Crespino, John U. Bacon, Sean Cassidy, Ellis Henican, and Christine Brennan helped me navigate the unfamiliar world of book publishing. Though many friends read bits and pieces of the work, I am particularly grateful to Michael Diesenhof, Hunter Smith, David Lloyd, Mike Decourcy, and Professor Ronald A. Smith, who each went through the full manuscript and contributed valuable feedback.

I am fortunate to have two incredible agents. Chris Park of Foundry Literary has been an absolute joy to work with. She "got" this story from the get-go, but constantly pushed me to make it better. When Chris told me it was good, I knew it was—because there were many times when she said just the opposite. I feel very fortunate to have found her.

Steve Herz of IF Management has represented me in the television business since 1996, and I sometimes think he believes in me more than I believe in myself. He has always been my champion, and this project was no exception. In addition to reading the manuscript at several different stages, he has been a great sounding board and resource throughout. Josh Santry in the IF office also provided valuable help.

I could not have asked for a better editor than Keith Wallman at Lyons Press. From the first time we started to discuss this book, it felt like a true partnership. His insights were unfailingly dead on, his commentary was always sharp, and his attention to detail was remarkable. I also greatly appreciate his willingness to alter his traditional editorial schedule to fit my unusual professional life. Thanks too to Lyons project editor Meredith Dias, designer Bret Kerr, and publicist Sharon Kunz.

Finally, none of this would have been possible without the support of my family. My mother, Barbara Revsine—an accomplished writer herself—was always there to lend an ear and a critical eye. My sister, Pam, a proud Badger, was kind enough to read the manuscript as well. My three wonderful daughters—Meredith, Abigail, and Caroline—all accepted the time I devoted to this project and even made occasional inquiries, such as, "Oh yeah, how's that thing going?" and "Do you really think anyone's going to read it?" Perhaps unknowingly, they provided the balance and perspective I needed. They are my inspiration.

As for my wife, Michele—what can I say? She was enthusiastic about this idea from the moment I told her about it, never wavering even when it proved to be a more formidable task than either of us could have ever imagined it would be. She shared my excitement when I regaled her with tales of small discoveries along the way and helped pick me up when the journey proved bumpy. Basically, she did what she does every day. I couldn't ask for a better spouse—or friend, for that matter.

Sources and Notes

Preface

III. *"scares me as a dad.":* Warner made the comments on *The Dan Patrick Show,* May 3, 2012.

III. *over violence and concussions:* Barney's comments were made at a youth camp on June 14, 2013, and were widely quoted. See, for instance, http://tracking.si.com/2013/06/14/ lem-barney-football-deadly.

III. *". . . worried about college players.":* Franklin Foer and Chris Hughes, "Barack Obama Is Not Pleased," *New Republic,* January 27, 2013.

III. *"shocking apathy of conscience.":* Charles Grosvenor Osgood, *Lights in Nassan Hall: A Book of the Bicentennial, Princeton, 1746–1946* (Princeton, NJ: Princeton University Press, 1951), 31.

IV. *". . . strain that football demands.":* John Sayle Watterson, *College Football: History, Spectacle, Controversy* (Baltimore: Johns Hopkins University Press, 2000), 76.

IV. *a list of Americans' favorite sports:* Michael McCarthy, "Look Out, Baseball. College Football Is Hot on Your Cleats," *Advertising Age,* January 7, 2013; http://adage.com/article/news/ baseball-college-football-hot-cleats/239014.

IV. *ESPN paid $5.64 billion:* Rachel Bachman, "ESPN Strikes Deal for College Football Playoff," *Wall Street Journal,* November 21, 2012; http://online.wsj.com/article/SB1000142412788732485170457813 3223970790516.html.

CHAPTER 1

1. *largest in the nation:* Descriptions of Edwards and Hoffman House are from Henry Collins Brown, *Valentine's Manual of Old New York* (New York: Valentine's Manual, 1922), 126–31.

1. *in a championship match: New York Clipper Annual* (New York: Frank Queen Publishing Company, 1893), 68.

2. *". . . don't light your nose.":* This was a favorite quote of the Hoffman House employees, as documented in "Art: Tales of the Hoffman House," *Time,* January 25, 1943. I cannot say definitively that Edwards uttered it on this particular night.

2. *"sis boom bah" of Princeton:* "Princeton's Great Victory," *New York Herald,* December 1, 1893.

2. *best-known bookie:* Richard Harding Davis, "The Thanksgiving Day Game," *Harper's Weekly,* December 9, 1893, 1170.

3. *five times their face value:* Michael Oriard, *Reading Football: How the Popular Press Created an American Spectacle* (Chapel Hill: University of North Carolina Press, 1993), 90, and "Gross Receipts about $41,000," *New York Sun,* December 1, 1893, 3.

3. *". . . over a whitewashed line.":* Richard Harding Davis, "The Thanksgiving Day Game," *Harper's Weekly,* December 9, 1893, 1170.

3. *". . . people bow down to him.":* "Princeton's Great Victory," *New York Herald,* December 1, 1893.

3. *". . . will not do.":* Editorial Article 1 (No Title), *New York Times,* December 1, 1893.

4. *far more luxuriously:* Descriptions of Tally-hos in next two paragraphs from "Some Went in Tally-hos," *New York Sun,* December 1, 1893, 3; and Richard Harding Davis, "The Thanksgiving Day Game," *Harper's Weekly,* December 9, 1893, 1170.

4. *farther away from the field:* "Going to the Game," *New York Times,* December 1, 1893.

4. *began to overflow:* Description of elevated cars: "Enthusiastic and Loyal," *New York Sun,* December 1, 1893, 2.

5. *". . . single play was made.":* Ibid.

5. *estimated at 50,000:* Descriptions of the crowd from Richard Harding Davis, "The Thanksgiving Day Game," *Harper's Weekly,* December 9, 1893, 1170; "Princeton's Great Victory," *New York Herald,* December 1, 1893; and "The Orange above the Blue," *New York Times,* December 1, 1893.

5. *into the upper forties:* New York State Weather Bureau, Report for the Month of November 1893, 7.

6. *had taken the field:* "Spectators Come to Blows," *New York Sun,* December 1, 1893, 3.

6. *its fine aroma:* "The Orange above the Blue," *New York Times,* December 1, 1893.

6. *1,285 to 6:* Yale year-by-year results from www.yalebulldogs.com/sports/m-footbl/2011-12/files/Year_by_Year_Results_through_2011.pdf.

6. *better than two to one:* "Now the City Is Football Mad," *New York Herald,* November 30, 1893.

6. *Tiger halfback Ledu Smock:* Alexander M. Weyand, *The Saga of American Football* (New York: Macmillan, 1955), 17. It is important to note that the word "smock," describing a loose-fitting outer garment, is well more than 1,000 years old and predates this use of the word. That both refer to shirts is a coincidence.

7. *amount they felt comfortable with:* Details on protective equipment from "Football Armor," *Chicago Daily Tribune,* October 3, 1897, 38.

7. *grand-nephew of the famous poet:* Detail on Poe and Balliett from Weyand, 37.

7. *for several years:* Ibid., 46.

7. *". . . concussion of the brain.":* "Ready for the Great Struggle," *New York Times,* November 30, 1893.

7. *". . . any football player in the country.":* "Ibid."

7. *on this Thanksgiving Day:* New York Sun staffing detailed in Richard Harding Davis, "The Thanksgiving Day Game," *Harper's Weekly,* December 9, 1893, 1170.

8. *"wearing a nose mask. . . .":* "Princeton's Game 6 to 0," *New York Sun,* December 1, 1893, 1.

8. *was a risky one:* "Princeton's Great Victory," *New York Herald,* December 1, 1893; "Princeton's Game 6 to 0," *New York Sun,* December 1, 1893, 1; "Princeton's Clever Play," *New York Times,* December 1, 1893; "The Orange above the Blue," *New York Times,* December 1, 1893; and Richard Harding Davis, "The Thanksgiving Day Game," *Harper's Weekly,* December 9, 1893, 1170–71.

8. *". . . remembered it for years.":* Parke H. Davis, *Football, the American Intercollegiate Game* (New York: C. Scribner's Sons, 1911), 97.

9. *and his right ear:* Princeton's Game 6 to 0," *New York Sun,* December 1, 1893, 2.

9. "*. . . let us get to work.":* "Princeton's Clever Play," *New York Times,* December 1, 1893.

9. *"Four, four, four yards more!":* Ibid.

10. "*. . . dead silence prevailed.":* "Like a Thunderbolt," *New York Times,* December 1, 1893.

10. "*. . . baffled and chagrined.":* "Princeton's Game 6 to 0," *New York Sun,* December 1, 1893, 2.

11. "*. . . the big Princeton centre.":* Ibid.

11. "*. . . were a necessary adjunct,":* Ibid.

11. "*. . . the men who conquer.":* Richard Harding Davis, "The Thanksgiving Day Game," *Harper's Weekly,* December 9, 1893, 1171.

11. "*. . . did play so well.":* "Battered and Joyful," *New York Sun,* December 1, 1893, 3.

11. "'*. . . I have nothing to say.'":* Ibid.

12. *the game's impact:* "More Than Fifty Arrests," *New York Sun,* December 1, 1893, 1.

12. "*. . . Princeton is everywhere.":* "Princeton Students to Celebrate," *New York Times,* December 2, 1893.

12. *at the New York Stock Exchange:* $100,000 figure comes from "Like a Thunderbolt," *New York Times,* December 1, 1893. This article cites $25,000 changing hands at the Stock Exchange and a smaller amount at the Hoffman House; "The Odds Were Too Great," *New York Sun,* December 1, 1893, 3.

CHAPTER 2

13–20. Wisconsin 47, Northwestern 0—Game descriptions taken from the following sources: "Routs Purple Team," *(Chicago) Daily Inter Ocean,* November 25, 1898; "Northwestern Was Easy," *Daily Cardinal,* November 28, 1898, 1; "O'Dea Great Kicker," *Fort Worth Star Telegram,* November 16, 1906; "Analysis of Evanston Game," *Chicago Daily Tribune,* November 25, 1898, 2; "Story of Purple's Downfall," *Chicago Daily Tribune,* November 25, 1898, 2; Caspar Whitney, "Amateur Sport," *Harper's Weekly,* November 25, 1898, 1301; "O'Dea Kicks a 60-Yard Goal," *Milwaukee Sentinel,*

November 25, 1898, 1; "O'Dea the Hero of the Field," *Chicago Times-Herald*, December 1, 1898, 1.

13. *"Nine, ten."* Detail on the signal taken from "Modern Punters Were Dubs Compared to Old Pat O'Dea," *(Butte) Montana Standard*, October 22, 1934, 7.

14. *"abnormally long and wonderfully developed.":* This note and the rest of the physical description of Pat O'Dea is from George F. Downer, "Pat O'Dea's Kicking Feats Still Amaze Football Fans," *Souvenir Program and Athletic Review*, November 17, 1934, 9.

14. *". . . we ever have played.":* "Enthusiastic at Madison," *Chicago Daily Tribune*, November 11, 1898, 4.

15. *". . . attraction of the day,":* "Stagg Returns Today," *Chicago Daily Tribune*, November 21, 1898, 4.

15. *". . . all the champagne you can drink.":* Phil King speech is paraphrased from "Modern Punters Were Dubs Compared to Old Pat O'Dea," *(Butte) Montana Standard*, October 22, 1934, 7. "Coach King had promised the squad all the champagne we could drink if we scored in the first two minutes."

15. *most prominent citizens:* Descriptions of Sheppard Field are taken from the author's observations of photographs in Northwestern University Archives.

16. *fraternities and sororities:* "Chaos for the Purple," *Chicago Chronicle*, November 25, 1898, 4.

16. *"Then shot it down again.":* "Songs for the Thanksgiving Game," *The Northwestern*, November 17, 1898.

17. *"All 187 had been from the East.":* Alexander M. Weyand, *The Saga of American Football* (New York: Macmillan, 1955), 200–5.

17. *well below freezing:* US Department of Agriculture, Report for November 1898, Illinois Section.

17. *shores of Lake Michigan:* "Chaos for the Purple," *Chicago Chronicle*, November 25, 1898, 4.

17. *jump at the pigskin:* Description of O'Dea's kicking style from Harry Grayson, "Pat O'Dea Wrecked Minnesota with 60 Yard Drop Kick on Run," *Milwaukee Journal*, October 15, 1943, 2.

18. *300-yard hurdles:* "Are Good Jumpers," *Milwaukee Journal*, May 12, 1897, 7.

18. *sprinted down the gridiron at the snap:* "O'Dea Great Kicker," *Fort Worth Star Telegram,* November 16, 1906.

19. *Spanish–American War:* "O'Dea Kicks a 60-Yard Goal," *Milwaukee Sentinel,* November 25, 1898, 1.

19. *". . . big Thanksgiving game.":* Ibid.

19. *". . . most ardent supporters.":* "Analysis of Evanston Game," *Chicago Daily Tribune,* November 25, 1898.

19. *"Pat O'Dea is king.":* "King of Kickers," *Duluth News Tribune,* November 25, 1898.

20. *". . . from the sixty-yard line.":* "O'Dea the Hero of the Field," *Chicago Times-Herald,* December 1, 1898, 1.

20. *". . . of this new record.":* Ibid.

20. *". . . at making the goal,":* Ibid.

20. *the All-American team:* Camp's 1898 All-American team included Herschberger of Chicago on the first team. Steckle and Cunningham of Michigan, Kennedy of Chicago, and O'Dea were on the second team. Weyand, 205.

Chapter 3

21. *around to see it:* Alexander M. Weyand, *The Saga of American Football* (New York: Macmillan, 1955), 1.

21. *". . . as the foot-ball":* Andy Mitten, *The Rough Guide to Cult Football* (London: Rough Guides, 2010), 4.

21. *kick it into the river:* "Foot-Ball," *Harper's Weekly,* December 20, 1879, 986.

21. *prohibition with expulsion:* Ronald A. Smith, *Sports and Freedom: The Rise of Big-Time College Athletics* (New York: Oxford University Press, 1988), 68.

22. *". . . were mind and soul.":* Francis A. Walker. "College Athletics," *Harvard Graduates' Magazine* (September 1893), 3.

22. *". . . slighter hold upon the men.":* Michael S. Kimmel, *Manhood in America: A Cultural History* (New York: Free Press, 1996), 176.

22. *". . . soft, doelike eyes.":* Ibid.

22. *"Have we a Religion for Men?":* Ibid.

22. *". . . sacred and the muscular.":* Ibid., 177.

23. "... *men or affairs.*": Josiah Strong, *Religious Movements for Social Betterment* (New York: League for Social Service, 1900), 29–30, as quoted in Clifford Putney, *Muscular Christianity: Manhood and Sports in Protestant America, 1880–1920* (Cambridge, MA: Harvard University Press, 2001), 42.

23. "... *in this period.*": Elmer L. Johnson, *The History of YMCA Physical Education* (Chicago: Association, 1979), 47, as quoted in Putney, 46.

23. "... *searched for students to serve.*": Guy Maxton Lewis, "The American Intercollegiate Football Spectacle, 1869–1917" (dissertation, University of Maryland, 1964), 16.

23. *all of Europe combined:* Burton J. Bledstein, *The Culture of Professionalism: The Middle Class and the Development of Higher Education in America* (New York: Norton, 1976), 241.

23. "... *rise of intercollegiate athletics.*": Merle Curti and Vernon Carstensen, *The University of Wisconsin 1848–1925: A History* (Madison: University of Wisconsin Press, 1949), 694.

24. *the latter were conincidental:* Descriptions of the first intercollegiate football game are taken from the following sources: Dean Hill, *Football Thru the Years* (New York: Gridiron Pub., 1940), 11; Weyand, 4; Lewis, 12–15; Frank Presbrey and James Hugh Moffatt, *Athletics at Princeton: A History* (New York: Frank Presbrey, 1901), 271.

24. *for the game:* Weyand, 2; Lewis, 11–12.

24. "... *if they can.*": As quoted in Presbrey and Moffatt, 271.

25. *on the results:* Ibid.

25. *had ever seen before:* Lewis, 28.

25. "... *on the part of any.*": *Yale Courant,* October 14, 1876, 1.

25. "... *team to represent us.*": *Yale Courant,* November 2, 1878, 40.

25. *miss class for games:* Lewis, 33.

26. *respect of his teammates:* Camp description from John Stuart Martin, "Walter Camp and His Gridiron Game," *American Hertiage* 12, no. 6 (October 1961).

26. "... *He always won.*": Ibid.

26. "... *by our men.*": As quoted in Weyand, 11–12.

26. "... *sold Rugby to the American colleges.*": Weyand, 14.

27. *play rugby, rather than soccer, going forward:* Weyand, 16. Yale initially refused to join the association due to a disagreement about the number of players on the field, though the school was brought into the fold several years later.

27. *". . . went the ball into scrummage.":* Amos Alonzo Stagg and Wesley Winans Stout, *Touchdown!* (New York: Longmans, Green and Co., 1927), 56. To Stagg's point, the games were often quite boring. For instance, the *New York Times* described a dissatisfied and hissing crowd watching a ten-minute scrummage during the Yale–Princeton game in 1879. See "Kicking the Leather Egg," *New York Times,* November 28, 1879.

27. *American football was born:* Weyand, 21.

27. *snapping and downing the ball:* See, for example, the *New York Times* description of the 1880 Yale–Princeton matchup: "A Princeton player would roll the ball six inches over the foul-line so that another could snatch it and bring it back, only to repeat the act. This was allowable, of course, but it looked a good deal like cowardice, and the crowd took it that way. No amount of hissing could make Princeton change her safe policy, however." "Vain Work at Football," *New York Times,* November 26, 1880.

27. *three downs to make five yards:* David M. Nelson, *The Anatomy of a Game: Football, the Rules, and the Men Who Made the Game* (Newark: University of Delaware Press, 1994), 49–50.

28. *converted the kick:* Scoring as described in this paragraph is from Weyand, 22–25.

28. *". . . agitate a bag of wind.":* Ibid.

29. *". . . hitting, gouging and howling.":* "Mighty Savage Football," *New York Sun,* November 28, 1884, 1. The original sentence read, "All of the maddened giants of both the teams were in it and they lay heaped, kicking, chocking, hitting, gouging and howling." I have changed "chocking" to "choking" for clarity.

29. *". . . by the opposite side.":* Stagg and Stout, 78.

29. *the school banned the game:* "The Documents of the Football Question," *Harvard Graduates' Magazine* (June 1894), 520.

29. *". . . elements of manhood may emerge.":* "Speech of Professor Francis L. Patton, DD, LLD, President-Elect of Princeton College at the Annual Dinner of the Princeton Club of New York," March 15, 1888, 5, 7, as quoted in Lewis, 84.

29. *". . . apathy of conscience."*: Charles Grosvenor Osgood, *Lights in Nassan Hall: A Book of the Bicentennial, Princeton, 1746–1946* (Princeton, NJ: Princeton University Press, 1951), 31.

30. *". . . behind Yale in no gift."*: "Speech of Professor Francis L. Patton," as quoted in Lewis, 84.

30. *more than thirteen-fold:* Lewis, 68. The rise in football-related profits was even more pronounced. The 1885 team made a profit of $19.49. The 1893 team finished $22,898.59 in the black. As cited in Richard P. Borkowski, *The Life and Contributions of Walter Camp to American Football* (thesis, Temple University, 1979), 84.

30. *". . . in any other way."*: *Weekly University Courier,* January 17, 1891. As quoted in John Sayle Watterson, *College Football: History, Spectacle, Controversy* (Baltimore: Johns Hopkins University Press, 2000), 45.

30. *more than doubled:* Weyand, 37.

30. *". . . science of the game."*: Parke H. Davis, *Football: The American Intercollegiate Game* (New York: Charles Scribner's Sons, 1911), 93.

30. *". . . What will you give [?]"*: Telegram from Corbin to Camp, November 4, 1889. Walter Chauncey Camp Papers, Yale University Archives, box 7, reel 6.

31. ON THE GRIDIRON: "Gone Football Mad," *Galveston Daily News,* October 25, 1894, 10.

31. *". . . he is the president of the university."*: Walter Harding Davis, "A Day with the Yale Team," *Harper's Weekly,* November 18, 1893, 1110.

31. *". . . enhanced her appearance."*: "Society Enjoys the Game," *New York Herald,* November 25, 1894.

31. *". . . and a spotted veil. . . ."*: Ibid.

CHAPTER 4

33. *was virtually shut down:* P. F. O'Dea details in the first two paragraphs, including story of his funeral, from *Kilmore (Victoria) Free Press,* December 2, 1880, as excerpted on November 23, 2002, by Dianne Le Quiniat, President, Kilmore Historical Society; from the files of Michael D. Shutko.

33. *next to his business:* "Pat O'Dea," *Kilmore (Victoria) Free Press,* October 11, 1934, 4.

33. *jailed for stealing caps:* www.historyaustralia.org.au/twconvic/
Katherine+Stewart+Forbes+1830.

34. *among the survivors:* There are several excellent accounts of the massacre: "A Glimpse of Past History," *Euroa Advertiser,* October 19,
1906, 3; R. M. McGowan, "The Story of Faithfull's Massacre," *(Melbourne) Argus,* July 8, 1950, 15; and Judith Bassett, "The Faithfull
Massacre at the Broken River, 1838," *Journal of Australian Studies*
13:24, 18–34.

34. *in the new village of Kilmore:* "Pat O'Dea," *Kilmore (Victoria) Free
Press,* October 11, 1934, 4.

34. *an area that is now known as Victoria:* "Kilmore," *Sydney Morning
Herald,* March 7, 2005.

34. *ideal for farming and grazing:* The best description of Kilmore comes
from Maya V. Tucker, *Kilmore on the Sydney Road* (Kilmore, Victoria: Shire of Kilmore, 1988).

34. *operating the flour mill in Kilmore:* Details of Patrick Flannery
O'Dea's life are from Andrew M. O'Dea, "Football's Longest
Kicker," *Big Ten Weekly,* October 22, 1925, 10–11.

34. *seven of whom survived infancy:* Elizabeth Kraus, "Known Des-
candants of Patrick O'Dea and Ann Flannery," from the files of
Michael D. Shutko.

34. *to have arrived a day later:* Pat O'Dea Birth Certificate, Office of
Government Statist, Melbourne, Australia; from the files of Michael
D. Shutko.

34. *scattered among nearly 300 dwellings:* Tucker, 130.

34. *a number of churches:* Ibid., 108, 144.

34. *town proper until 1888:* Ibid., 125–26.

34. *". . . against any epidemic.":* Ibid., 136.

35. *"particularly worth stopping for.":* Ibid., 126.

35. *shores of Port Phillip Bay:* "Another Bathing Fatality," *(Melbourne)
Age,* January 4, 1888, 5.

35. *". . . bringing her to shore.":* "Drowning of a Lady at Mordialloc,"
(Melbourne) Argus, January 4, 1888, 6.

35. *while interviewing O'Dea:* Details in this paragraph taken from
"Kicker O'Dea," *Milwaukee Journal,* November 24, 1897, 8.

36. *were his creation:* Bill Leiser, "O'Dea, Lost Grid Immortal, Comes to
Life," *San Francisco Chronicle,* September 19, 1934, 1.

36. *. . . died of a heart attack.":* "Kangaroo Kicker," *Melbourne (Australia) Herald-Sun,* December 1, 2007, 94. The same account appears in the 1962 Xavierian yearbook.

36. *focused on sports:* Elizabeth Kraus, "The Mysterious O'Dea Brothers," unpublished research article, from the files of Michael D. Shutko.

36. *with a goose quill:* Andrew M. O'Dea, "Football's Longest Kicker," *Big Ten Weekly,* October 22, 1925, 10.

36. *either end of the field:* Detail on needing to bounce the ball every 7 yards is from "Capt. Pat O'Dea Talks about His Football Career and His Future," *Milwaukee Journal,* December 5, 1899, 10.

37. *All-Victorian team in 1894:* "Intercolonial Football," *(Adelaide) South Australian Register,* July 14, 1894, 7.

37. *". . . with his debut.":* "The Game of the Season," *(Melbourne) Argus,* June 17, 1895, 5–6.

37. *broke off from Slavin:* George F. Downer, "Pat O'Dea's Kicking Feats Still Amaze Football Fans," *Souvenir Program and Athletic Review,* November 17, 1934, 9.

37. *". . . Wisconsin's crew coach in 1895:* Ibid.

37. *trickier propositions than they are today:* There were two ways to convert the goals after touchdowns. The first involved walking the ball out on a straight line from the spot where it crossed the goal line. In other words, if the touchdown was made close to the sideline, the kick had to be attempted from that angle. Alternatively, the scoring player could kick the ball out from behind the goal line back onto the field of play. If one of his teammates caught the ball, that player could attempt the kick from the spot where he caught it.

38. *bit slow to develop:* The best explanation of the early rules of football comes from David M. Nelson, *The Anatomy of a Game: Football, the Rules, and the Men Who Made the Game* (Newark: University of Delaware Press, 1994).

38. *legalized tackling below the waist:* Ronald A. Smith, *Sports and Freedom: The Rise of Big-Time College Athletics* (New York: Oxford University Press, 1988), 90.

38. *four or five blockers on the same play:* A variety of different versions of the "guards back" play are diagrammed in Walter Camp, Amos Alonzo Stagg, Lorin F. Deland, and Henry L. Williams, *The*

American Football Trilogy (Newbury Park, CA: Lost Century of Sports Collection, 2010), 349–51.

39. *launching the runner around end:* Alexander M. Weyand, *The Saga of American Football* (New York: Macmillan, 1955), 48.

39. *"... something once seen, never forgotten.":* Ibid., 40.

39. *"... That halted the wedge.":* Ibid., 32.

39. *was in his thirties:* Camp et al., About the Authors."

39. *applied to the football field:* Weyand, 45; and Joseph Hamblen Sears, "A Football Scientist," *Harper's Weekly,* December 2, 1893, 1147.

40. *... before they were downed.":* "Rah! Rah! Rah! Yale!" *New York Times,* November 20, 1892.

40. *kicking team could recover:* Nelson, 67.

40. *five yards behind the play:* Ibid., 73.

40. *vivid in their descriptions:* Accounts of the game taken from the following sources: "Yale Again Triumphant," *New York Times,* November 25, 1894; "Blue above the Crimson," *New York Herald,* November 25, 1894, 1; "Yale 12, Harvard 4," *Boston Sunday Globe,* November 25, 1894, 1.

41. *that he had died:* "Yale Again Triumphant," *New York Times,* November 25, 1894.

41. *"... the destructiveness of [to]day's game,.":* Ibid.

41. *"... game should be continued or not.":* "Yale 12, Harvard 4," *Boston Sunday Globe,* November 25, 1894, 1.

41. *"... free from objectionable features, the game must stop.":* "Harvard Has No Excuse" *Boston Sunday Globe,* November 25, 1894, 2.

41–42. *"... unfit for college use.":* "President Eliot's Report," *Harvard Graduates' Magazine* (March 1895), 369.

CHAPTER 5

43. *gazing at the choppy water:* Details of rowing accident are from the following sources: "A College Oarsmen Drowned," *New York Times,* April 8, 1896; "John Day Drowned in a Madison Lake," *Janesville Daily Gazette,* April 8, 1896, 2; "Drowned in Mendota," *Weekly Wisconsin,* April 11, 1896; "Drowned at Madison." *Daily (Oshkosh, WI) Northwestern,* April 7, 1896, 4; *Daily Cardinal,* April 8 and 9, 1896; "Pat O'Dea Visits McConville, Friend of His Student Days at Wisconsin," *Wisconsin State Journal Sports,* December 3, 1934, 1.

44. "...*Australian stroke 'Yarra-Yarra' at Wisconsin.*": Bonnie Ryan, "O'Dea Devoted to U.W." *(Madison, WI) Capital Times*, April 5, 1962, 1.

44. *through the town's streets:* Stuart D. Levitan, *Madison: The Illustrated Sesquicentennial History* (Madison: University of Wisconsin Press, 2006), 135.

44. *double during the next four years:* David V. Mollenhoff, *Madison: A History of the Formative Years* (Madison: University of Wisconsin Press, 2003), 196.

44. *its streets and homes:* Ibid., 200.

44. *"covered with fecal matter in varying stages of decay."*: Ibid., 212.

44. *few hundred yards from the university campus:* Levitan, 111,118.

44. *more than 50 percent over the previous four years:* "Enrollments 1888 to Present, Office of the Registrar, University of Wisconsin–Madison." http://registrar.wisc.edu/enrollments_1888_to_present.htm, June 20, 2013.

45. *"Well this is a good place."*: Bonnie Ryan, "O'Dea Devoted to U.W." *(Madison, WI) Capital Times*, April 5, 1962, 1.

47. "...*once you get to shore.*": Quote is from paraphrased text in a newspaper article: "O'Dea refused to be taken into the boat until McConville was taken off, after which he insisted that Wheeler should row ashore and come back for him." "Lost in Lake Mendota," *Daily Cardinal*, April 8, 1896, 1.

49. *O'Dea responded hesitantly:* Quotes are from paraphrased text in Ken Blanchard, "Fabulous O'Dea Visits La Crosse," *La Crosse Tribune*, September 29, 1957; and Bonnie Ryan, "O'Dea Devoted to U.W." *(Madison, WI) Capital Times*, April 5, 1962, 1.

49. *of the Wisconsin football team:* Kevin O'Kreisman, "O'Dea Would Have Been 100 Today!" *(Madison, WI) Capital Times*, March 17, 1972, 1–2.

49. *"deplored college athletics."*: Merle Curti and Vernon Carstensen, *The University of Wisconsin 1848–1925: A History* (Madison: University of Wisconsin Press, 1949), 693.

49. "...*very decidedly athletically wrong.*": Ibid.

49. "...*defeats in funereal-black borders.*": Ibid., 698.

49. *shot in the foot:* Ibid., 533.

50. "...*and the second half playing.*": Bonnie Ryan, "O'Dea Devoted to U.W." *(Madison, WI) Capital Times*, April 5, 1962, 1.

50. *". . . 20 or 24 points to nothing."*: "Varsity to Win 20 to 0." *Daily Cardinal,* October 10, 1896, 1.

50. *". . . where O'Dea stood when they fell on it."*: "Varsity Did Win 34 to 0," *Daily Cardinal,* October 12, 1896, 1.

50. *third-longest of O'Dea's career: 2012 Wisconsin Football Fact Book,* 149.

51. *". . . missed by barely three feet."*: "Varsity Did Win 34 to 0," *Daily Cardinal,* October 12, 1896, 1.

51. *". . . a student at the university."*: "'Twas Not Andy O'Dea," *Minneapolis Journal,* October 14, 1896.

51. *". . . then fell on my arm."*: "O'Dea's Arm Broken," *Daily Cardinal,* October 13, 1896, 3.

51. *"famous as a great punter."*: "Football Player Laid Up," *Eau Claire (WI) Leader,* October 14, 1896, 1.

Chapter 6

52. *simply to ignore the rules:* Michael Oriard, *Reading Football: How the Popular Press Created an American Spectacle* (Chapel Hill: University of North Carolina Press, 1993), 155.

53. *". . . post-graduate course is to play football."*: Frank Presbrey and James Hugh Moffatt, *Athletics at Princeton: A History* (New York: Frank Presbrey, 1901), 578.

53. *before the Harvard game:* Monte Cash details from Ibid., 577, and Mark F. Bernstein, *Football: The Ivy League Origins of an American Obsession* (Philadelphia: University of Pennsylvania Press, 2001), 30.

53. *". . . best treatment of any of the colleges."*: Details on the Harvard–Princeton dispute come from Presbrey and Moffatt, 578–85.

54. *for the next five years:* Bernstein, 30–31.

54. *". . . no organizations to enforce any."*: Allan Nevins, *Illinois* (New York: Oxford University Press, 1917), as cited in Carl D. Voltmer, *A Brief History of the Intercollegiate Conference of Faculty Representatives, with Special Consideration of Athletic Problems* (thesis, Columbia University, 1935), 2.

54. *"No one thought of inquiring about their standing,"*: Frazier Harrison, "Ferry Field Passes at Ann Arbor," *Big Ten Weekly,* February 10, 1927, 6.

54. *". . . to maintain classroom standing."*: Caspar Whitney, "Amateur Sport," *Harper's Weekly,* November 4, 1899, 1122.

54. *finish off his career at West Virginia:* Ronald A. Smith, *Sports and Freedom: The Rise of Big-Time College Athletics* (New York: Oxford University Press, 1988), 139.

55. *". . . from taking root at colleges?":* Caspar Whitney, "Amateur Sport," *Harper's Weekly,* December 2, 1893, 1161–62.

55. *friendly, collegial student matches:* Smith, 172–73.

55–56. *". . . the price of purity in college sport.":* Caspar Whitney, "Amateur Sport," *Harper's Weekly,* January 14, 1899, 53–54.

56. *"There are no degrees of amateurism.":* Ibid.

56. *for the season ahead:* Caspar Whitney, "Amateur Sport," *Harper's Weekly,* October 24, 1896, 1061–62. Whitney published the school's response two weeks later. See Caspar Whitney, "Amateur Sport," *Harper's Weekly,* November 7, 1896, 1109–10.

56. *". . . the game mere means to that end.":* Caspar Whitney, "Amateur Sport," *Harper's Weekly,* October 24, 1896, 1062.

56. *the domain of the captain:* Oriard, 38.

56. *". . . from the side receiving coaching.":* Caspar Whitney, "Amateur Sport," *Harper's Weekly,* December 30, 1899, 1330.

57. *was even the coach in those years:* The five-year figure is from Yale's official records. Smith, 85.

57. *". . . advice and direction for the team.":* Ibid.

57. *"Dear Oligarch.":* Guy Maxton Lewis, *The American Intercollegiate Football Spectacle, 1869–1917* (dissertation, University of Maryland, 1964), 73.

57. *". . . Latin, Greek, Sanskrit and Gothic.":* Robin Lester, *Stagg's University: The Rise, Decline, and Fall of Big-Time Football at Chicago* (Urbana: University of Illinois Press, 1995), 2.

58. *". . . select circle of higher education.":* Ibid., xix.

58. *". . . cutting wood, [and] beating carpets.":* Amos Alonzo Stagg and Wesley Winans Stout, *Touchdown!* (New York: Longmans, Green and Co., 1927), 50.

58. *off-campus in an unheated attic:* Ibid., 52–53.

58. *". . . pitch like that going to be a minister.":* Ibid., 104.

58. *". . . undoubtedly is Pitcher Stagg.":* Ibid., 108.

58. *". . . tone of the game was smelly.":* Ibid., 104.

58. *by an incredible 698–0:* Yale University website: www.yalebulldogs .com/sports/m-footbl/2011-12/files/Year_by_Year_Results_ through_2011.pdf.

58. *great deal of public speaking:* Stagg and Stout, 130

58. *basketball there a year later:* Ibid., 131.

60. *"We will give them a palace car and a vacation too.":* Lester, 19.

60. *". . . to turn the latches.":* Stagg and Stout, 154.

60. *". . . our good athletes were few.":* Voltmer, 2.

60. *"We will have a college here soon if this keeps up.":* Lester, 25.

60. *". . . the leaders in athletic games.":* Ibid.

61. *". . . for horses and cows and grain.":* Caspar Whitney, "Amateur Sport," *Harper's Weekly,* November 23, 1895, 1123.

61. *in Ann Arbor for $600:* Ibid.

61. *the end "of modern civilization.":* Voltmer, 3.

61. *coaches could not play:* Ibid., 4–5.

61. *". . . clarified era in Western college sport,.":* Ibid., 11.

CHAPTER 7

62. *put to the test:* "Rules in Suspense," *Daily Cardinal,* October 9, 1896, 1.

62. *would not abide by it:* "To Retain the Rule," *Daily Cardinal,* October 6, 1896, 1.

63. *". . . about the hiring of players came out.":* Ibid.

63. *". . . applaud and support Wisconsin.":* "Caspar Whitney Commends," *Daily Cardinal,* October 10, 1896, 1.

63. *". . . champion of the west very bright.":* "Rule Not in Force," *Daily Cardinal,* October 10, 1896, 1.

63. *". . . postponement of a lecture for a football game.":* Charles Forster Smith, *Charles Kendall Adams: A Life-Sketch.* (Madison: University of Wisconsin Press, 1924), 67.

64. *"Now go in and win.":* Ibid.

64. *help reschedule the lecture:* Ibid., 68.

64. *". . . they should be enforced.":* "The 'Six Months' Rule," *Daily Cardinal,* October 10, 1896, 2.

64. *"Wisconsin stands disgraced before the college world.":* Caspar Whitney, "Amateur Sport," *Harper's Weekly,* October 31, 1896.

64. *". . . the highest officials of the university!":* Ibid.

65. *payments to top players:* Information contained in an e-mail between the author and Ryan Larkin, media relations director for the Melbourne Football Club, with information provided by the club's historian, June 24, 2013.

65. *". . . to discharge their veterans."*: "President Replies," *Daily Cardinal,* October 30, 1896, 1.

65. *". . . it is big enough to rule the west."*: "New Rules Tonight," *Daily Cardinal,* October 14, 1896, 1.

66. *". . . and were not stout-hearted."*: "Now for Nov. 21 and 26," *Daily Cardinal,* November 11, 1896, 1.

66. *". . . number of yards to gain."*: "Some More 'Doubt,'" *Daily Cardinal,* November 6, 1896, 1.

66. *". . . neglect of the men in charge is lamentable,"*: Untitled editorial, *Daily Cardinal,* November 9, 1896, 3.

66. *game-winning touchdown in the final minute:* "Badgers Win the Game," *Chicago Daily Tribune,* November 22, 1896, 3.

67. *"the Minnesota game knocked us to pieces."*: "Comment of Wisconsin's Captain," *Chicago Daily Tribune,* November 27, 1896, 1.

67. *adopted and ignored the year before:* "New Athletic Rules," *Daily Cardinal,* November 30, 1896, 1.

67. *the season was over:* University of Wisconsin Faculty Minutes, November 30, 1896, University of Wisconsin Archives.

68. *"finally settles the question of the western championship."*: "To Play the Indians," *Daily Cardinal,* December 4, 1896, 1.

68. *". . . quite out of the ordinary,"*: "Will Play at Night," *Daily Cardinal,* December 7, 1896, 1.

68. *". . . nothing short of marvelous."*: "Left for Chicago," *Daily Cardinal,* December 18, 1896, 1.

68. *late that afternoon:* Details in this paragraph from ibid. and "Ready for the Game," *Daily Cardinal,* December 19, 1896, 1.

69. *". . . on the part of the players."*: "Indians Get the Scalps," *Chicago Daily Tribune,* December 20, 1896, 1.

69. *". . . just for practice."*: Ibid.

69. *". . . for nearly half an hour"*: Ibid.

69. *victim of circumstance:* December 19, 1896: Carlisle 18, Wisconsin 8. Details of the game taken from "Indians Get the Scalps," *Chicago Daily Tribune,* December 20, 1896, 1, and "The Carlisle Game," *Daily Cardinal,* December 21, 1896, 1.

69. *". . . evoked the wildest applause."*: "The Carlisle Game," *Daily Cardinal,* December 21, 1896, 1.

69. *". . . wishes of a rabble crowd."*: Ibid.

69. *". . . dropped it to the ground."*: Arthur Daley, "The Customers Always Write," *New York Times*, March 4, 1896, 20.
69. *knocked the ball back down:* Ibid.
69. *". . . would have won easily,"*: "The Carlisle Game," *Daily Cardinal*, December 21, 1896, 1.
70. *". . .at their own game."*: "Indians Get the Scalps," *Chicago Daily Tribune*, December 20, 1896, 1.
70. *". . . not eligible for any athletic team."*: University of Wisconsin Faculty Minutes, March 13, 1897, University of Wisconsin Archives.

CHAPTER 8

71. *". . . which make life worth living."*: The Merriwell story is from Burt L. Standish, "Frank Merriwell's High Jump," *Tip Top Weekly*, Number 242, December 1, 1900.
74. *seven million Merriwell books every year:* Stewart H. Holbrook, "Frank Merriwell at Yale Again and Again and Again," *American Heritage* 12, no. 4 (June 1961). Standish himself reportedly estimated that 200,000 Merriwell books were sold per week, which would put the figure at more than ten million copies per year. The publishers put a total estimate on Merriwell sales at 500 million in a span of less than twenty years. By comparison, the American Bible Society estimated that, in a span of 143 years, just over 545 million "Bibles . . . Testaments and other Biblical supplements" were sold in the United States. Burt L. Standish and Harriett Hinsdale, *Frank Merriwell's "Father"; an Autobiography* (Norman: University of Oklahoma Press, 1964), xiii–xiv.
75. *". . . put away that flask."*: Standish and Hinsdale, xiii–xiv.
75. *toward the upper classes:* Will Irwin, "The American Newspaper," *Collier's*, February 4, 1911, 15.
75. *was forever changed:* "A Pioneer in Journalism," *New York Times*, December 22, 1899.
75. *". . . the first on our soil."*: Will Irwin, "The American Newspaper," *Collier's*, February 4, 1911, 15.
76. *"I renounce all so-called principles."*: Ibid. 16.
76. *". . . and to print it first."*: Ibid.
76. *official government transmissions:* Ibid.

76. *". . . the business of a newspaper."*: Ibid.
76. *". . . all public attention."*: "The Recent Tragedy," *New York Herald*, April 12, 1836, 1.
76. *the sporting world for him:* William Henry Nugent, "The Sports Section," *American Mercury* (March 1929), 335.
77. *just days later:* "Sporting Intelligence," *New York Herald*, May 14, 1847, 1.
77. *8,000 copies per hour:* Will Irwin, "The American Newspaper," *Collier's*, February 4, 1911, 16.
77. *just sixty years earlier:* Will Irwin, "The American Newspaper," *Collier's*, February 18, 1911, 14.
77. *tripled to 12,000:* Guy Maxton Lewis, *The American Intercollegiate Football Spectacle, 1869–1917* (dissertation, University of Maryland, 1964), 123.
77. *". . . sinks into insignificance."*: J. W. Keller, "Journalism As a Career," *Forum* (August 1893), 696.
77. *swelled to 90 percent:* Lorin Fuller Deland, *At the Sign of the Dollar, and Other Essays* (New York: Harper & Brothers, 1917), 1.
78. *". . . instincts and business energy."*: Frank Munsey, "The Journalists and Journalism of New York," *Munsey's Magazine* (January 1892).
78. *expanded fifteen-fold:* Jno. Gilmer Sneed, "Do Newspapers Now Give the News?" *Forum* (August 1893), 707.
78. *". . . quadrupled the space."*: William Henry Nugent, "The Sports Section," *American Mercury* (March 1929), 336.
78. *". . . was simply a beneficiary."*: Michael Oriard, *Reading Football: How the Popular Press Created an American Spectacle* (Chapel Hill: University of North Carolina Press, 1993), 60.
78. *"football was simply available for promotion."*: Ibid., 70.
79. *". . . emulate the social elite."*: Ibid., 61.
79. *than actually see it:* Ibid.
79. *". . . on professional football in the 1950s and 1960s."*: Ibid., 57.
80. *". . . were greatly pleased."*: Lewis, 118.
80. *more than 1,800 by 1900:* James Playsted Wood, *Magazines in the United States* (New York: Ronald, 1956), 99–100, 103.
80. *nearly 300 percent:* Frank Presbrey, *The History and Development of Advertising* (Garden City, NY: Doubleday, 1929), 353.
80. *". . . and cut recitations."*: Richard Harding Davis, "The Story of Two Collegains," *Harper's Weekly*, July 4, 1891.

80. *". . . strength of a gentleman.":* Ibid.

80. *". . . of the 1890s.":* Oriard, 187.

CHAPTER 9

82. *on the Badgers' prospects:* "Football Prospects," *Milwaukee Sentinel,* September 27, 1897, 2.

82. *". . . remains somewhat problematical.":* Roy L. Foley, "Willie Hoppe Had Nothing on O'Dea Putting 'English' on Ball," *Wisconsin News,* December 1, 1934, 12.

82. *one that now appeared "strong.":* "All O.K. at Madison," *Minneapolis Journal,* October 2, 1897.

83. *". . . solved the fullback problem for Wisconsin.":* Ibid.

83. *basic tackling techniques:* "Battle for Victory," *Daily Cardinal,* September 29, 1897, 1.

83. *". . . invited his charges to throw him.":* "Great Day at Hand," *Minneapolis Journal,* October 28, 1897.

83. *". . . with the armor used.":* Ibid.

83. *"plan worked admirably.":* Ibid.

84. *"Play up sharp, Charley!":* John Stuart Martin, "Walter Camp and His Gridiron Game," *American Hertiage* 12, no. 6 (October 1961).

84. *who would carry the ball:* Alexander M. Weyand, *The Saga of American Football* (New York: Macmillan, 1955), 33.

84. *a part of the varsity team:* Amos Alonzo Stagg and Wesley Winans Stout, *Touchdown!* (New York: Longmans, Green and Co., 1927), 125.

84. *". . . in mental arithmetic.":* Ibid., 127.

84. *look slow by comparison:* For a rough idea of what the game looked like, see www.youtube.com/watch?v=YHBNu-qzGNE.

85. *"Pat O'Dea is a wonderful kicker.":* "Train Up Kickers," *Chicago Daily Tribune,* October 4, 1897, 4.

85. *". . . to achieve this end.":* "Is Wisconsin to Win?" *Daily Cardinal,* October 27, 1897, 1.

85. *". . . than it did a week ago.":* "Same Story over Again," *Daily Cardinal,* October 26, 1897, 2.

85. *". . . towards the Varsity eleven.":* "Is Wisconsin to Win?" *Daily Cardinal,* October 27, 1897, 1.

85–86. *". . . in the Old Town Tonight.":* Ibid.

86. *those didn't catch on:* Ibid., and "The Cheers and Songs," *(Milwaukee) Sunday Sentinel,* October 31, 1897, Part Four, 1.

86. *team marched in single file:* "'Twas the Best of All," *Daily Cardinal,* October 28, 1897, 1.

86. *"... to win the game!":* Pyre's speech is paraphrased from ibid. Pyre "reviewed the team in a rapid manner, concluding with O'Dea, of whom he said that it would not be necessary for Wisconsin to make any touchdowns, since he alone could kick enough goals from the field to win the game."

87. *"... forgive all his shortcomings.":* "Great Day at Hand," *Minneapolis Journal,* October 28, 1897.

87. *fifteen players apiece:* "A Royal Send-Off," *Daily Cardinal,* October 29, 1897, 1.

87. *"the West Hotel in downtown Minneapolis:* Wisconsin 39, Minnesota 0, October 30, 1897. Descriptions of the game taken from "O'Dea's Great Kick," *(Milwaukee) Sunday Sentinel,* October 31, 1897, 1; Dick Hyland, "The Hyland Fling," *Los Angeles Times,* February 6, 1949, 26; "Mourning at the U," *Saint Paul Globe,* October 31, 1897, 9; "Gophers' Waterloo," *Chicago Daily Tribune,* October 31, 1897, 5; and Roy L. Foley, "Pat O'Dea Disclaims Playing Hero's Role," *Wisconsin News,* 1934, excerpted from chapter two of Foley's twelve-chapter series on O'Dea.

88. *not a recent phenomenon:* "O'Dea's Great Kick," *(Milwaukee) Sunday Sentinel,* October 31, 1897, 1.

88. *"... a deaf and dumb man at a singing school.":* Ibid.

88. *"... a belligerent German at an Irish picnic.":* Ibid.

88. *"the really great spectacular event of the contest.":* Ibid.

89. *"... shot by rule and line.":* Ibid. In the original source of this quotation, the word "straight" appears as "straigth." For purposes of clarity, I have corrected the typographical error.

89. *twirled himself completely around:* "Mourning at the U," *Saint Paul Globe,* October 31, 1897, 9.

89. *"... 40 yards out on the dead run.":* Dick Hyland, "The Hyland Fling," *Los Angeles Times,* February 6, 1949, 26.

89. *"... O'Dea got it off.":* Ibid. In the original source of this quotation, the word "when" appears as "whe." For purposes of clarity, I have corrected the typographical error.

89. *rectified by game time:* "Is Wisconsin to Win?" *Daily Cardinal,* October 7, 1948, 1.

89. *". . . rustle the maples that day.":* Prescott Sullivan, "The Low Down," *San Francisco Chronicle,* October 7, 1898.

90. *". . . Ain't this a good enough game?":* "Mourning at the U," *Saint Paul Globe,* October 31, 1897, 9.

90. *". . . other things than punt.":* "O'Dea's Great Kick," *(Milwaukee) Sunday Sentinel,* October 31, 1897, 1.

90. *". . . pleased the watching thousands.":* "Gophers' Waterloo," *Chicago Daily Tribune,* October 31, 1897, 5.

90. *". . . even for a single minute.":* "O'Dea's Great Kick," *(Milwaukee) Sunday Sentinel,* October 31, 1897, 1.

90. *". . . against Minnesota in a football game.":* "Struggles of Past Years," *(Milwaukee) Sunday Sentinel,* October 31, 1897, Part Four, 1.

91. *red-clad revelers:* "O'Dea's Great Kick," *(Milwaukee) Sunday Sentinel,* October 31, 1897, 1.

91. *less than musical, din:* "Madison Goes Wild," *(Milwaukee) Sunday Sentinel,* October 31, 1897, Part Four, 1.

91. *well into the evening:* "A Grand Celebration," *Daily Cardinal,* November 1, 1897, 1.

91. *"waiting to glimpse the kicking kangaroo.":* Roy L. Foley, "Pat O'Dea Disclaims Playing Hero's Role," *Wisconsin News,* 1934, excerpted from chapter two of Foley's twelve-chapter series on O'Dea, unknown date.

91. *". . . lusty Wisconsin yells.":* "A Grand Celebration," *Daily Cardinal,* November 1, 1897, 1.

92. *slowly began to drift home:* Ibid.

Chapter 10

93. *". . . occurred in the South.":* "Virginia vs. Georgia," *Red and Black,* October 30, 1897, 1.

93. *". . . to win or die.":* Ibid.

93. *into the line:* Christopher C. Meyers, "'Unrelenting War on Football': The Death of Richard Von Gammon and the Attempt to Ban Football in Georgia," *Georgia Historical Quarterly* 93, no. 4 (Winter 2009), 388–407.

94. *". . . tripped and fell on him.":* *Atlanta Journal,* November 1, 1897, as quoted in Meyers.

94. *". . . got out of humor.":* George Magruder Battey, *A History of Rome and Floyd County, State of Georgia, United States of America: Including Numerous Incidents of More than Local Interest, 1540–1922* (Atlanta: Webb and Vary, 1922), 345.

94. *mitts and football equipment:* Ibid., 344.

94. *Daughters of the Confederacy:* "Gammon of the Georgia," *Macon Telegraph,* October 31, 1897, 18.

94. *freshly prepared sweets:* Battey, 344.

94. *the tree was spared:* Ibid., 348.

95. *to a nearby hospital:* "A Fatal Game in Atlanta," *New York Times,* October 31, 1897.

95. *father at his side:* Battey, 346.

95. *disband the University of Georgia football team:* "Colleges and Football," *Macon Telegraph,* November 2, 1897, 6.

95. *signature to become law:* Cal Powell, "The Day One Woman Saved Football," *Red and Black,* October 30, 1997, 1.

95. *". . . a great American game.":* All quotes in this paragraph from Meyers.

95. *". . . object of his life.":* Ibid., Powell.

96. *". . . principle of our government.":* Meyers.

96. *"The Woman Who Saved Southern Football.":* Ernie Harwell, "How a Woman Saved Southern Football," *Saturday Evening Post,* October 14, 1944.

97. *". . . for they did not beat Yale.":* Ralph J. Findlay, "The Abuses of Training," *Harvard Graduates' Magazine* (March 1894), 322–28.

97. *". . . eleven other youths dressed in blue.":* Frank W. Taussig, "A Professor's View of Athletics," *Harvard Graduates' Magazine* (March 1895), 308–9.

97. *"the ever present liability to death on the field.":* "President Eliot's Report," *Harvard Graduates' Magazine* (March 1895), 367.

97. *". . . gamblers and rowdies all contribute.":* Ibid.

97. *"There's murder in that game.":* Amos Alonzo Stagg and Wesley Winans Stout, *Touchdown!* (New York: Longmans, Green and Co., 1927), 91.

98. *to ban the game:* Albert Bushnell Hart, "The Documents of the Football Question," *Harvard Graduates' Magazine* (June 1895), 519–27.

98. *". . . the main purpose of college life.":* Ibid.

98. *the game should and would continue:* Ibid.

98. "*. . . because the risk exists.":* Theodore Roosevelt, "Value of an Athletic Training," *Harper's Weekly,* December 23, 1893, 1236.

98. "*. . . than give it up.":* Theodore Roosevelt to Walter Camp, March 11, 1895, Walter Chauncey Camp Papers, box 21, folder 593, Yale University Archives.

98. "*. . . for being world-conquerors.":* "Commencement. —The Alumni Dinner. Senator Lodge," *Harvard Graduates' Magazine* (September 1896), 66.

99. *the rise of bare-knuckle boxing:* Elliott Gorn, *The Manly Art: Bare-Knuckle Prize Fighting in America* (Ithaca, NY: Cornell University Press, 1986), 192, as quoted in Michael Kimmel, *Manhood in America: A Cultural History* (New York: Free Press, 1996), 118.

99. "*. . . that is what I want to preserve.":* Henry James, *The Bostonians* (New York: Modern Library, 2003), 325–26.

99. "*. . . conquests on the gridiron.":* Stephen Ducat, *The Wimp Factor: Gender Gaps, Holy Wars, and the Politics of Anxious Masculinity* (Boston: Beacon Press, 2004), 75.

99. "*. . . hit the line hard!":* Theodore Roosevelt, *The Strenuous Life* (New York: Review of Reviews, 1904), 137.

100. "*. . . vigorous and unsullied manhood,":* John Sayle Watterson, *College Football: History, Spectacle, Controversy* (Baltimore: Johns Hopkins University Press, 2000), 42. Article is clipped, without specifying origins in University of Chicago Archives, PDF file ofcpreshjb-0020-0080-01.pdf.

100. "*. . . all other agencies combined.":* Ibid.

100. "*. . . all the letters received . . . are printed.":* Walter Camp, *Football Facts and Figures. A Symposium of Expert Opinions on the Game's Place in American Athletics* (New York: Harper & Brothers, 1894), viii.

100. *responses were omitted:* Watterson, 33.

100. *"cooled my ardor for the game personally.":* Camp, 161, 164.

100. "*. . . nambypambyism, then play football.":* Ibid., 46.

101. "*. . . who has been seriously injured.":* Ibid., 209–10.

101. *fresh men into the game:* Quotes from captains all from "Opinions of Captains," *Chicago Daily Tribune,* November 11, 1897, 4.

101. "*. . . thirty thousand spectators.":* "Slugball Courage," *Chicago Daily Tribune,* December 9, 1896, 6.

101. *". . . crippled in the course of it."*: This is excerpted from a *New York Tribune* editorial, as quoted in "Slugball," *Chicago Daily Tribune,* November 9, 1897, 6.

102. *hence, the term "yellow."*: James McGrath Morris, *Pulitzer: A Life in Politics, Print, and Power* (New York: Harper, 2010), 330–31.

102. *". . . not fail to get a thrill of interest."*: Will Irwin, "The American Newspaper," *Collier's,* February 18, 1911, 16.

102. *". . . widely discussed newspaper in New York."*: Ibid., 14.

102. *". . . a temple of America's new mass media."*: Morris, 287.

102. *". . . even amplified Pulitzer's approach."*: Irwin, 22.

102. *". . . World and Journal became melodrama."*: Ibid.

103. *text of Georgia's antifootball bill*: Michael Oriard, *Reading Football: How the Popular Press Created an American Spectacle* (Chapel Hill: University of North Carolina Press, 1993), 205.

103. *". . . in every football game."*: Illustration, *New York. World,* November 14, 1897, 1.

103. *". . . campaigns for circulation."*: Oriard, 203.

103. *". . . being exposed as mayhem."*: Ibid.

103. *". . . savage instincts of onlookers."*: "Death on the Football Field," *New York Herald,* November 13, 1897, 4.

103. *that was plaguing the sport*: "Harvard or Yale the Cry To-Day," *New York Herald,* November 13, 1897, 4.

104. *all of them in 1897 alone*: Amos Alonzo Stagg Papers, University of Chicago Archives, various unlabeled newspaper clippings.

CHAPTER 11

105. *". . . black with people."*: "Chicago is Beaten," *Chicago Daily Tribune,* November 14, 1897, 3.

105. *packed into the grandstand*: "Madison, 23; Chicago, 8," *(Milwaukee) Sunday Sentinel,* November 14, 1897, 1.

105. *nothing but dread*: "Plotke Sees a Game," *Chicago Daily Tribune,* November 14, 1897, 4.

106. *". . . forehead in drops."*: All quotes in this paragraph from ibid.

106. *to the meeting*: "Alderman Killed," *Chicago Daily Tribune,* November 9, 1897, 1.

106. *election to the city council:* "Nathan M. Plotke," *Illinois Stats-Zeitung,* July 16, 1900, 5; http://flps.newberry.org/article/5418474_11_1584/.

106. *in the city's theaters:* "War on Theater Hats," *Chicago Daily Tribune,* January 5, 1897, 1.

106. *"the hat ordinance man.":* "Plotke Sees a Game," *Chicago Daily Tribune,* November 14, 1897, 4.

106. *between five and fifty dollars:* "Seeks to Bar Football," *Chicago Daily Tribune,* November 9, 1897, 1.

106. *". . . colleges a few years ago.":* "Abolish Slugball Now," *Chicago Daily Tribune,* December 6, 1896, 30.

107. *". . . for this elevating purpose.":* "The Slugball Season," *Chicago Daily Tribune,* September 26, 1897, 30.

107. *". . . often fatal practice.":* "He Defends Slugball," *Chicago Daily Tribune,* November 22, 1897, 9.

107. *". . . been severely injured.":* "More Slugball Casualties," *Chicago Daily Tribune,* November 12, 1897, 6.

107. SURE WISCONSIN AND CHICAGO LADS WILL INFLICT DEATH, *read another:* "Plotke Sees a Game," *Chicago Daily Tribune,* November 14, 1897, 4.

108. *". . . of the wounded, I suppose.":* Ibid.

108. *". . . Garibaldi and George Washington.":* Ibid.

108. *". . . on his way to a carriage.":* Ibid.

108. *". . . in football circles as at present.":* "Await the Kickoff," *Daily Cardinal,* November 10, 1897, 2.

108. *"over the heads of the baffled collegiate.":* "O'Dea's Day Again," *Milwaukee Sentinel,* November 7, 1897, 26.

109. *eighteen-member university band:* "Off for the Battle," *Daily Cardinal,* November 12, 1897, 1.

109. *a severe stomach ache:* Amos Alonzo Stagg and Wesley Winans Stout, *Touchdown!* (New York: Longmans, Green and Co., 1927), 207.

109. *"of no use to us.":* "Stagg Tells Grid Story," *Baltimore Sun,* November 6, 1957, S26.

109. *the Badgers struck:* Wisconsin 23, Chicago 8—November 13, 1897. Game descriptions taken from the following sources: Roy L. Foley, "Champions of the West in '97 —and Badgers Won Title for Gobbling Turkeys, Too," *Wisconsin News,* 1934, unknown date; "Chicago Is Beaten," *Chicago Daily Tribune,* November 14, 1897, 3; "Madison, 23; Chicago, 8," *(Milwaukee) Sunday Sentinel,* November 14, 1897,

1; "25 to 8," *Daily Cardinal,* November 13, 1897, 1; "Nothing to Nothing," *Sioux City Journal,* November 14, 1897; "The 'Kangaroo' Kicker," *Middleville (Michigan) Sun,* December 9, 1897.

110. *". . . It had enough.":* "Chicago Is Beaten," *Chicago Daily Tribune,* November 14, 1897, 3.

110. *". . . they do the game.":* "Madison, 23; Chicago, 8," *(Milwaukee) Sunday Sentinel,* November 14, 1897, 1.

110. *". . . in the house.":* Ibid.

111. *"all the loose wood at Ladies' hall.":* "Red Fire in Madison," *(Milwaukee) Sunday Sentinel,* November 14, 1897.

111. *"one man's toe settled the struggle.":* "Chicago Is Beaten," *Chicago Daily Tribune,* November 14, 1897, 3.

111. *". . . brilliant feature of the day.":* "Madison, 23; Chicago, 8," *(Milwaukee) Sunday Sentinel,* November 14, 1897, 1.

111. *". . . for such a move.":* "Will Refuse," *Milwaukee Journal,* November 15, 1897, 1.

112. *defeated 57 to 5:* "Plotke Fails at Tackle," *Chicago Daily Tribune,* November 16, 1897, 1.

112. *loss of the season:* "Varsity Defeated," *Daily Cardinal,* November 22, 1897, 1.

112. *". . . a bunch of quitters.":* Meir Z. Ribalow, "Phil King '93, Little Big Man," *Princeton Alumni Weekly,* September 26, 1977, 19.

112. *". . . length and beauty.":* "Kicker O'Dea," *Milwaukee Journal,* November 24, 1897.

113. *". . . he gave it up.":* Ibid.

113. *". . . at a bench show.":* Ibid.

113. *". . . peculiar side movement.":* Ibid.

113. *cruised to a 22–0 win:* "Badgers Head List," *Duluth News Tribune,* November 26, 1897.

113. *turkey disappeared quickly:* Roy L. Foley, "Champions of the West in '97 —and Badgers Won Title for Gobbling Turkeys, Too," *Wisconsin News,* 1934, unknown date.

113. *". . . all the others.":* "Easy for Wisconsin," *Daily Cardinal,* November 29, 1897, 1. Note: Accounts of the period did not capitalize team names. I have capitalized team names throughout the text to adhere to modern usage.

114. *"... wonderful leg of Pat O'Dea.":* Quote from the *Chippewa Falls Herald* appeared in "Football's New Friends," *Daily Cardinal,* November 19, 1897, 2.

114. *"... make the game less rough.":* "No More Slugball," *Chicago Daily Tribune,* November 27, 1897, 1.

114. *"but it cannot be continued as at present.":* Ibid.

114. *"... in a much-needed reform.":* Ibid.

114–115. *for their "impertinence.":* Stagg and Stout, 209.

115. *"... What are they doing?":* "Where Are Those Reforms?" *Chicago Daily Tribune,* January 16, 1898, 30.

CHAPTER 12

116. *"... honest university sport.":* Caspar Whitney, *A Sporting Pilgrimage; Riding to Hounds, Golf, Rowing, Football, Club and University Athletics. Studies in English Sport, Past and Present* (New York: Harper, 1895), 113.

116. *limitations of the cameras:* John Adams Blanchard, *The H Book of Harvard Athletics 1852–1922* (Cambridge, MA: Harvard Varsity Club, 1923), 392.

116. *$3 million in today's currency:* John Sayle Watterson, *College Football: History, Spectacle, Controversy* (Baltimore: Johns Hopkins University Press, 2000), 17.

116. *"The P. T. Barnum of education.":* Robin Lester, *Stagg's University: The Rise, Decline, and Fall of Big-Time Football at Chicago* (Urbana: University of Illinois Press, 1995), 18.

117. *at least one against Stanford:* Amos Alonzo Stagg and Wesley Winans Stout, *Touchdown!* (New York: Longmans, Green and Co., 1927), 189.

117. *a seat at the Chicago-Michigan game:* Ibid., 91.

117. *75 percent of the gate receipts:* "Stagg's Eleven May Go to California," *Chicago Daily Tribune,* December 10, 1894, 11.

117. *"... for 50 per cent.":* "Chicago Varsity Team Is Made Up," *Chicago Daily Tribune,* December 15, 1894, 3.

117. *"we could use the advertising.":* Stagg and Stout, 191.

117. *"... university's name in print.":* Ibid.

118. *for a nominal fee:* "Chicago Varsity Team Is Made Up," *Chicago Daily Tribune,* December 15, 1894, 3.

118. *in anticipation of the trip:* Stagg and Stout, 193.
118. *for the luggage and food:* "Given a Big Send Off," *Chicago Times,* December 20, 1894, 6.
118. *". . . who are to be its occupants.":* Lester, 29.
118. *". . . as a culinary artist.":* "Given a Big Send Off," *Chicago Times,* December 20, 1894, 6; "Off for the Coast," *Chicago Herald,* December 20, 1894, 5.
118. *of the train car:* "Stagg's Eleven on Its Way West," *Chicago Daily Tribune,* December 20, 1894, 11.
118. *". . . we reach the Golden Gate.":* "Chicago Varsity Team Is Made Up," *Chicago Daily Tribune,* December 15, 1894, 3.
118. *he recalled many years later:* Stagg and Stout, 193.
119. *". . . burnt to a crisp.":* Ibid., 194.
119. *"a picnic.":* Lester, 29.
119. *". . . did not have to chew.":* Stagg and Stout, 197.
119. *which totaled $136:* Ibid., 199.
119. *". . . characterized by inter-regional play.":* Lester, 131.
120. *". . . were celebrated like the Second Coming.":* Milton Mayer, "Portrait of a Dangerous Man," *Harper's* (July 1946).
120. *". . . we do have it.":* Stagg and Stout, 203.
120. *". . . both students and financial support.":* Michael Oriard, *Reading Football: How the Popular Press Created an American Spectacle* (Chapel Hill: University of North Carolina Press, 1993), 173.
120. *". . . Go out and win.":* Charlie Brown Hershey, *Colorado College, 1874–1949* (Colorado Springs: Colorado College, 1952), 82.
121. *in the* Harvard Graduates' Magazine *in 1895:* Robert W. Emmons, "Needed Football Reforms," *Harvard Graduates' Magazine* (March 1895), 319.
121. *". . . at such institutions as Harvard and Yale.":* "President Eliot's Report for 1892–'93," *Harvard Graduates' Magazine* (March 1894), 377.
121. *". . . the increasing glorification of college athletics.":* Edwin Godkin, "The Glorification of Athletics," *Nation,* December 1, 1892, 406.
121. *". . . for the treasury of the university.":* "Slugball Courage," *Chicago Daily Tribune,* December 9, 1896, 6.
121. *". . . over the western world and to 'lick' Michigan.":* Lester, 137.
121. *to declare themselves candidates for a degree:* Caspar Whitney, "Amateur Sport," *Harper's Weekly,* December 2, 1899, 1217.

122. *". . . not a half a mile away.":* Ibid.
122. *rules for Chicago athletes:* See, for instance, Stagg to J. C. Knowlton, January 9, 1897, and Knowlton to Stagg, January 14, 1897. Amos Alonzo Stagg Papers, University of Chicago Archives, box 90, folder 1. Stagg asked Knowlton for an exception to the rules to allow one of Chicago's players to participate despite his ineligibility. Knowlton responded that they had many men in similar situations, but that Michigan would not allow them to play. "I must say Professor Stagg, that any exception of any kind whatsoever, to any of these rules, cannot be made in the interest of pure athletics."
122. *"needs thorough shaking up.":* Caspar Whitney, "Amateur Sport," *Harper's Weekly,* December 2, 1899, 1217.
122. *"Last year cost us $1100.":* "The Athletic Controversy," Amos Alonzo Stagg Papers, University of Chicago Archives, box 88.
122. *". . . enough to make all share alike.":* Clipping from an unnamed newspaper, Stagg Papers, University of Chicago Archives, box 88.
124. *distorting the world of college football:* "The Athletic Controversy," Amos Alonzo Stagg Papers, box 88.
124. *". . . of a big successful business?":* Caspar Whitney, "Amateur Sport," *Harper's Weekly,* October 21, 1899, 1073.
124. *to have seen the men compete:* "Must Answer Charges," *Chicago Daily Tribune,* May 26, 1898, 4.
124. *Western Intercollegiate Amateur Athletic Association:* "Colleges in a Row," *Chicago Daily Tribune,* June 4, 1898, 7.
124. *scheduled for the fall of 1898:* Insinuated in Adams to Harper letter of July 16, 1898: "In cancelling the football game scheduled for the fall of 1898, Chicago has either broken a written contract, or has indicated that she regards a written contract of no binding force." This is in digital files of University of Chicago Archives, ofcpreshjb-0020-0090-01.
124. *". . . as unsportsmanlike and childish.":* "Fight for Control," *Chicago Daily Tribune,* June 6, 1898, 9.
124. *had refused to hear the information:* Ibid.
125. *"whether their course is right or wrong.":* Ibid.
125. *that lacked both "comity" and "courtesy.":* Adams to Harper letter of July 16, 1898. This is in digital files of University of Chicago Archives, ofcpreshjb-0020-0090-01.

Chapter 13

126. *not far from Madison:* "Takes Radical Action," *Chicago Daily Tribune*, September 24, 1898, 4.

127. *". . . had played under assumed names.":* "Important Letters," *Daily Cardinal*, September 28, 1898, 1, 3.

127. *which they had already earned:* "Much Sympathy for Maybury," *Chicago Daily Tribune*, September 25, 1898, 6.

127. *felt was appropriate against them:* "Takes Radical Action," *Chicago Daily Tribune*, September 24, 1898, 4.

127. *". . . in favor of their encouragement and support.":* "Important Letters," *Daily Cardinal*, September 28, 1898, 1, 3.

128. *eagerly awaited a response:* "Accepts Chicago Conditions," *Chicago Daily Tribune*, September 23, 1898, 4.

128. *properly from the outset:* "Much Sympathy for Maybury," *Chicago Daily Tribune*, September 25, 1898, 6.

128. *". . . we care what happens [with Wisconsin]?":* "Will Bury the Hatchet," *Chicago Daily Tribune*, September 28, 1898, 4.

128. *". . . than any occurrence in years.":* "Much Sympathy for Maybury," *Chicago Daily Tribune*, September 25, 1898, 6.

128. *come up with new solutions:* "Colleges Are at Peace," *Chicago Daily Tribune*, September 29, 1898, 4.

128. *far from a guarantee of success:* "Sporting," *Los Angeles Times*, October 10, 1898, 7.

128. *"never been tested in an executive position.":* "Pat O'Dea for Captain," *Milwaukee Sentinel*, September 12, 1898, 2.

129. *would be returning to play for the Badgers:* Ibid.

129. *the Chicago Tribune reported:* "Birge Tells Them to Quit," *Chicago Daily Tribune*, September 20, 1898, 4.

129. *early portions of the season:* "True State of Affairs," *Daily Cardinal*, October 27, 1898, 3.

129. *". . . and the disbanding of the team.":* "Important Mass Meeting To-Night!" *Daily Cardinal*, October 27, 1898, 1.

129. *". . . WE MUST HAVE MORE CANDIDATES OUT FOR PRACTICE.":* "Deplorable Lack of Football Material," *Daily Cardinal*, October 27, 1898, 1.

129. *". . . not come out for one night, then quit.":* "Outlook Disheartening," *Daily Cardinal*, October 27, 1898, 1.

129. *". . . know the formations and signals.":* "Coach King's Opinion," *Daily Cardinal,* October 27, 1898, 1.

130. *would not be able to play against Minnesota:* Roy L. Foley, "O'Dea Gets Pair of Kangaroo Hide Shoes—Score of Next Game: 76 to 0," *Wisconsin News,* unknown date, 1934, chapter ten of twelve-chapter O'Dea series.

130. *from earlier in the week:* "Ready for Battle," *Daily Cardinal,* October 28, 1898, 1.

130. *". . . lethargy proved most effectual.":* "Football Practice," *Daily Cardinal,* November 1, 1898, 3.

130. *". . . while he was in grammar school.":* "Stagg May Retain Rogers," *Chicago Times-Herald,* November 5, 1898.

130. *Minds kept the information to himself:* "Evidence against Holmes," *Chicago Daily Tribune,* November 11, 1898, 4; "Maroons Are Under Fire," *Chicago Times-Herald,* November 6, 1898.

131. *". . . for the purpose of drawing spectators.":* Ibid.

131. *". . . Holmes had wrestled with professionals.":* "Holmes Gives Flat Denial," *Chicago Times-Herald,* November 7, 1898.

131. *the school's captain, Walter Kennedy:* "Maroons Are Under Fire," *Chicago Times-Herald,* November 6, 1898.

131. *later in the week:* Ibid.

131. *after playing for Beloit:* "Answer to Wisconsin," *Chicago Chronicle,* November 5, 1898.

132. *". . . every member of the Maroon team.":* "To Meet No More," *Chicago Times-Herald,* November 8, 1898. The original sentence read "every member of the maroon team." I have capitalized Maroon for the sake of clarity.

132. *withdrew from the team:* "Clarke Quits the Team," *Chicago Daily Tribune,* November 2, 1898, 4.

132. *". . . Again the poorer team won.":* "Football Song," *Daily Cardinal,* October 28, 1898, 1.

133. *". . . more pure and high-minded than their instructors?":* "As Others See Us," *Daily Cardinal,* October 12, 1898, 3, quoting an editorial from *Milwaukee Sentinel,* date unknown.

133. *in a secret location:* "Evidence against Holmes," *Chicago Daily Tribune,* November 11, 1898, 4.

133. *". . . boarded a street car and disappeared.":* "Spies on Stagg's Tactics," *Chicago Chronicle,* November 23, 1898.

133. *". . . such giants of the pigskin met on the gridiron."*: "May Be the Last," *Chicago Times-Herald,* November 12, 1898.

134. *inside the gymnasium due to field conditions:* "Practice in the Park," *(Chicago) Daily Inter Ocean,* November 11, 1898; "Ready for the Game," *(Chicago) Daily Inter Ocean,* November 12, 1898.

134. *". . . gone over with a steam roller."*: "Big Gridiron Game Today," *Chicago Chronicle,* November 12, 1898, 10.

134. *simply hoped for the best:* "Maroons Take the Game," *Chicago Chronicle,* November 13, 1898.

134. *"A pair of heroic limbs had gone wrong."*: "Maroons Best Badger Men," *Chicago Times-Herald,* November 13, 1898, 1.

134. *the* Daily Inter Ocean *reported:* "Chicago Men Win," *(Chicago) Daily Inter Ocean,* November 13, 1898, 1.

134. *King said afterward:* "Maroons Take the Game," *Chicago Chronicle,* November 13, 1898.

135. *". . . to make the field passably good,"*: Roy L. Foley, "O'Dea Gets Pair of Kangaroo Hide Shoes—Score of Next Game: 76 to 0," *Wisconsin News,* unknown date, 1934, chapter ten of twelve-chapter O'Dea series.

135. *". . . in the previous year."*: Caspar Whitney, "Amateur Sport," *Harper's Weekly,* December 31, 1898, 1301.

135. *". . . for the future."*: "Feeling Is High," *Chicago Times-Herald,* November 9, 1898.

135. *after he intentionally kicked O'Dea:* Roy L. Foley, "O'Dea Gets Pair of Kangaroo Hide Shoes—Score of Next Game: 76 to 0," *Wisconsin News,* unknown date, 1934, chapter ten of twelve-chapter O'Dea series; and "Chicago Men Win," *(Chicago) Daily Inter Ocean,* November 13, 1898, 1.

135. *". . . begotten of praise."*: "Roses for Pat O'Dea," *Milwaukee Sentinel,* November 15, 1898, 6.

135. *". . . performances of its kind in football annals."*: Caspar Whitney, "Amateur Sport," *Harper's Weekly,* December 31, 1898, 1301.

135. *"sixty-two yards to cover."*: Ibid.

135. *the longest field goal in the school's history: Wisconsin Football Fact Book,* 2011 edition, 129.

136. *". . . has immortalized himself in the annals of football."*: "Capt. O'Dea Breaks Two World's Records, Kicking Goal from the Sixty-Yard Line," *Chicago Times-Herald,* November 25, 1898.

136. *a few others broke through in that 1898 season:* Alexander M.Weyand, *The Saga of American Football* (New York: Macmillan, 1955), 197.

136. *". . . the unthinking pupil of the East.":* Caspar Whitney, "Amateur Sport," *Harper's Weekly,* December 17, 1898, 1248.

CHAPTER 14

137. *to see them off:* "Off for New Haven," *Daily Cardinal,* October 16, 1899, 1.

137. *"crude blacksmiths, miners and backwoodsmen.":* As quoted in Caspar Whitney, "Amateur Sport," *Harper's Weekly,* November 13, 1895, 1124.

138. *". . . like changing caste in India.":* "A Forecast of the Football Season," *Outing, an Illustrated Monthly Magazine of Recreation* (November 1899), 172.

138. *the Badgers taking on Yale:* Ibid.

138. *a dangerous attitude to take:* Walter Camp, "Watch Western Teams," *Chicago Daily Tribune,* October 8, 1899, 20.

138. *". . . The interesting question is, 'How soon?'":* Ibid.

138. *remembered many years later:* Henry J. McCormick, ". . . Henry J. McCormick Means No Foolin'!" *Wisconsin State Journal,* November 11, 1940, 11.

138. *to protect them against bad luck:* "Badgers in Form," *(Chicago) Daily Inter Ocean,* October 14, 1899.

139. *". . . we shall surely come back winners.":* "Off for New Haven," *Daily Cardinal,* October 16, 1899, 1.

139. *". . . the anticipation of the game itself.":* "Football Contrasts," *(New Haven) Evening Leader,* October 21, 1899, 11.

139. *letters from flirtatious women:* Betty Cass, "Madison Day by Day," *Wisconsin State Journal,* September 28, 1934, 1, Part 2.

139. *". . . Send up a carriage right away!":* Ibid. I have italicized "Pot" to highlight the writer's mimicking of O'Dea's accent.

140. *". . . its fullness, richness and purity.":* "'Lucia' at the Opera," *New York Times,* December 5, 1893.

140. *and the queen of England: Australian Dictionary of Biography,* vol. 10; http://adb.anu.edu.au/biography/melba-dame-nellie-7551.

140. *well-known claimant to the French throne:* Ibid.

140. *the paper explained:* "Chumming with Melba," *New York World,* February 27, 1899, 4.

140. WITHSTOOD THE PRIMA DONNA'S APPEAL: "Melba and Pat O'Dea," *St. Paul Globe,* March 5, 1899, 10.

140. *". . . of one of its particular stars.":* Ibid.

140. *". . . you are playing here in America.'":* Ibid.

140. *". . . from the field as good as dead.":* Ibid.

140. *ran 100 yards for a touchdown:* Roy L. Foley, "Rip Van Winkle of the Grid," *Wisconsin News,* December 8, 1934, 12, chapter eleven of twelve-chapter O'Dea series. Foley was quoting an unspecified newspaper article from O'Dea's time: "The principal feature of the game was the phenomenal run of O'Dea who sprinted down the field covering 100 yards and making a touchdown." O'Dea's run is not listed in the Wisconsin record book.

141. *". . . got it on a fumble.":* "Badgers' Easy Victory," *Chicago Daily Tribune,* October 15, 1899, 17.

141. *"made only by the wonderful punting of Captain O'Dea.":* Ibid.

141. *". . . push the Badgers all over the field.":* "Badgers' Easy Game," *Sunday (Chicago) Times-Herald,* October 15, 1899; "Badgers' Easy Victory," *Chicago Daily Tribune,* October 15, 1899, 17.

141. *important contest was still a week away:* "Badgers' Easy Game," *Sunday (Chicago) Times-Herald,* October 15, 1899.

141. *". . . appeared to be saving himself.":* Ibid.

141. *". . . would be disastrous.":* "Score, 38 to 0 for Wisconsin," *(Milwaukee) Sunday Sentinel,* October 15, 1899, 1.

141. *". . . continued so in part of the second.":* Ibid.

142. *". . . better condition to meet Yale.":* Ibid.

142. *took a few minutes to run around:* "Badgers Enroute," *Daily Cardinal,* October 17, 1899, 1.

142. *down to New Haven on Saturday morning:* "Journey Is Ended," *Daily Cardinal,* October 18, 1899, 1.

142. *prevent them from spying on Wisconsin:* "Trinity Interferes," *Daily Cardinal,* October 19, 1899, 1.

142. *proceedings through binoculars:* "Spies See Badgers Work," *Chicago Chronicle,* October 19, 1899.

142. *"an unusually fast, snappy team.":* "Badgers at Hartford," *Chicago Daily Tribune,* October 19, 1899, 4.

142. *"kicking was a revelation to the onlookers."*: Ibid.

142. *his ability to snap the ball:* Ibid.

142. *during the course of the week:* Unheadlined article datelined "New Haven, Conn., Oct 18," *Daily Cardinal,* October 19, 1899, 4. Article is credited to the *Chicago Times-Herald.*

142. *"modestly declined even to hazard a guess.":* "Yale–Wisconsin Game," *(New Haven) Morning Journal Courier,* October 20, 1899.

142–143. *". . . cannot be a shadow of a doubt.":* "Yale Tomorrow," *Daily Cardinal,* October 20, 1899, 1.

143. *as Wisconsin's greatest strength:* "Yale Practice Is Secret," *Chicago Chronicle,* October 16, 1899.

143. *was at an all-time high:* All details on arrangements to follow the game in Madison are from "Reports from Yale," *Daily Cardinal,* October 18, 1899, 1.

143. *didn't confine his ingenuity to baseball:* Peter Morris, *A Game of Inches: The Stories Behind the Innovations That Shaped Baseball: The Game on the Field* (Chicago: Ivan R. Dee, 2006), 293.

143. *"a great 'Educator' of football.":* Reprinted letter from Phil King to Arthur Irwin, *Daily Cardinal,* October 19, 1899, 4.

143. *thirteen hundred seats in advance:* "Many Games Today," *(New Haven) Evening Leader,* October 21, 1899.

143. *the* Daily Cardinal *reported:* "Yale Tomorrow," *Daily Cardinal,* October 20, 1899, 1.

143. *Saturday to head to New Haven:* Andrew M. O'Dea, "Badgers at Work at Hartford," *Chicago Daily Tribune,* October 20, 1899, 4.

144. *until after the game:* "Aftermath," *Daily Cardinal,* October 24, 1899, 1; "Three Players Injured," *Milwaukee Sentinel,* October 25, 1899, 6.

144. *hampered his movements:* Ibid.

144. *heard above the din:* "The Football Bets," *(New Haven) Evening Leader,* October 21, 1899, 1.

144. *adorned with Yale flags and banners:* This and the pregame descriptions that follow are taken from "Eastern Opinions," *Daily Cardinal,* October 25, 1899, 1.

144. *"a fat little dago.":* Ibid.

145. *earlier in the decade:* Alexander M. Weyand, *The Saga of American Football* (New York: Macmillan, 1955), 206.

145. *as the Badgers brought:* "Yale Wins but a Close Shave," *(Milwaukee) Sunday Sentinel,* October 22, 1899, 1.

145. *"seemed unconscious of the interest he aroused,":* "Eastern Opinions," *Daily Cardinal,* October 25, 1899, 1.

145. *". . . such prominent newspaper men.":* "Came with Wisconsin Team," *New Haven Evening Register,* October 23, 1899, 1.

145. *at its back for the first half:* Wisconsin vs. Yale. October 21, 1899. The account of the game is drawn from the following sources: "Yale Wins but a Close Shave," *(Milwaukee)Sunday Sentinel,* October 22, 1899, 1; "O'Dea the Whole Thing," *Milwaukee Sentinel,* October 24, 1899, 4; "Badgers Lose to Yale," *Daily Cardinal,* October 21, 1899, 1; "Aftermath," *Daily Cardinal,* October 24, 1899, 1; "Eastern Opinions," *Daily Cardinal,* October 25, 1899, 1; "Few Famous Kickers," *Washington Post,* December 25, 1910, 53; "Yale Beats Badgers," *Philadelphia Inquirer,* October 22, 1899; "Yale, 6; Wisconsin, 0," *New York Times,* October 22, 1899, 4; "Barely Wins Out," *Boston Globe,* October 22, 1899, 16; "In the Football World," *New York Sun,* October 27, 1899, 5; "Football," *(New Haven) Morning Journal Courier,* October 23, 1899, 1; "Yale's Crack Player," *(New Haven) Evening Leader,* October 23, 1899, 1; "Holds Badgers Safe," *(Chicago) Daily Inter Ocean,* October 22, 1899; "Westerners Win Defeat," *Omaha World Herald,* October 22, 1899; "Three Players Injured," *Milwaukee Sentinel,* October 25, 1899, 6; "Yale's Great Victory Saturday Men Were in Splendid Condition," *(New Haven) Evening Leader,* October 23, 1899; "Great Interest in Chicago," *(Milwaukee) Sunday Sentinel,* October 22, 1899, 11; "Eager Interest at Madison," *(Milwaukee) Sunday Sentinel,* October 22, 1899, 11.

145. *". . . blocking of drop kicks an easy matter.":* "Few Famous Kickers," *Washington Post,* December 25, 1910, 53.

146. *". . . We've got the wind and the game.":* "Yale's Great Victory Saturday Men Were in Splendid Condition," *(New Haven) Evening Leader,* October 23, 1899.

146. *". . . unexpected mettle and speed.":* "Great Interest in Chicago," *(Milwaukee) Sunday Sentinel,* October 22, 1899, 11.

146. *". . . we hope you will score.":* "Badgers Lose to Yale," *Daily Cardinal,* October 21, 1899, 1.

146. *"terrific plunges into the scrub line.":* "Yale's Crack Player," *(New Haven) Evening Leader,* October 23, 1899, 1.

147. *". . . never been equaled on the Yale field.":* "Yale, 6; Wisconsin, 0," *New York Times,* October 22, 1899, 4.

147. *"the house fairly went crazy.":* "Eager Interest at Madison," *(Milwaukee) Sunday Sentinel,* October 22, 1899, 11.

147. *". . . to bowl over with his free arm.":* "Yale Wins but a Close Shave," *(Milwaukee)Sunday Sentinel,* October 22, 1899, 1.

148. *". . . failed to bring down his man.":* "Aftermath," *Daily Cardinal,* October 24, 1899, 1.

148. *". . . ever witnessed on the Yale gridiron.":* "Yale, 6; Wisconsin, 0," *New York Times,* October 22, 1899, 4.

148. *". . . known enough to 'tackle low.'":* "Barely Wins Out," *Boston Globe,* October 22, 1899, 16.

148. *". . . under similar circumstances.":* "In the Football World," *New York Sun,* October 27, 1899, 5.

148. *". . . game of his life notwithstanding.":* "Aftermath," *Daily Cardinal,* October 24, 1899, 1.

148. *"marvelous man.":* Both quotes in this sentence are from "O'Dea the Whole Thing," *Milwaukee Sentinel,* October 24, 1899, 4. This article quoted various Eastern papers on O'Dea's performance.

148. *". . . great punter he was reported to be.":* Ibid.

148. *". . . O'Dea is a wonder.":* "Barely Wins Out," *Boston Globe,* October 22, 1899, 16.

148. *"O'Dea's punting for Wisconsin was marvelous.":* "Yale Beats Badgers," *Philadelphia Inquirer,* October 22, 1899.

148. *the* Globe *stated:* "Barely Wins Out," *Boston Globe,* October 22, 1899, 16.

148. *in the entire game:* "Yale, 6; Wisconsin, 0," *New York Times,* October 22, 1899, 4.

148. *". . . whatever danger she was in.":* As quoted in "O'Dea the Whole Thing," *Milwaukee Sentinel,* October 24, 1899, 4.

149. *". . . of the smaller New England colleges.":* Ibid.

149. *". . . the result will be reversed.":* "In the Football World," *New York Sun,* October 27, 1899, 5.

149. *"and the Badgers found it out today.":* As quoted in "O'Dea the Whole Thing," *Milwaukee Sentinel,* October 24, 1899, 4.

149. *The* Philadelphia Inquirer *called that part of his game "a disappointment.":* "Yale Beats Badgers," *Philadelphia Inquirer,* October 22, 1899.

149. *"terribly overrated" as a drop-kicker:* As quoted in "O'Dea the Whole Thing," *Milwaukee Sentinel,* October 24, 1899, 4; and "Barely Wins Out," *Boston Globe,* October 22, 1899, 16.

149. *made a "poo fizzle" of a third:* "Barely Wins Out," *Boston Globe,* October 22, 1899, 16.

150. *". . . with vividness for such a long period?":* Malcolm McLean, "Malcolm McLean Has Inside Dope on the Sport World Doings," *Atlanta Constitution,* May 28, 1917, 7.

150. *later in newspapers across the country:* For example, see "O'Dea and Haxall Greatest Kickers," *Oneonta (New York) Star,* November 4, 1929.

150. *". . . hit the crossbar against Yale from 64 yards.":* Grantland Rice, "The Greatest Kicker," *Atlanta Constitution,* January 30, 1944, 9B.

151. *described in the game reports:* 2012 Wisconsin Football Fact Book, 147.

151. *". . . was credited with another kick of 110 yards.":* Allison Danzig, "On College Gridirons," *New York Times,* November 13, 1934, 25.

151. *". . . to Yale's 5 yard line.":* "O'Dea Great Kicker," *Fort Worth Star Telegram,* November 16, 1906.

151. *". . . 1899 that went 117 yards.":* "Modern Punters Were Dubs Compared to Old Pat O'Dea," *(Butte) Montana Standard,* October 22, 1934, 7.

151. *". . . groaned a unanimous groan and sat down!":* Kenneth E. Kennedy, "Pat O'Dea Returns from Self-Imposed Exile," *Wisconsin State Journal,* November 15, 1934, 4.

151. *". . . on any gridiron in the world.":* "O'Dea Kicks a 60-Yard Goal," *Milwaukee Sentinel,* November 25, 1898, 1.

151. *"on decent ground.":* "O'Dea the Hero of the Field," *Chicago Times-Herald,* November 25, 1898.

151. *the gridiron was in "fine condition.":* "Story of Purple's Downfall," *Chicago Daily Tribune,* November 25, 1898, 2.

151. *in the three days before the contest:* "US Department of Agriculture, Illinois Section of the Climate and Crop Service, Report for November 1898," December 19, 1898.

152. *". . . from the sidelines with a slippery ball.":* George F. Downer, "Pat O'Dea's Kicking Feats Still Amaze Football Fans," *Wisconsin Athletic Review,* November 17, 1934, 12; "Modern Punteres Were Dubs Compared to Old Pat O'Dea," *(Butte) Montana Standard,* October 22, 1934, 7.

152. *"on the run from scrimmage" when he kicked it:* "Patrick O'Dea, 90, of Gridiron Dead," *New York Times*, April 5, 1962.

152. *". . . it became stabilized . . . at six inches.":* John Lardner, "Ruth Didn't Call That Home Run," *New York Times*, January 16, 1955.

152. *"was made from relatively bare ground.":* Ibid.

152. *"easily an 80 yard drop.":* "O'Dea Great Kicker," *Fort Worth Star Telegram*, November 16, 1906.

152. *"a kick of 80 yards.":* "Badgers Lose to Yale," *Daily Cardinal*, October 21, 1899, 1.

153. *which is the 77-yard boot described earlier:* Ibid.

153. *". . . to Yale's 8 yard line.":* "Barely Wins Out," *Boston Globe*, October 22, 1899, 16.

153. *". . . 95 yds for a touchdown.":* "Yale Beats Badgers," *Philadelphia Inquirer*, October 22, 1899; "Badgers Lose to Yale," *Daily Cardinal*, October 21, 1899, 1.

154. *". . . considerably above average.":* "Yale Beats Badgers," *Philadelphia Inquirer*, October 22, 1899.

154. *". . . the greatest kicker who ever played football.":* As quoted in "O'Dea the Whole Thing," *Milwaukee Sentinel*, October 24, 1899, 4.

154. *the* New York Sun *concluded:* As quoted in "Three Players Injured," *Milwaukee Sentinel*, October 25, 1899, 6.

154. *". . . no difference between the east and the west.":* "Fisher on the Game," *Daily Cardinal*, October 24, 1899, 4.

155. *". . . of the tradition is still convincing.":* "Wisconsin Kicks a Hole in a Football Tradition," *Milwaukee Sentinel*, October 24, 1899, 4.

155. *". . . strongest team of the East.":* Ibid.

CHAPTER 15

156. *". . . condition myself for athletic contests.":* "Pat O'Dea to Retire," *Milwaukee Sentinel*, October 25, 1899, 6.

156. *"had no time to call on girls.":* "Capt. Pat O'Dea Talks about His Football Career and His Future," *Milwaukee Journal*, December 5, 1899, 10.

156. *as Dallas, New Orleans, and Boston:* See, for instance, "Pat O'Dea to Retire from Gridiron," *Dallas Morning News*, November 26, 1899.

157. *". . . should be done, if he desires it.":* "O'Dea May Be Coach," *Minneapolis Journal*, November 16, 1899.

157. *". . . I have learned from Phil King."*: "Capt. Pat O'Dea Talks about His Football Career and His Future," *Milwaukee Journal,* December 5, 1899, 10.

157. *perhaps as a kicking coach:* "Pat O'Dea to Retire," *Milwaukee Sentinel,* October 25, 1899, 6.

157. *boycott of the Maroons in March of 1899:* "Boycott the Maroons," *Chicago Daily Tribune,* March 14, 1899.

157. *Wisconsin manager John Fisher said:* "Would Like to Meet the Chicago Eleven," *Milwaukee Sentinel,* October 25, 1899.

157. *". . . comprised in Manager Fisher's statement."*: Ibid.

157. *scoffed at as "socialistic philanthropy."*: Caspar Whitney, "Amateur Sport," *Harper's Weekly,* October 21, 1899, 1073.

157. *on the part of the Chicago coach:* Adams to Harper, March 12, 1899. Filed digitally at University of Chicago Archives, ofcpreshjb-0020-009-02.pdf, p. 4.

157–158. *would come to be known as the Cubs:* "Wisconsin Is the Champion," *Milwaukee Sentinel,* December 1, 1899, 1.

158. *"had enough of Stagg and Staggism."*: "New Alliance Possible," *Chicago Chronicle,* November 26, 1898.

158. *to mark the spot of the catch:* "O'Dea Made Sixty-Yard Dropkick While on Run," (*Zanesville, Ohio*) *Signal,* October 20, 1943.

158. *". . . trying to score in this wind."*: Jack Newcombe, *The Fireside Book of Football* (New York: Simon and Schuster, 1964), 171.

159. *he later recounted:* "Patrick O'Dea, 90, of Gridiron Dead," *New York Times,* April 5, 1962.

159. *". . . landed outside the park."*: Joseph Coughlin, "Roundy Says," *Wisconsin State Journal,* November 16, 1934.

159. *to have traveled roughly 75 yards:* Dave Lewis, "Once Over Lightly," (*Long Beach, California*) *Independent,* July 30, 1950, 22-A.

159. *"O'Dea's kick was wonderful."*: "Badger Team Wins," *Chicago Chronicle,* November 12, 1899; "Wisconsin Wins," *Daily Cardinal,* November 11, 1899, 1.

159. *". . . near the edge of the field."*: Unlabeled newspaper clipping, Amos Alonzo Stagg Papers, University of Chicago Archives, box 58, folder 1. In the original source of this quotation, the word "marvelous" appears as "marvellous." For purposes of clarity, I have corrected the typographical error.

159. *"... as ever happened on a football field.":* "O'Dea Wins for Badgers," *Chicago Daily Tribune,* November 12, 1899, 17.

159. *"to have not the slightest idea what to do.":* Ibid.

159. *"the greatest individual play he ever saw.":* "O'Dea Made Sixty-Yard Dropkick While on Run," (*Zanesville, Ohio*) *Signal,* October 20, 1943.

160. *"... was running to his left.":* Ibid.

160. *"... will always stay with me.":* Hank Casserly, "Hank Casserly Says," (*Madison*) *Capital Times,* November 21, 1941, Sports, 1.

160. *"... Wisconsin had a score, 5–0.":* "The Kangaroo Kicker," *Wisconsin Football Facts 1954, Wisconsin Athletic Review,* 1954, 36.

161. *he had miscalculated:* Unlabeled newspaper clipping, Amos Alonzo Stagg Papers, University of Chicago Archives, box 58, folder 1.

161. *at between 13,000 and 22,000:* "Colleges Sign New Pact," *Chicago Chronicle,* December 2, 1899; "Wisconsin, 17; Michigan, 5," *Chicago Daily Tribune,* 3.

161. *a football game in the West:* This claim is asserted in both "Wisconsin Vanquishes Michigan, Though O'Dea Is Ordered Off Field," *Milwaukee Journal,* November 30, 1899, 1, and "Wisconsin Is the Champion," *Milwaukee Sentinel,* December 1, 1899, 1.

161. *numbering less than 8,000:* Caspar Whitney, "Amateur Sport," *Harper's Weekly,* December 23, 1899, 1305.

161. *that wouldn't be possible:* "Wisconsin Is the Victor," *Chicago Chronicle,* December 1, 1899.

161. *and even an occasional cowbell:* "Badgers Triumph over Men of Michigan," *Los Angeles Times,* December 1, 1899, 4; "Wisconsin Is Victor," *Chicago Chronicle,* December 1, 1899, 1.

161. *decorated in school colors:* "Wisconsin Is the Champion," *Milwaukee Sentinel,* December 1, 1899, 1.

161. *and the other in left center field:* "Gridiron at the West Side Ballpark," *Chicago Chronicle,* November 28, 1899.

161. *behind the home plate area:* Ibid.

161. *ever for a football game in Chicago:* "Colleges Sign New Pact," *Chicago Chronicle,* December 2, 1899.

162. *pay off the debt from the journey:* "When Wisconsin Last Met Michigan," *Milwaukee Sentinel,* December 1, 1899, 2.

162. *"... famous kicking leg to advantage in scoring.":* "Pat O'Dea's Leg Will Govern Play," *Milwaukee Journal,* November 28, 1899, 10.

162. *". . . offensive work has suffered."*: "Michigan a Slight Favorite," *Chicago Daily Tribune,* November 30, 1899, 6.

162. *"O'Dea is our greatest fear."*: Unlabeled newspaper clipping, Amos Alonzo Stagg Papers, University of Chicago Archives, box 58, folder 1.

162. *". . . get me out of the game," he said afterward:* "O'Dea Defends His Act," *Chicago Chronicle,* December 1, 1899.

162. *"and tackled the Australian foully."*: "Wisconsin Is the Victor," *Chicago Chronicle,* December 1, 1899.

162. *". . . seemed almost stereotyped."*: Ibid.

162. the Chronicle *observed:* Ibid.

163. *". . . without actual slugging."*: As quoted in "Pat O'Dea," *Milwaukee Sentinel,* December 2, 1899, 4.

163. *his pleas were ignored:* "O'Dea Defends His Act," *Chicago Chronicle,* December 1, 1899, 4.

163. *". . . into his ribs with terrific force."*: "Wisconsin Is the Champion," *Milwaukee Sentinel,* December 1, 1899, 1.

163. *". . . and ordered O'Dea out of the game."*: Ibid.

163. *"autocratic and unjust."*: Ibid.

163. *". . . than was O'Dea at this time."*: As quoted in "Pat O'Dea," *Milwaukee Sentinel,* December 2, 1899, 4.

163. *". . . in the eyes of his admirers."*: Ibid.

163. *glancing fondly at his star player:* Details and quotes regarding the celebration are taken from "Wisconsin Rooters Celebrate the Victory," *Milwaukee Sentinel,* December 1, 1899, 2.

164. *be guaranteed at least $1,000:* Caspar Whitney, "Amateur Sport," *Harper's Weekly,* December 23, 1899, 1305.

164. *". . . larks in this agreement."*: Ibid.

165. *". . . which way the wind is blowing," Whitney observed:* Ibid.

165. *". . . color dear to Wisconsin men."*: "Victory for Maroons," *Sunday (Chicago) Inter Ocean,* December 10, 1899, 1.

165. *". . . bewildered their opponents."*: Ibid.

165. *". . . the attack of Chicago . . . was directed."*: "Analysis of Chicago's Victory," *Chicago Daily Tribune,* December 10, 1899, 18.

165. *Stagg observed afterward:* "Opinions of the Chicago Players," *Chicago Daily Tribune,* December 10, 1899, 18.

165. *"and many of his punts fell woefully short."*: "Victory for Maroons," *Sunday (Chicago) Inter Ocean,* December 10, 1899, 1.

165. *"O'Dea's kicking was poor.":* "Opinions of the Chicago Players," *Chicago Daily Tribune,* December 10, 1899, 18.

166. *"... and protested such righteousness.":* Caspar Whitney, "Amateur Sport," *Harper's Weekly,* December 23, 1899, 1305.

CHAPTER 16

168. *in* McClure's Magazine *in 1905:* Henry Beach Needham, "The College Athlete. How Commercialism Is Making Him a Professional," *McClure's Magazine* (June 1905), 118.

168. *"... to support athletics in general.":* Ibid.

168. *"... is an honor to other universities.":* "Columbia Beats Yale at Football," *New York Times,* October 29, 1899.

168. *only score of the game:* Ibid. The *New York Sun* reported the run at 70 yards: "Columbia Victorious," *New York Sun,* October 29, 1899, 9.

168. *other than Harvard or Princeton had beaten Yale:* "Columbia Beats Yale at Football," *New York Times,* October 29, 1899.

168. *"... I played in that game.":* Ibid.

168. *"... throughout the United States.":* "Columbia Victorious," *New York Sun,* October 29, 1899, 9.

168. *box office revenues of $12,000:* Ibid.

169. *Whitney wrote in* Harper's Weekly*:* Caspar Whitney, "Amateur Sport," *Harper's Weekly,* November 4, 1899, 1122.

169. *solely due to their football ability:* Ibid.

169. *funneled to the school as tuition payments:* "Report to the Advisory Committee of the Columbia Athletic Association," March 6, 1900, Columbia University Archives.

169. *"... as a favor to Columbia.":* "Larendon and Miller Write a Letter—Say They Played As a Favor to the University," *New York Daily Tribune,* March 24, 1900, 4.

169. *"were subjected to the deepest mortification and humiliation.":* Pine to Hutton, September 13, 1900, Columbia University Archives.

169. *He got a raise:* Henry Beach Needham, "The College Athlete. How Commercialism Is Making Him a Professional," *McClure's Magazine* (June 1905), 118.

170. *"... five and a half feet off the ground.":* Alexander M. Weyand, *The Saga of American Football* (New York: Macmillan, 1955), 67.

170. *his father found work as a stonemason:* "James J. Hogan Dead—Was Football Star," *New York Times,* March 21, 1910.

171. *". . . amusing at times to watch him.":* William Hanford Edwards, *Football Days; Memories of the Game and of the Men behind the Ball* (New York: Moffat, Yard, 1916), 449.

171. *when the moment got particularly tense:* Edwards, 279; Allison Danzig, *The History of American Football: Its Great Teams, Players, and Coaches* (Englewood Cliffs, NJ: Prentice-Hall, 1956), 163.

171. *free tuition and spending money:* Henry Beach Needham, "The College Athlete. How Commercialism Is Making Him a Professional," *McClure's Magazine* (June 1905), 124.

171. *". . . degrading to amateur sport.":* Ibid., 115.

172. *". . . I am sure that Hogan is.":* Ibid., 124.

172. *"the filth of the floor.":* Robert G. Torricelli and Andrew Carroll, *In Our Own Words: Extraordinary Speeches of the American Century* (New York: Kodansha International, 1999), 13.

173. *in her autobiography:* Ida M. Tarbell, *All in the Day's Work* (New York: Macmillan, 1939), 25.

173. *write a piece on Standard Oil:* Tarbell background from Steve Weinberg, *Taking on the Trust: The Epic Battle of Ida Tarbell and John D. Rockefeller* (New York: W. W. Norton, 2008).

173. *". . . production and efficient distribution.":* James Playsted Wood, *Magazines in the United States, Their Social and Economic Influence* (New York: Ronald, 1949), 133. Wood's contention that Tarbell was not originally looking to expose Standard Oil were confirmed by Steve Weinberg in an e-mail exchange in May 2013.

173. *". . . by fair means and foul.":* Wood, 133.

173. *". . . on the minds of their readers.":* Ibid., 145.

174. *". . . and its evils to be incurable.":* Kirchwey to Butler, July 14, 1902, Columbia University Archives.

174. *". . . and pays the athletes.":* Henry Beach Needham, "The College Athlete. How Commercialism Is Making Him a Professional," *McClure's Magazine* (June 1905), 126. Emphasis is Needham's.

174. *"class of students tainted with commercialism.":* Ibid., 123.

174. *". . . and covering many sins.":* Ibid.

174. *". . . sport is primary, winning secondary.":* Caspar Whitney, "Amateur Sport," *Harper's Weekly,* November 4, 1899, 1121.

175. *". . . Couldn't stand losing."*: Henry Beach Needham, "The College Athlete. How Commercialism Is Making Him a Professional," *McClure's Magazine* (June 1905), 117.

175. *". . . bought him a sixty-dollar overcoat."*: Ibid., 121.

175. *". . . sustain men by devious means."*: Edward S. Jordan, "Buying Football Victories," *Collier's*, November 11, 1905, 19.

175. *". . . conservation of academic ideals."*: Ibid.

175. *". . .required of athletes," Jordan wrote:* Ibid., 19.

176. *". . . according to [President] Harper's instructions."*: Robin Lester, *Stagg's University: The Rise, Decline, and Fall of Big-Time Football at Chicago* (Urbana: University of Illinois Press, 1995), 90.

176. *". . . what is necessary to be done."*: Ibid. 89.

176. *". . . You haven't got the money."*: John Sayle Watterson, *College Football: History, Spectacle, Controversy* (Baltimore: Johns Hopkins University Press, 2000), 85.

176. *a mark that stood for twenty-five years:* Lester, 55.

176. *final score was 105–0:* James Andrew Peterson, *Eckersall of Chicago* (Chicago: Hinckley & Schmitt, 1957), pages not numbered; and "Hyde Park 105; Brooklyn Poly 0," *Chicago Daily Tribune*, December 7, 1902, 9.

176. *a campus visit to Ann Arbor:* Lester, 56.

176. *". . . most poorly prepared freshman."*: Edward S. Jordan, "Buying Football Victories," *Collier's*, November 11, 1905, 19.

177. *full load of courses that quarter:* Lester, 52.

177. *". . . 'he never appeared in class.'"*: Ibid., 57.

177. *Eckersall, 15; Wisconsin, 6:* Ibid.; Peterson, no page number.

177. *"service in the University."*: Lester, 60.

177. *". . . in the Univ. again—for cause."*: Ibid.

177. *". . . had completed his college career."*: Ibid., 61.

178. *". . . and that is enough."*: Edward S. Jordan, "Buying Football Victories," *Collier's*, November 11, 1905, 19.

178. *". . . great annual game with Kansas."*: Edward S. Jordan, "Buying Football Victories," *Collier's*, November 25, 1905, 21.

178. *". . . not to be counted as sinless."*: Ibid.

178. *". . . Heston was well paid."*: Ibid.

178. *"took care of Heston while in college."*: "Former Michigan Regent, James Murfin Dies at 65," *Milwaukee Journal*, July 12, 1940, 9.

178. *". . . see that boy hit the line."*: Edward S. Jordan, "Buying Football Victories," *Collier's*, November 25, 1905, 22.

179. *assistant coach at Minnesota:* Edward S. Jordan, "Buying Football Victories," *Collier's*, December 2, 1905, 20.

179. *the son of two former slaves:* Mark F. Bernstein, *Football: The Ivy League Origins of an American Obsession* (Philadelphia: University of Pennsylvania Press, 2001), 71.

179. *early years of the college game:* It should be noted that many of the black colleges in the South began fielding their own football teams at this time. See Charles H. Martin, *Benching Jim Crow* (Urbana: University of Illinois Press, 2010), 8.

179. *rooming for African Americans:* Ibid., 11; Henry Beach Needham, "The College Athlete. How Commercialism Is Making Him a Professional," *McClure's Magazine* (July 1905), 271.

180. *could continue with mass plays:* David M. Nelson, *The Anatomy of a Game: Football, the Rules, and the Men Who Made the Game* (Newark: University of Delaware Press, 1994), 92.

180. *more dangerous than mass plays:* "O'Dea on New Rules," *Dallas Morning News,* September 6, 1903.

180. *". . . he was one of the heirs."*: Orlando Burnett, "Madison Letter," *Eau Claire (Wisconsin) Leader,* April 25, 1900.

181. *southern portion of that continent:* "O'Dea Going to Africa," *Minneapolis Journal,* April 20, 1900.

181. *". . . He's a waiter."*: Red Salmon anecdote: Dick Hyland, "Hyland Fling," *Los Angeles Times,* February 12, 1949, B2.

181. *". . . to Coach O'Dea."*: "Our Gridiron Heroes," *Notre Dame Scholastic,* December 14, 1901, 227.

182. *Andrew Morrissey fired O'Dea:* Herb T. Juliano, *Notre Dame Odyssey: A Journey through Sports and Spirituality on the Notre Dame Campus* (Notre Dame, IN: Notre Dame Press, 1993), 279.

182. *in a sling for six weeks:* "Pat O'Dea Breaks Shoulder," *Chicago Daily Tribune,* December 5, 1901, 6.

182. *who proceeded to rob him:* "Chicago Highwaymen Set Upon Pat O'Dea," *Racine Daily Journal,* December 24, 1901, 7.

182. *". . . as well as one of his legs."*: "Coach O'Dea Is in Hostpital," *Chicago Daily Tribune,* January 16, 1902, 6.

182. *". . . they're wasting their time."*: Jack Newcombe, *The Fireside Book of Football* (New York: Simon and Schuster, 1964), 172.

182. *". . . of the Tigers next season."*: "New Coach for Missouri," *Omaha World Herald,* March 17, 1902.

182. *pistol in town for his safety:* Wendy Bolz, "The 'Kicking Kangaroo' and the 'Kangaroo Stroker,'" (unpublished family history), 6.

183. *". . . during the hurried ceremony."*: "Pat O'Dea Married," *Eau Claire (Wisconsin) Leader,* February 19, 1903, 4.

183. *the baby and her mother:* Wendy Bolz, "The 'Kicking Kangaroo' and the 'Kangaroo Stroker,'" (unpublished family history), 7.

183. *on three separate occasions:* Michael D. Shutko, "College Football at Its Best," *Now & Then. National Center for Osteopathic History* (Fall 2003).

184. *on the 1903–04 school year:* "The Evils of Football," *Harvard Graduates' Magazine* (March 1905), 385.

184. *". . . the business of teaching deception."*: Troy Soos, *Before the Curse: The Glory Days of New England Baseball, 1858–1918* (Jefferson, NC: McFarland & Company, 2006), 44.

184. *experienced by the New Haven school:* Bill Reid and Ronald A. Smith, *Big-Time Football at Harvard, 1905: The Diary of Coach Bill Reid* (Urbana: University of Illinois Press, 1994), xv.

184. *behind only Columbia's Sanford:* Ronald A. Smith, *Sports and Freedom: The Rise of Big-Time College Athletics* (New York: Oxford University Press, 1988), 156.

184. *". . . Harvard's president since 1869."*: Ibid.

185. *". . . would have considered possible."*: Reid and Smith, 12.

185. *". . . things except loud women."*: Ibid., 14.

185. *installing telegraph lines:* Ibid., 15.

185. *". . . try to get him eligible."*: Ibid., 78.

185. *". . . fellows is disgustingly ludicrous."*: Ibid., 80.

186. *to work on a sheep ranch:* Background on LeMoyne: Myron Finkbeiner, *From Harvard to Hagerman: An Incredible Journey of an Unknown Athlete: Harry LeMoyne* (Boise, ID: Borderline Pub., 2012).

186. *LeMoyne stayed in Idaho:* Reid and Smith, 11–12.

CHAPTER 17

187. *a summit with President Theodore Roosevelt:* Bill Reid and Ronald A. Smith, *Big-Time Football at Harvard, 1905: The Diary of Coach Bill Reid* (Urbana: University of Illinois Press, 1994), 193.

187. *". . . you will be able to come.":* Letter from Theodore Roosevelt to Walter Camp, October 2, 1905, Walter Chauncey Camp Papers, Yale University Archives, box 21, folder 593. I am assuming the timeline and wording of the letters were similar to all the coaches and administrators.

187. *headed toward the nation's capital:* Reid and Smith, 193.

187. *weakness in their archrivals:* Ibid.

187. *a visit to the top of the Washington Monument:* Ibid.

188. *were greeted at the entrance:* Descriptions of the 1905 White House from "The White House—A Home of Stately Dignity and Beauty," *Washington Post*, March 5, 1905, 14, and a postcard of the Dining Room from the White House Archives.

188. *made the journey from New Jersey:* Reid and Smith, 193–94.

188. *appealed to the magazine not to publish them:* John Sayle Watterson, *College Football: History, Spectacle, Controversy* (Baltimore: Johns Hopkins University Press, 2000), 66.

188. *after the exposé was published:* Theodore Roosevelt and E. E. Morison, *The Letters of Theodore Roosevelt* (Cambridge, MA: Harvard University Press, 1951), 1280–82.

188. *suggested a meeting of the "Big Three.":* Ibid., 94.

189. *". . . the athletic spirit has saved us.":* Letter from Theodore Roosevelt to Walter Camp, March 11, 1895, Walter Chauncey Camp Papers, Yale University Archives, box 21, folder 593.

189. *". . .an occasional bruise or cut," he wrote:* Ibid.

189. *". . . honorable limits, is an advantage.":* Letter from Theodore Roosevelt to Walter Camp, March 11, 1895, Walter Chauncey Camp Papers, Yale University Archives, box 21, folder 593.

189. *". . . both in letter and spirit?":* H. F. Manchester, "Reveals How College Football Was Saved in 1905," *Boston Herald*, October 17, 1926, 7.

189. *". . . to carry out these obligations.":* Reid and Smith, 194–95.

189. *thanked the men for their service:* Telegram, Roosevelt to Camp, October 11, 1905, Walter Chauncey Camp Papers, Yale University Archives, box 21, folder 593.

190. *in eliminating the game's brutality:* "Civilizing Football," *New York Times,* October 12, 1905; "Reforming Football to Reduce Injuries," *New York Times,* October 15, 1905.

190. *". . . responsible for their continuance.":* "Hard Job to Reform It, Eliot Says," *New York Times,* October 11, 1905.

190. *". . . are all dealt with in the rules.":* Reid and Smith, 207.

190. *". . . college sport is doomed.":* As quoted in "Princeton for Reform," *New York Times,* October 15, 1905.

190. *". . . practice of the game itself.":* Ibid.

190. *"merely a tool of Camp's.":* Reid and Smith, 34.

190. *". . . demanded by public sentiment.":* Letter from Francis Bangs to Nicholas Murray Butler, October 28, 1905, Columbia University Archives, Athletics Folder, 1–2.

191. *". . . existing irresponsible committee on rules.":* Letter from Butler to Bangs, November 2, 1905, Columbia University Archives, Athletics Folder.

191. *". . . not likely to be cured at his age.":* Ibid.

191. *in the school's athletics operation:* Letter from William Beebe to Arthur Hadley, September 27, 1905, Walter Chauncey Camp Papers, Yale University Archives, box 3, reel 2.

191. *of the school's athletic finances:* Richard P. Borkowski, *The Life and Contributions of Walter Camp to American Football* (thesis, Temple University, 1979), 177.

191. *". . . extravagance in connection with athletics.":* "Light on Yale Athletics," *New York Times,* October 29, 1905.

191. *". . . voted to abolish football.":* H. F. Manchester, "Reveals How College Football Was Saved in 1905," *Boston Herald,* October 17, 1926, 7.

192. *". . . ought to be radically changed.":* Ibid.

192. *Bartol Parker, fought back:* Ibid.

192. *". . . appetites are like, you know.":* Ibid.

193. *Harvard's loss to Yale:* John J. Miller, *The Big Scrum: How Teddy Roosevelt Saved Football* (New York: Harper Collins, 2011), 197.

193. *Harvard guard in the face:* Reid and Smith, 316.

193. *the game's power brokers:* Guy Lewis, "Theodore Roosevelt's Role in the 1905 Football Controversy," *Research Quarterly* (December 1969), 723.

193. *adopt that country's game:* Theodore Roosevelt to Walter Camp, August 21, 1906, Walter Chauncey Camp Papers, Yale University Archives, box 21, folder 593.

193. *". . . abide by whatever you do.":* Theodore Roosevelt to Walter Camp, October 11, 1905, Walter Chauncey Camp Papers, Yale University Archives, box 21, folder 593.

193. *". . . venture to make a suggestion.":* Ibid.

193. *". . . not a crucial one.":* Guy Lewis, "Theodore Roosevelt's Role in the 1905 Football Controversy," *Research Quarterly* (December 1969), 724.

194. *suffered a cerebral hemorrhage:* "Football Player Killed," *New York Times,* November 26, 1905.

194. *put the toll at eighteen:* Nineteen number is from "The Homicidal Pastime," *New York Times,* November 29, 1905; eighteen number is from John S. Watterson, "The Gridiron Crisis of 1905: Was It Really a Crisis?" *Journal of Sport History* (Summer 2000), 294.

194. *". . . very bad thing for his health.":* "The Homicidal Pastime," *New York Times,* November 29, 1905.

194. *". . . distinction of supremacy.":* Ibid.

194. *". . . it is all in the game.":* Ibid.

194. *"but so does war.":* "Favor Revision of Rules," *New York Times,* November 27, 1905. Watterson, 87.

194. *". . . disliked the existing gridiron system.":* John S. Watterson, "The Gridiron Crisis of 1905: Was It Really a Crisis?" *Journal of Sport History* (Summer 2000), 298.

195. *". . . dangerous to human life.":* "Football Is Abolished by Columbia Committee," *New York Times,* November 29, 1905.

195. *the paper editorialized:* Untitled Editorial, *Columbia Spectator,* November 29, 1905, 2.

195. *he wrote to MacCracken:* "Football Is Abolished by Columbia Committee," *New York Times,* November 29, 1905.

195. *". . . profitable is the main evil.":* Ibid.

195. *rather than abolish the game:* Guy Lewis, "Theodore Roosevelt's Role in the 1905 Football Controversy," *Research Quarterly* (December 1969), 721.

195. *meeting in late December:* Watterson, *College Football,* 74.

195. *". . . to this narrow committee.":* "Oligarchy of Football," *New York Daily Tribune,* December 21, 1905, 10.

196. *also sent representatives:* Watterson, *College Football,* 77–78.

196. *before agreeing to combine forces:* Ibid., 81.

196. *found guilty of foul play:* Ibid., 82.

196. *just one rule change—the 10-yard rule:* Ibid., 101.

196. *". . . alter the present style of the game.":* "Changes in Football Promise a Deadlock," *New York Times,* January 9, 1906.

197. *". . . will be dealt to the game.":* H. F. Manchester, "Reveals How College Football Was Saved in 1905," *Boston Herald,* October 17, 1926, 7.

197. *it would be on Harvard's terms:* Ronald A. Smith, *Sports and Freedom: The Rise of Big-Time College Athletics* (New York: Oxford University Press, 1988), 203–05.

197. *The fund now totaled nearly $100,000:* Clarence Deming, "Mr. Camp's Financiering," *(New York) Evening Post,* January 18, 1906.

198. *under the heading of "maintenance.":* Ibid.

198. *on page one the next day:* "Deming after Walter Camp," *New Haven Evening Register,* January 19, 1906, 1.

198. *". . .commercialism which has brutalized" football:* As quoted in "Radical Football Reform," *(New Haven) Evening Leader,* January 25, 1906.

198. *". . . expense of the associations.":* "Yale Faculty Divided," *New York Times,* January 21, 1906.

198. *$8 each to support athletics:* Ibid.

198. *broader issues the sport was facing:* "President Hadley on Football," *Yale Daily News,* January 20, 1906.

198. *". . . overwhelming physical danger.":* Ibid.

199. *". . . rules as we please.":* Hadley to Camp, February 2, 1906, Walter Chauncey Camp Papers, Yale University Archives, box 11, reel 9.

199. *". . . ought to be spanked this time.":* Murphy to Curtis, January 22, 1906, Walter Chauncey Camp Papers, Yale University Archives, box 20, reel 14.

199. *resulted in a turnover:* David M. Nelson, *The Anatomy of a Game: Football, the Rules, and the Men Who Made the Game* (Newark: University of Delaware Press, 1994), 123–25.

199. *limiting eligibility to three years total:* "The Overseers Permit Football," *Harvard Graduates' Magazine* (June 1906), 694.

200. *to continue at the school:* Ibid.

200. *". . . may develop in each institution.":* Merle Curti and Vernon Carstensen, *The University of Wisconsin 1848–1925: A History* (Madison: Univsity of Wisconsin Press, 1949), 538.

200. *". . . sport, manliness, and decency.":* Ibid., 540.

200. *including Michigan's Yost, were grandfathered in:* Carl D. Voltmer, *A Brief History of the Intercollegiate Conference of Faculty Representatives, with Special Consideration of Athletic Problems* (thesis, Columbia University, 1935), 19.

201. *burned effigies of Turner and two other Wisconsin professors:* Description of student protests in Madison from Ray Allen Billington, *Frederick Jackson Turner: Historian, Scholar, Teacher* (New York: Oxford Univsity Press, 1973), 273.

201. *". . . I now tackle thee.":* Quotes in this paragraph from "Mr. Camp's New Rules," *Yale Daily News,* February 1, 1906, 1.

201. *". . . at Harvard and elsewhere.":* "Football Differences," *New York Times,* September 30, 1906.

CHAPTER 18

202. *instruments in hand, lingered alongside:* Descriptions of funeral from "Cadet Byrne's Body Is Placed in Grave," *New York Times,* November 3, 1909.

203. *to his final resting place:* "Cadet Near Death from Football Hurt," *New York Times,* October 31, 1909.

203. *to witness a game at West Point:* "Injury to Cadet Stops Harvard Game," *New York Times,* October 31, 1909.

203. *in the final ten minutes of play:* Alexander M. Weyand, *The Saga of American Football* (New York: Macmillan, 1955), 93.

203. *Byrne didn't move:* Descriptions of the injury from "Cadet Near Death from Football Hurt," *New York Times,* October 31, 1909.

203. *ten of them college players:* John S. Watterson, "The Gridiron Crisis of 1905: Was It Really a Crisis?" *Journal of Sport History* (Summer 2000), 294.

203. *perished just a year earlier:* Ibid.

203. *". . . Foot Ball in popular favor.":* Weyand, 87.

203. *". . . improved by the new rules.":* "Rational College Sports," *Harvard Graduates' Magazine* (March 1907), 385.

204. *"Overhead Projectile Spiral Pass.":* Weyand, 85.

204. *"a remarkable development of the forward pass.":* "Iowa Beats the Illini," *Chicago Daily Tribune,* November 10, 1907, C1.

204. *Northwestern's newly reinstated team:* "Illini Swamp the Purple," *Chicago Daily Tribune,* November 22, 1908, B3.

204. *days after Christian's fatal injury:* "Stop the Mass Plays," *New York Times,* November 16, 1909.

204. *". . . before the next boy is killed.":* Ibid.

204. *". . . henceforth a doomed sport.":* Both quotes in this paragraph from "Sympathy at Harvard," *New York Times,* November 1, 1909.

205. *". . . pushing and pulling of the runner.":* John Sayle Watterson, *College Football: History, Spectacle, Controversy* (Baltimore: Johns Hopkins University Press, 2000), 121.

205. *". . . individuals as well as for the game.":* Amos Alonzo Stagg to Walter Camp, November 20, 1909, Walter Chauncey Camp Papers, Yale University Archives, box 23, folder 651.

205. *open up the game dramatically:* Weyand, 94. Potential impact of the new rules discussed in "Future of the Changed Football Rests with Coaches and Officials," *New York Times,* September 18, 1910.

205. *refused to sign the new rules:* Watterson, *College Football,* 128.

206. *facilitating the passing game:* David M. Nelson, *The Anatomy of a Game: Football, the Rules, and the Men Who Made the Game* (Newark: University of Delaware Press, 1994), 158.

206. *hoping to secure a game:* Frank P. Maggio, *Notre Dame and the Game That Changed Football: How Jesse Harper Made the Forward Pass a Weapon and Knute Rockne a Legend* (New York: Carroll & Graf, 2007), 83.

206. *shutout win over Tufts:* "Army Escapes a Tie," *New York Times,* October 26, 1913.

206. *"simply ran wild.":* "Thorpe's Indians Crush West Point," *New York Times,* November 10, 1912.

206. *$1,000 for its troubles:* Maggio, 87.

207. *". . . a bottle of iodine.":* Ibid., 104.

207. *". . . probably thought we were crazy.":* Ibid., 100.

207. *"... the entire squad," Harper recalled:* Ibid., 101.

207. *the* Chicago Tribune *reported:* "It Takes the Aftermath to Show How Sincere the Noise Really Is," *Chicago Daily Tribune,* November 1, 1913, 17.

207. *"... what it consists of.":* "Army Wants Big Score," *New York Times,* November 1, 1913.

207. *between 25 and 40 yards:* "Notre Dame's Open Play Amazes Army," *New York Times,* November 2, 1913; Maggio, 111.

207. *"... touchdown by rapid transit.":* Maggio, 111.

208. *"... of the Indiana collegians.":* "Notre Dame's Open Play Amazes Army," *New York Times,* November 2, 1913.

208. *"... a state of perfection.":* Ibid.

208. *declined to just one by 1912:* John S. Watterson, "The Gridiron Crisis of 1905: Was It Really a Crisis? *Journal of Sport History* (Summer 2000), 294.

208. *the same three-year span:* Watterson, *College Football,* 401.

208. *committee on casualties:* Ibid., 136.

208. *gate receipts and glory:* Robert M. Hutchins, "Gate Receipts and Glory," *Saturday Evening Post,* December 3, 1938, 23.

EPILOGUE

209. *"... Paul Bunyan that the game has produced.":* John Lardner, "Legends about O'Dea Pale Beside His Saga," September 20, 1934, unknown newspaper, from the University of Notre Dame Archives, via the files of Michael D. Shutko.

209. *back in front of the reverent masses:* Tom Butler, "O'Dea Put the Foot into Badger Football," *Wisconsin State Journal,* September 3, 1988, 2C.

210. *"... knew and loved years ago.":* Descriptions of scene in Madison from Morris H. Rubin, "Glory of Old Lives Again for O'Dea as Thousands Roar Welcome in Firelight," *Wisconsin State Journal,* November 17, 1934, 1.

210. *"... years of study at Madison.":* "Sporting Facts and Fancies," *Kansas City Star,* December 10, 1905.

210. *"... mercantile field for the Japanese.":* Ibid.

210. *"a failure as a coach.":* Newspaper clipping, unknown paper, September 15, 1908, from the files of Michael D. Shutko.

210. *showed up to court drunk:* Wendy Bolz, "The 'Kicking Kangaroo' and the 'Kangaroo Stroker,'" (unpublished family history), 10.

210. *law in California:* "Roll of Attorneys Admitted to Practice in the Supreme Court of the State of California," from the files of Michael D. Shutko.

211. *he held for one season:* "Stanford Gossip," *Los Angeles Times,* June 19, 1913, V23.

211. *". . . than Miss Zwillinger.":* "How Society Girl Beat Boston Rival," *Los Angeles Times,* May 13, 1913, 11.

211. *antecedent to Sunsweet:* "O'Dea Is Fugitive," *San Jose Evening News,* May 8, 1919.

211. *fled to Seattle:* "Former Association Man Now a Fugitive," *San Jose Mercury News,* May 8, 1919.

211. *". . . where I will find rest.'":* "Athlete Faces Embezzlement Charge: Missing," *San Francisco Chronicle,* May 6, 1919, 6.

211. *was all along:* Bolz, 10.

211. *". . . another name than their own.":* Correspondence, Dick Pershing to Tim Purdy, University of Wisconsin Archives, Pat O'Dea file.

212. *lumber-camp folk hero:* Tim Purdy, *Red River: The Early Years* (Susanville, CA: Lahotan Images, 2011), 115–24.

212. *they were immediately fired:* Message board post authored by Red River expert Tim Purdy: http://archiver.rootsweb.ancestry.com/th/read/NORCAL/1999-04/0924128460.

213. *". . . at his lumber mill," Bruhn recalled:* "O'Dea Mystery Deepens," *Wisconsin Rapids Daily Tribune,* April 9, 1962, 7.

213. *O'Dea told Bruhn:* Ibid.

213. *member of the community:* Correspondence, Dick Pershing to Tim Purdy, University of Wisconsin Archives, Pat O'Dea file.

213. *several other publications:* Joseph H. Hunter, "Westwood Cal., Thrills to Find Hero in Midst," *Wisconsin State Journal,* October 21, 1934, 2.

213. *". . . O'Dea in California.":* Roy L. Foley, "Pat O'Dea Disclaims Playing Hero's Role," *Wisconsin News,* unknown date, 1934, chapter two of twelve-chapter O'Dea series.

213. *newspapers to which he subscribed:* Information on phonograph from Correspondence, Dick Pershing to Tim Purdy, University of Wisconsin Archives, Pat O'Dea file. Information on newspaper

subscriptions from Roy L. Foley, "Wisconsin's Great Gridder Got Hoarse Talking of Exploits," *Wisconsin News,* unknown date, 1934, chapter four of twelve-chapter O'Dea series.

214. *greatest kicker in football history:* "Live Tips and Topics," *Boston Daily Globe,* November 27, 1924, 17.

214. *". . . an egg and spoon race.":* Frank Getty, "Coaches Want Accurate Kickers," *Atlanta Constitution,* November 22, 1925, A3. In the original article, the word "shooting" appears as "shotting." For purposes of clarity, I have changed the spelling.

214. *Isn't Life Tough?:* Al Demaree, "Hero One Day—Bum the Next—Isn't Life Tough?" *Washington Post,* December 18, 1925, 19.

214. *"just flickered and died.":* Irwin M. Howe, "Hot Stove League," *Washington Post,* January 15, 1926, 17.

214. *". . . he is an unknown soldier.":* "Pat O'Dea, Rugby's Gift to Football," *Literary Digest,* March 17, 1934, 28.

214. *". . . never been in the army!":* Correspondence, Dick Pershing to Tim Purdy, University of Wisconsin Archives, Pat O'Dea file.

215. *". . . that did ensue.":* "From the Shadowland Where Great Deeds Sleep Walks a Gridiron Legend to Live Again," *Wisconsin State Journal,* November 16, 1934, 1, photo caption. In the original piece, the word "furor" appears as "furore." For purposes of clarity, I have changed the spelling.

215. *the scoop of his career:* Bill Leiser, "O'Dea, Lost Grid Immortal, Comes to Life," *San Francisco Chronicle,* September 19, 1934, 1.

216. *". . . from followers of opposing teams.":* "Pat O'Dea, Gridiron Immortal, Alive in San Francisco, Newspaper Claims," *Wisconsin State Journal,* September 19, 1934, 1.

216. *to verify the man's identity:* "Older Brother Does Not Think Pat O'Dea, of Grid Fame, Is Alive," *Oshkosh (Wisconsin) Northwestern,* September 20, 1934, 15.

216. *to prove his identity:* Harry L. Smith, "Chronicle Scribe's Story Ends Earth Wide Search for 'Superman' O'Dea," *San Francisco Chronicle,* September 20, 1934.

217. *". . . would know the answers.":* Henry J. McCormick, "'Mitchell' Provides Definite Proof He Is Pat O'Dea," *Wisconsin State Journal Sports,* September 21, 1934, 1.

217. *". . . of that being Pat O'Dea.":* Ibid.

217. *". . . hero of long ago.":* "The Story of Pat O'Dea," *New York Times,* September 21, 1934.

217. *"it ought to be.":* Ibid.

217. *". . . to carry through life.":* "Pat O'Dea—Star," *La Crosse (Wisconsin) Tribune and Leader-Press,* September 27, 1934, 3.

217. *". . . It began to annoy me.":* "O'Dea Tells Own Story of Why He Disappeared," newspaper clipping, unknown paper, 1934, from the files of Michael D. Shutko.

218. *had any intent to deceive:* "Pat O'Dea," *Kilmore (Victoria) Free Press,* October 11, 1934, 4.

218. *". . . was his famous opponent.":* "Incognito Hero Drops His Name to Dodge Public," *Nevada State Journal,* November 15, 1934, 6.

218. *"recognized his writing instantly.":* Ibid.

218. *". . . I do not want to interfere.":* "Brother Admits Pat's Identity," *La Crosse (Wisconsin) Tribune and Leader-Press,* November 14, 1934, 12.

218. *". . . do the thing up right.":* Henry J. McCormick, "O'Dea to Return as Guest of U.W.," *Wisconsin State Journal Sports,* September 23, 1934, 1.

218. *". . . brings them in the dough.":* Joseph Coughlin, "Roundy Says," *Wisconsin State Journal,* November 10, 1934.

218. *". . . reaching a crescendo today.":* Betty Cass, "Madison Day by Day," *Wisconsin State Journal,* November 16, 1934, 1, part 2.

218. *". . . Pat O'Dea is coming.":* Ibid.

218. *". . . gridiron heroes of all time.":* Allison Danzig, "On College Gridirons," *New York Times,* November 13, 1934, 25; Fred Bailey, "Gala Welcome Awaiting Pat O'Dea at Wisconsin," *Los Angeles Times,* November 14, 1934, A13.

219. *". . . know it's the one?":* "Pat O'Dea Criticizes the Huddle," *Oshkosh (Wisconsin) Northwestern,* November 15, 1934, 16.

219. *"crowds gathered at railroad stations to cheer him" along the way:* "Pat O'Dea Is Man of Hour As He Returns to Wisconsin," *Syracuse Herald,* November 16, 1934, 29.

219. *gathered to welcome him:* Sanford Jarrell, "Lost Dropkicker Ends Anonymity," *Baltimore Sun,* November 23, 1934, 13.

219. *with the famous Aussie:* Details on Crystal Ball Room celebration from "Fabulous Pat O'Dea Dies at 90," *(Madison) Capital Times,* April 5, 1962, Sports 1.

219. *". . . in Wisconsin and her achievements.":* Wallace Meyer, "Pat O'Dea's Day in Chicago," *Wisconsin Alumni Magazine* (December 1934), 100.

219. *". . . glad he's back when you see him.":* Monte McCormick, "Football Legend Pat O'Dea Dies," *Wisconsin State Journal,* April 5, 1962, Section 3: 1, 3.

219. *". . . broke into a pealing serenade.":* Morris H. Rubin, "Glory of Old Lives Again for O'Dea As Thousands Roar Welcome in Firelight," *Wisconsin State Journal,* November 17, 1934, 1.

220. *". . . to glory and to victory.":* Ibid., 10.

220. *". . . connected with the homecoming celebration.":* Ibid.

220. *"Auld Lang Syne.":* "Badger Gridders Play Great Game for Pat O'Dea," *Oshkosh (Wisconsin) Northwestern,* November 17, 1934, 1.

220. *". . . virtually every imaginable pose.":* Rubin H. Morris, "Patrick John O'Dea, Benched by Time, Sees Phantom Gridders March Again to Victory," *Wisconsin State Journal,* November 18, 1934, 1.

220. *"Chief Four Leaf Clover.":* Paul Mickelson, "Badgers Score Homecoming Victory over Illinois," *La Crosse (Wisconsin) Tribune and Leader-Press,* November 18, 1934, 11.

220. *". . . no more than useless.":* Rubin H. Morris, "Patrick John O'Dea, Benched by Time, Sees Phantom Gridders March Again to Victory," *Wisconsin State Journal,* November 18, 1934, 1.

220. *a 7–3 defeat:* www.collegepollarchive.com/football/ap/research/1934-11-15_poll.cfm#.Uaj9Upw9-So.

220. *the season finale against Minnesota:* Henry J. McCormick, "Badger Ticket Sales Force Gets Still Monday Drill," *Wisconsin State Journal Sports,* November 20, 1934, 1.

220. *pass to a streaking receiver:* Art Krenz, "Winning Plays of 1934," *La Crosse (Wisconsin) Tribune and Leader-Press,* November 18, 1934, 11.

220. *boasted a capacity of 78,000:* John Sayle Watterson, *College Football: History, Spectacle, Controversy* (Baltimore: Johns Hopkins University Press, 2000), 156.

220. *sign a professional contract:* "738,555 Persons Have Seen Grange Make Football History," *New York Times,* November 25, 1925.

222. *pocketed $30,000 in gate receipts:* Richards Vidmer, "70,000 See Grange in Pro Debut Here," *New York Times,* December 7, 1925.

222. *was pondering his football future:* "Has Prospect of a Fortune," *New York Times,* November 19, 1925.

222. *coach Columbia in 1925:* Watterson, 150.

222. *subsidized their athletes in some form:* Howard J. Savage, *American College Athletics* (Princeton, NJ: *Carnegie Foundation for the Advancement of Teaching,* 1929), 241–42.

223. *Rice was twelfth, Louisiana State thirteenth, and Southern Methodist fifteenth:* www.collegepollarchive.com/football/ap/research/1934-11-15_poll.cfm#.Uaj9Upw9-So.

223. *on the sport in later years:* Watterson, 182.

224. *". . . give up the gate receipts.":* Robert M. Hutchins, "Gate Receipts and Glory," *Saturday Evening Post,* December 3, 1938, 23.

224. *upon his departure:* Henry McCormick, "No Foolin' Now," *Wisconsin State Journal Sports,* January 7, 1936, 1.

224. *Stanford hired a new coach:* "Stuhldreher Has Revived Badgers for Grid Games," *Freeport Journal-Standard,* October 22, 1936, 17.

225. *". . . standing by, awaiting orders.":* Prescott Sullivan, "The Low Down," *San Francisco Chronicle,* October 7, 1948.

225. *". . . fun for anything," O'Dea said:* "Legendary Pat O'Dea to Attend Rose Bowl," *Wisconsin State Journal,* November 30, 1952, 1.

225. *while at his alma mater:* "Pat O'Dea Returns As Hall of Famers Are Saluted," *Wisconsin Alumnus* (November 1959), 25; Letter from Mrs. E. Wynona Hauser to Wynona Hauser Murray, September 30, 1959, from the files of Michael D. Shutko.

225. *in Pasadena for the game:* Frank Finch, "Bruhn Predicts Tight Game, Badger Victory," *Los Angeles Times,* December 31, 1959, C1.

225. *Wisconsin's Athletic Hall of Fame:* Dave Lewis, "Once Over Lightly," *(Long Beach, California) Independent,* July 30, 1950, 22-A.

225. *at a gathering in 1957:* Warner note is from "Warner Takes Dim View of Platoon System," *Los Angeles Times,* November 8, 1952, B2; Stagg note is from "Stagg Tells Grid Story," *Baltimore Sun,* November 6, 1957, S26; Hope note is from Neil Kearney, "Kangaroo Kicker," *Melbourne (Australia) Herald-Sun,* December 1, 2007, 94.

225. *"the patron saint of all kickers.":* Jim Day, "Pipefuls," *Bakersfield Californian,* January 6, 1953, 15.

225. *". . . game of football has ever known.":* Dave Lewis, "Once Over Lightly," *(Long Beach, California) Independent,* July 30, 1950, 22-A.

225. *". . . most trying of circumstances.":* Monte McCormick, "The Legend of Pat O'Dea," *Wisconsin State Journal,* April 6, 1962, Section 3, 1.

226. *have ever been located:* Dick Nolan, *San Francisco Chronicle,* June 17, 1958.

226. *he was recovering well:* Bonnie Ryan, "O'Dea Shelved by Taxi," *Wisconsin Capital Times,* January 24, 1961, S1.

226. *so many years before:* Wendy Bolz, "The 'Kicking Kangaroo' and the 'Kangaroo Stroker,'" (unpublished family history), 15.

226. *". . . will be on your feet again.":* "Wrote JFK to Pat O'Dea," *San Francisco Chronicle,* March 23, 1962.

226. *might call to wish him well:* Lew Cornelius, "Lew Cornelius' Scorebook," *Capital Times,* April 3, 1962, 15.

226. *"brightened his final days.":* "O'Dea Disappeared For 17 Long Years," *Capital Times,* April 5, 1962, S1.

226. *"he was hard to find.":* "O'Dea Mystery Deepens," *Wisconsin Rapids Daily Tribune,* April 9, 1962, 7.

AFTERWORD

228. *student body as a whole:* Graduation success rates are published on the NCAA website NCAA.org.

229. *came with plenty of controversy:* "Texas, ESPN Announce New Network," espn.com, January 19, 2011; http://sports.espn.go.com/espn/news/story?id=6037857.

229. *onset dementia, and depression:* Mark Fainaru-Wada, Jim Avila, and Steve Fainaru, "Doctors: Junior Seau's Brain Had CTE," espn.com, January 11, 2013; http://espn.go.com/espn/otl/story/_/id/8830344/study-junior-seau-brain-shows-chronic-brain-damage-found-other-nfl-football-players.

Index

About the Author

Dave Revsine has been the lead studio host of the Big Ten Network since its inception in 2007. Before that, he spent more than a decade as a studio anchor at ESPN. He lives in suburban Chicago with his wife and three daughters.